Tiann Horng Wenn
E. L.

Jiann Horng Wenn
EL.

5-17-1981   PP ²¹¹

6800

clnk

C

A, S7
A'

S7 ALU

$$\uparrow \text{memory Buft}$$

SC PC P
AC SC I
JC I S

D b

HOME COMPUTERS
Volume 1

HOME COMPUTERS:
2^{10} Questions & Answers
Volume 1: Hardware

Rich Didday

dilithium PRESS P.O. Box 92, Forest Grove, Oregon 97116

The technical information, statements about specific products, and descriptions of specific computer languages in this book are based on fact and are believed to be accurate. The characters are fictional, and are not intended to portray any real persons, living or dead. Some fragments of conversations are based on real conversations.

HOME COMPUTERS: 2^{10} QUESTIONS AND ANSWERS
Volume 1: Hardware

Rich Didday

ISBN 0-918398-00-2

®Copyright 1977 by dilithium Press, P.O. Box 92, Forest Grove, Oregon 97116

10   9   8   7   6   5   4   3   2

Library of Congress Cataloging in Publication Data

Didday, Richard L
    Home computers.

    Bibliography: p.
    Includes index.
    CONTENTS: v. 1. Hardware.—v. 2. Software.
    1. Microcomputers—Miscellanea. I. Title.
TK7885.4.D53   001.6'4'04   77-9285
ISBN 0-918398-00-2 (v. 1)
ISBN 0-918398-01-0 (v. 2)

PRINTED IN THE UNITED STATES OF AMERICA

CONTENTS

PREFACE

What's in this book,

This is the first volume of the two-volume set **Home Computers: 2^{10} Questions and Answers.** This book has two main purposes. First, it's intended to give you a real feeling for what's involved in home computing so you can make rational decisions about what way you want to go *before* you trade your hard-earned cash for equipment. Second, it's intended to give people who come with an interest, but no specialized knowledge, a general background in computing in general and microcomputers in specific. Enough of a background so that you'll have no trouble understanding articles about advanced projects in the computer hobbyist magazines, ads for home computing equipment, and people who do have specialized computing knowledge. There is *no* intent to push any specific products, nor is there an attempt to cover advanced esoteric hardware or software techniques. The whole idea is to get you to the point where you can make your own, informed decisions about what to get and what projects to attempt.

A glance at the Table of Contents and a few minutes of flipping through the book will show you how these purposes are accomplished. The book is expressed in the form of a dialog. One participant (A) has a substantial background in computing and home computing, the other (Q) is a bright, interested newcomer. In addition, an Editor adds occasional fine points and clarifications. Diagrams, Tables, and Appendices are used to provide additional information in a compact form.

Although there is a definite structure to the whole book, so that by reading from start to finish, you will find an orderly progression of material (general overview of microcomputing including both hardware and software → number systems → digital logic notation → understanding different kinds of diagrams → assembling a computer from a kit → details of special microprocessors), the book is also designed to make it easy to skip around, covering topics of special interest to you (see Figure O). Regardless of your specific background, I'm sure you'll find many topics of

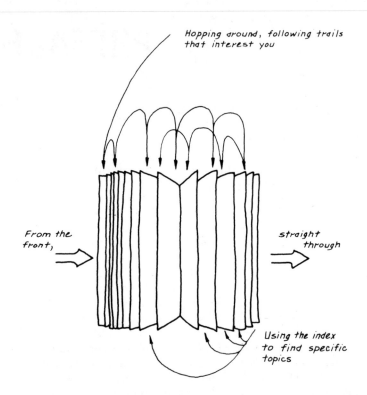

Hopping around, following trails that interest you

From the front,

straight through

Using the index to find specific topics

Figure 0   Different Ways of Using this Book

interest, simply because computing itself is such a rich, fascinating, lively activity.

And how I came to write it.

I've been interested in computing for a long time (I wrote my first programs in 1964, soldered my first digital logic chips together in 1965), and when affordable computers became available, I jumped at the opportunity to have my own system, free from the constraints imposed by the companies and universities whose computers I had been using. As I went around talking to people, dropping into newly opened computer stores, going to conventions, I was struck by the high proportion of people I met who had substantial backgrounds in electronics and computer hardware — there seemed to be relatively few newcomers. "Why is that?", I wondered. Further investigation revealed what should have been obvious. Although dealing with computers is inherently no more difficult than working on your car, and although programming in a language like Basic is easily and commonly taught to children, the mystique and special jargon built up around computers serves as a barrier. People can't be expected to take a deep interest in computing if they can't really understand what's being talked about and if they have no way of knowing what they're in for.

My first plan was to produce a short book of answers to questions like "What is a buffer?", "What is an interface?", "What is the difference between static and dynamic memory?", "What is assembly language?", etc. That failed because the terms, although each one is simple in itself, are densely interrelated and make little sense out of context. The solution was to write a more extensive book consisting of coherent conversations involving the terms to be explained. But now another problem arose. If enough material was included to make the book of real use to people with wide differences in background, the cost to the purchaser would be objectionably high. Fortunately, the material lent itself quite naturally to being divided in two, so the person who is interested mainly in hardware aspects of home computing as well as the person who is interested mainly in programming can each find the material they want in a moderately priced book (Vol. 1 and Vol. 2, respectively).

Overall, it turned out to be much more work than I'd bargained for, but I feel it will be well worth the effort if it succeeds in helping people over the initial barriers, enabling them to discover the joys and excitements of computing.

Thanks to . . .

Many, many thanks to "Nick" Nichparenko, Dan Ross, Dennie Van Tassel, John Craig, the Byte Shop of Santa Cruz, Merl Miller, Rob Walker of Intel, Margaret Kinstler, Raymond Langsford, the late Walter Orvedahl, Rex Page, the lady in Albuquerque, and William Makepeace Thackeray.

EDITOR'S INTRODUCTION

This book and the companion volume *Home Computers: 2¹⁰ Questions and Answers, Volume 2: Software* represent a heavily edited transcription of nine days of conversation focusing on home/hobby computing. Among the steps taken to create a useful book from the raw recordings are these:

- —each Day's conversation has been grouped into sections, and each section given a title.
- —presentable figures have been drawn from the rough sketches provided by the participants.
- —editorial insertions (denoted by [square brackets]) have been made to explain fine points or to correct potentially misleading statements.
- —an extensive set of Appendices, a Bibliography, and an Index have been provided.
- —much of the conversation has been condensed. Some has been converted into tabular form. Portions of questionable relevance have been deleted. In other cases, material representing qualifications of previous statements has been made into parenthetical phrases and inserted at the appropriate points.
- —a numbering scheme has been placed on the material. Questions are numbered only where either the question or the answer (or both) add substantively to the discussion. Unnumbered material has been retained where necessary for continuity or where it gives an indication of the nature of the interaction between the participants.

The conversations divided into two self-sufficient volumes very naturally, with a few minor exceptions. The switch from a concern with hardware issues to a concentration on software occurs very gradually during Day 5, so gradually that there seems to be no single point at which the change can be said to occur. For this reason, the first three sections of Day 5 have been included in both volumes. In addition, some material, notably the discussion of binary, octal, and hexadecimal number systems, is needed in both volumes. Hence, a summary of the relevant information from the first five days has been included in the last five days. In addition, there is a duplication of some of the Appendices, the Bibliography, and the Index. This last duplication is intended to aid those readers who possess both volumes.

The Editor

DAY 1: OVERVIEW

What are we doing here?

Q   . . . recorder is finally working, so I guess we can get started.

A   OK, ask me a question. Anything you want.

Q   Before we get going, there's something I've been wondering about ever since you called to ask if I'd do this.

A   Well?

Q   You said you wanted to do a book of conversations about home computers, and you wanted to call it (if I remember right) 124 or 256 or 1028 Questions and Answers About Home Computers.

A   Right . . . I want to call it 128 or 256 or 512 or 1024 Questions and Answers, depending on how many we wind up with.

Q 1   But every other book like this is called 101 or 1001 Questions and Answers About Aardvarks, or whatever.

A   Ah. But I want the number we use to be a power of two. See, 128 is two to the seventh, 256 is 2^8, 512 is 2^9, 1024 is 2^{10} . . .

Q 2   Oh. Because computers work with binary numbers. Is that the idea?

A   Right. I thought it would tie in with computers better. Make sort of a snazzy title. People who work with computers are always coming across powers of two because digital computers are made up to two-state elements, and . . .

Q 3   Wait — I have lots of questions about what you just said. Like, why *two*-state elements, and what does **state** mean, for that matter, and do I have to learn trivia like the powers of two to get anything out of computers, and . . .

A   Hold It! Let's not get too far ahead of ourselves. No, you don't have to memorize the powers of two if you don't want to. There are so many aspects of computing that you *can't* learn everything right at the start. Designing, building, using, and thinking about computers can be done separately or in various combinations, and each phase requires different skills. You can start with the areas that seem most interesting to you, and not bother with things that seem boring. If you find that you need to know something you skipped over earlier, when you go back

Table 1 — To Do This,... You Need →

Column key (To Do):

1. design and implement your own computer language
2. Q 904-963
3. design and write major programs (record keeping, accounting, simulations,...)
4. Q 203-228
5. write "systems programs" (monitor, handling I/O,...)
6. do arithmetic (say balancing your checkbook, computing interest payments) Q784-812
7. send program, messages to friends Q821-861
8. design and write your own game programs Q827-861
9. design and write your own game programs QB19-826
10. play a wide variety of games on a microcomputer Q908-915
11. use a computer to control something (a burglar alarm, a furnace,) Table 6
12. component port Q445-465; Table 6
13. design and build your own component part Q445-465
14. add an already assembled component part to your system (say more memory) Table 5
15. design and build your own microcomputer
16. Troubleshoot your microcomputer Q583-600
17. build a microcomputer from a kit Q548-582 Figure 58

You Need → / To Do	1	2	3	4	5	6	7	8	9	10	11	12	13	14	15	16	17
be able to solder, do wiring Q536-546; Q576-593											●	●			●	●	●
be able to read circuit diagrams, manufacturer's literature Day 3											●	●		●	●	●	●
understand some digital logic, electronics											●				●		
understand a lot about digital logic, electronics											●	●			●		
learn the binary number system Q238-308	●		●								●	●			●	●	●
understand computer principles of operation Day1, Day 5	●		●								●	●	●		●	●	●
have expensive test equipment Q600														●		●	
learn to program in machine or assembly language Day 6	●		●		●						●						
learn to program in Basic Day 8	●		●			●	●	●									
understand data structures (arrays, stacks, etc) Q656-667 Q840-842	●		●		●			●									
study uses of computers in commercial & scientific applications	●		●														
buy already-written programs (including a Basic interpreter)	●		●			●	●	●	●								
have a terminal of some sort Table 5	●		●			●	●	●	●								
have a "hard-copy" terminal Table 5	●		●														
have a tape recorder system hooked to your microcomputer	●		●					●									

over it, it won't seem boring any more.

Q 4   I presume that we're going to go into all the things mentioned in Table 1?*

A   If you ask all the right questions, I suppose we will.

Q   In detail?

A   Well, I don't think we'll have time for complete detail on every aspect of home computers. My idea was that since you've just developed an interest in computers, and you seem to have bought every piece of literature you could find in the local computer store . . . Good grid! What all do you have in that bag?

Q 5   Here. Have a look.

A   Hmmm. An issue of Kilobaud, an issue of Popular Electronics, Byte, 73, Interface, Radio-Electronics, Microtrek, Computer, a bunch of sales literature, the People's Computer Company Newsletter, Dr. Dobb's Journal, Personal Computing, Computer Notes**,. . .*Swank?*

Q 6   Ooops! How did that get in there?

A   Quite a pile.

      Anyway, my idea was that I could provide some background, cover the main ideas, help you over some of the hurdles to understanding what they're talking about in the articles, help you understand how to read the ads. I thought I could tell you what's involved in putting a computer kit together, and what it really feels like to program. Generally what I thought I could do is give you a feeling for what it's all about, so you'll have some basis for making a decision before you go rushing off to buy a lot of equipment, or start tackling some big project.

Q 7   I have a feeling already that I'm going to have to ask you questions to figure out what *you're* talking about — there are a lot of terms in Table 1 that I'm not sure about.

A   Well, there's no way around that. There are a lot of inter-related concepts in computing. We'll just have to start in somewhere, and then go back and keep filling in the parts you don't understand. Today, let's try to stay pretty general so you get an overview of all aspects of home computers. Then we can take a day or so going into detail on each of the major topics.

      Want to go back now to your question about **state**?

Q 8   All right. Well, before that, why don't you tell me why you're calling these things **home computers**. I've

---

* Table 1 shows what different sorts of skills and knowledge are needed for a range of different activities.

** descriptions of these and other relevant publications appear in the Bibliography skimmed through some of the magazines, and they use terms like **microcomputers, microprocessors, personal computers,** . . .

A   OK. Calling them **home computers** may just be my own little idiosyncrasy. A **microprocessor** is one of the key parts of a **microcomputer**. A **microcomputer** is called that because it's much smaller in physical size (but not necessarily in capabilities) than older computers. **Home computers** or **personal computers** are computers (almost always microcomputers) that people use in their home, with friends, or in small businesses, that is, that aren't used in industry or universities for scientific or engineering problems or for large commercial data processing jobs. I use the term **home computers** just because **personal computer** makes me think of a pocket calculator, and **microcomputer** makes them sound insignificant. No big deal.

Q 9   Are we starting at the right place? I'd really just like to ask "what's a home computer, what can you do with it, and how do you do it?", but I realize that's a pretty broad question.

A   Well, hopefully, you'll know all that after all our conversations. Some of this will probably be familiar at first, because it's all assumed in the magazines, but . . .

Q 10   That'll be all right, I think. Sometimes when I look at them it just seems like a jumble of unrelated things.

A   Ask me how computers work.

Q 11   All right, how do computers work?

A   By the hour, with no time off for lunch, and no old-age pension plans.

Q   Very funny.

A   OK. Let's start at the most general level.

The general organization of computer systems

There are two major categories of things associated with all computers, namely **hardware** and **software. Hardware** refers to the parts of a computer system that you can touch. Actual physical devices. The chips containing the electronics, the wires, the switches, lights, power supply, terminal, plugs, sockets, tape recorders, the boxes the parts are mounted in, etc.

Software refers to things that exist as patterns, namely programs, data, stored values.

There are three major sub-parts of a computer's hardware, which I'll call the **controller** (or **processor**), the **memory,** and **input/output devices**. (Incidentally, **input/output** is always abbreviated as **i/o**.)

When you use a computer, you enter a **program** (which is a piece of software), and cause it to be carried out (by the hardware). A **program** causes the computer to go through some sort of symbol manipulation process, possibly to accept data from you, and certainly to output information in some form that you can use. The **memory** stores the program, data, and partial results. The **controller** interprets and carries out the instructions in a program. (That's what a **program** is — a sequence of instructions to the controller.) The **i/o devices** permit communication between the controller and the ''outside world''.

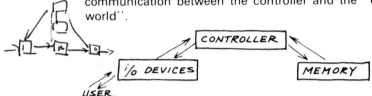

Figure 1   The Conceptual Computer

To give you a feeling for how all these parts interact, let me talk through what happens when you write a program and run it.

Q 12   All right. But I'm going to start writing questions down to ask later.
Where do you start?

A   Let's see. First, you need a computer.

Q   I think I could have figured that part out.

A   Then we would write a program. That involves having some task or problem in mind, figuring out (in detail) how to solve it, and then translating our solution into some language the computer is equipped to accept.

Q 13   That depends on what brand the computer is?

A   Not necessarily. There are some languages, called **higher-level languages*** that are accepted by a wide range of different computers. Anyway, once we have our program written, we enter it into the machine through some sort of **i/o device**.

Q 14   For instance?

A   The most commonly used i/o devices on home computers are the **switches** on the front panel of the microcomputer itself, a **keyboard** used in conjunction with a TV set, and the ever-popular **Teletype**.

*higher level languages Q 185-189

Q 15   But not all computers have switches on the front. I've seen ads for several that don't. Why not? Is that bad?

A   We're getting a little off the track, but I'll try to answer you. You can use a microcomputer which has panel switches without having to buy any kind of terminal, because you can enter programs and inspect values in memory by flipping the appropriate switches and looking at the lights. If the computer doesn't have front panel switches, you've got to have some kind of terminal to do anything with it (besides use it as a paper weight).

Q 16   So it *is* bad if it doesn't have switches.

A   No, it all depends on what you want to do. You'd go bananas doing anything but really small programs through the switches, so you need a terminal anyway. Also, the microcomputers that don't have front panels usually come equipped with a permanently stored program that lets you inspect specific values in memory, enter programs, generally do all the things you can do using switches, right from the terminal.

Q 17   So now you're saying it's a waste of money to have the switches?

A   No, I'm saying that it's a matter of taste. Some people feel more comfortable with switches and lights on the front panel, and some people feel it's more convenient to be able to do everything form the terminal and don't care if they have the switches at all.

Q 18   What do you think I'd like better?

A   Don't know. Go to your local computer store and play around with one of each type. [Editor's note: The trend seems to be away from front panels.] Let's see. Where were we?

Q   I think we were entering the imaginary program into the computer.

A   Oh, right. OK. So we have the program written, and then we'd enter it, one character at a time . . .

Q 19   Do you mean anything special by that?

A   No, I mean that just as you type one letter at a time on a typewriter, you enter one character at a time into the computer. As each character enters, it goes to the controller (processor) and then gets stored in memory, one by one. Of course, it's an electrical signal that we're talking about, a coded form of the characters. We'll . . .

Q   I know. We'll get to that later.

A   OK. So once we're through entering our program, and it's neatly stored away in memory, we cause the controller to start **running** or **executing** it.

Q 20   How do you do that?

A   Depends on the details of the particular system. Either
        you type in one last thing, or you flip some switches.
        Now comes the key part to understand. A program, as
        I said before, is a sequence of commands or instructions
        to the controller. To **run** a program, the controller brings
        one instruction at a time from memory, and then carries
        it out. Then it fetches the next instruction from memory,
        carries it out, and so on.

Q 21   Wait a minute . . . it doesn't sound like you're really telling
        me very much. What are these instructions like?

A   OK. Here's what some typical instructions do:
        Get a value from a particular place in memory and bring
        it into the controller.
        Store a value in a particular place in memory.
        Stop.
        Form the sum of two values.
        Accept a value from a specific i / o device.
        Test a value to see if it's zero, and if it is, take the next
        instruction from some specific place in memory.

Q 22   Those don't sound very exciting.

A   Maybe not, but by putting them together in the right order,
        you can create programs that do myriad and marvelous
        things. That is, you can do that once you understand two
        things. First, you need to understand what each type of
        instruction actually does, that is, how the various instruc-
        tions make the parts of the computer system (**controller,
        memory,** and **i / o**) perform and interact. Second, you need
        to learn how to make correspondences between parts of
        the problem you're trying to solve and things going on
        in the computer.

Q 23   Is it hard to learn to program?

A   Depends on you and how deeply you want to get into
        it. Most people I know think it's really fun. I know I do.

Q 24   Now that I think about it, I'm not sure I understand what
        your second thing was. The thing about correspondences
        between your problem and the computer. If the controller
        carries out instructions, it must know what the corre-
        spondences are. How else would it know what to do?

A   Ooosh. I guess I've been too sloppy in explaining this
        so far. There's a really important idea to get here, so you
        don't go around thinking computers are magic. See, when
        I say things like "the controller fetches an instruction,
        figures out what it is, and carries it out", that's just a
        colorful way of speaking. It's not as if there's a tiny person
        in there who thinks about what to do. Hmmm . . .

Q   Don't be ridiculous! Of *course* I don't think there's a tiny
     . . .

A   Here. Here's the crux of the thing. You know those signs
     in radio stations that light up and say "ON THE AIR"?

Q   I've seen them in movies, I know what you mean.

A   OK. When a sign like that lights up, and we look at it,
     we say that it "means" something, right? But we know
     that what it means isn't in the sign itself, right? The sign
     itself is either on or off, that's all. We interpret the sign
     to mean that the station is operating, and that we should
     be quiet, or whatever.

Q   Sure, sure.

A   OK. When a computer prints out some sequence of letters,
     say, uh, "YES, I UNDERSTAND.", it can look meaningful
     to us, and it may well *be* meaningful to us, but the meaning
     doesn't arise mysteriously from within the computer cir-
     cuitry, it comes from the way the designer of the computer
     and the programmer assigned **symbols** (in this case **let-
     ters,** in other cases, **numbers**) to processes going on in
     the computer.

Q 25 But wait a minute. Computers *can* make decisions, right?
     One of the instructions you listed a while back decided
     whether or not some number was zero, right?

A   Yes and no. Computers "decide" to do something in the
     same sense that a light "decides" to go on depending
     on whether or not the switch is thrown or not. Here. Let
     me draw out a little example that shows how meanings
     get assigned to events in electrical circuits.

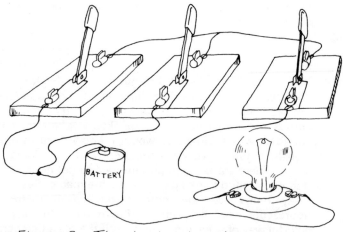

Figure 2 The basic circuit

Tell me what this circuit does.

Q 26   Let's see. The light bulb lights if the switch on the right is closed, and at least one of the two switches to the left is closed.

A   Right. No magic, no "electronic brain", just a simple electrical circuit.

Now suppose I take the exact same circuit and lean some signs up against the switches and in front of the light bulb.

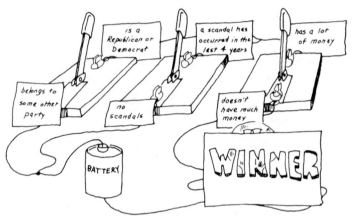

Figure 3   The Prognosticator begins to take form

In fact, just to get carried away, why don't we put the circuit in a nice looking box, and let the switches stick out of it, and put a fancy name on the front.

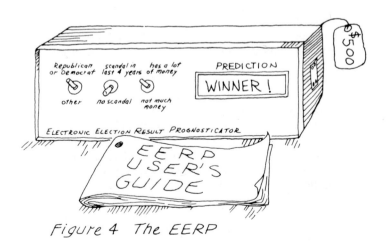

Figure 4   The EERP

Now suppose I hadn't told you anything about what was inside the box, but just walked up to you with it.

"Here's how you use it" (I'd say). "You enter the data on the candidate of your choice by setting the switches, and the machine will *predict* if he or she will be a WINNER in the next election."

Suppose that we entered the data for a candidate, say, one Milton P. Waxley, the WINNER light came on, and in the fall elections, Waxley actually won. We could hold a press conference and announce that the Prognosticator's prediction powers had been proven.

Q 27 But it's just a stupid little bunch of switches and a light. It's not *predicting* anything.

A That may be true, but any fool can see that it says "WINNER" when the data for Milton P. Waxley is entered, and that the prediction turned out to be true!

Q 28 Now *you're* trying to put magic in it.

A Yeh. Actually, what's "made a prediction" or "made a decision" is the simple model that says that a candidate will win an election if he or she is in one of the major parties or there's been a recent scandal (or both), and he or she has a lot of money. The circuit is just a convenient way to figure out what that model predicts because the light bulb comes on only if the left switch is closed or the middle switch is closed (or both), and the right switch is closed. *We* assigned the meanings just by slapping the signs on the switches and the light bulb. Obviously the circuit works the same way no matter *what* signs we put on it.

Q 29 And I gather that you're telling me that that's the way it is with computers.

A In essense.

We could keep playing around with switches and light bulbs to show some other things, but maybe it's time to start getting more specific.

First, let's distinguish between a **special purpose computer** and a **general purpose computer.**

A 30 The Prognosticator must be a special purpose computer?

A Right. Its capabilities are limited to computing that one expression — left or middle switch (or both) thrown and right switch thrown. You can put different signs on the switches all day long, but it still does just the one thing. A **general purpose computer,** on the other hand, can be used to solve any problem you can write a program for. All the microcomputers you're likely to come across as a hobbyist are general purpose computers.

Q 31   Why would you ever want a special purpose computer anyway?

A   Cost, speed. For example, a group of people around MIT is building a special purpose computer which analyzes chess positions. It goes much faster than any commercially available general purpose computers could (parts of it operate in parallel).

Q 32   In parallel as opposed to . . . ?

A   Ah. Good. That's another hardware distinction we can make. Microcomputers are **serial** computers. That means they carry out one instruction after another, one at a time. A **parallel** machine has a number of processors, all of which can be carrying out instructions simultaneously. The computers we'll be talking about here are all **general purpose, serial, digital computers.**

[Editor's note: Like many other terms in the computing field, **serial** and **parallel** do not have single, precise definitions. The way A has used them here is the way they are most commonly used today. Thus, a system which has one "central" processor, that is, a system in which no more than one instruction can be carried out at a time, is said to be a **serial** computer. A system which has many processors, each of which can carry out instructions independently (such as the Illiac IV and other experimental machines) is said to be a **parallel** computer, or to be capable of **parallel processing**.

An older sense of the words, one which is still seen occasionally, is this: if in carrying out an instruction, the processor is able to operate on all bit positions (in the accumulator, say) at once it is said to operate in **parallel**. If the processor cannot do this (if, for example, to add two 8 bit values it adds the rightmost two bits, then the next pair of bits, then the next, and so forth until it has built up the sum) it is said to operate **serially**. The word **sequential** was/is used to describe systems which carry out instructions one at a time, one after the next. Using the older terminology, we would say that microprocessor chips are **sequential, 8 bit-parallel processors**.]

       Those are all characteristics of the hardware. Then, of course, we have the distinction between hardware and software. Taken together, the hardware and the software associated with a specific machine are said to make up the **computer system.**

Q 33   I hear what you're saying, but I don't really know what you're talking about . . .

A   Tell you what. Let me sketch out the typical pieces of hardware that you'll find in any home computer and go over them. Maybe we were getting a little too abstract.

Q 34   All right. So we'll concentrate on hardware for a while.

A   Right. Here are the main pieces of hardware you'll come across. (See figure 5)

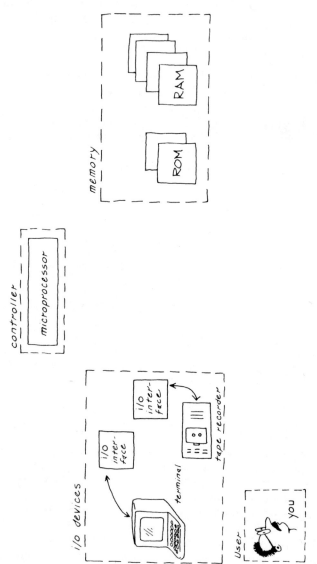

Figure 5 Major pieces of hardware in the conceptual computer

Q 35   I could swear I've seen a picture something like this in one of the magazines, . . . but . . . Oh! I know what's different. Instead of **controller,** they called it a **cpu.** What's the difference?

A   No difference. **Cpu** stands for Central Processing Unit. It's a term from the old days. **Controller, processor, cpu** — take your choice.

How is memory organized?

Q 36   Also, I've come across the terms you've written in the memory box there. **ROM** stands for read-only memory and **RAM** stands for random-access memory, right?

A   Right. Sort of strange, isn't it?

Q 37   What?

A   Well, computer memories are organized like the little mail boxes they used to have in post offices. There are a number of **locations,** each of which can hold a certain (fixed) amount of information. Each location has an **address** (a sort of a name) that can be used to refer to it.

Q 38   And ''certain amount of information'' means what?

A   OK. Let's see. In the Prognosticator, one of the basic units of information was whether one of the switches was thrown or not. Two possibilities, right?

Q 39   Yes. You're leading up to binary numbers, I bet.

A   In a way. We could just as well write down a **1** when a switch is closed and a **0** when it's open as to say ''thrown'' or ''not thrown'', right? It conveys the same information. In fact, we could use a shorthand way of referring to *all* the switches on the Prognosticator, and write, oh say, **011** to mean ''the left switch isn't thrown, the middle switch is thrown, and the right switch is thrown.'' Then we could see right away that there are exactly eight different possible settings of the switches, from 000 to 001 to 010 to 011 to 100 to 101 to 110 to 111. Since it doesn't matter what signs we put on the switches, we might as well think of the eight different switch settings as being eight different patterns of 1's and 0's, without caring what they ''mean''. If I asked you how the switches were set and you told me ''011'', then you would have given me three **bits** of information.

Q 40   I didn't follow all that. If I told you the settings of the three switches . . .

A   Before you tell me, all I know is that each switch might be thrown or not thrown, either **1** or **0.** In information theory terms, a **bit** is the amount of information required to answer a question which has two (equally likely) possible answers. Since in telling me "011" you answered three such questions, you gave me three **bits of information**.

Q 41 Where does the word **bit** come from? Does it just mean "small"?

A I think it's a contraction of **binary digit**. In our normal, **decimal** number system, there are ten digits, 0 1 2 3 4 5 6 7 8 9. In the **binary** number system, there are just two digits, 0 1. So one **bit**, or one **bit of information**, is just enough information to specify one of the two binary digits.*

Q 42 Why use binary numbers?

A Why don't you just write that down and ask it later? Let's not get in a jumble here — let's finish going over the basic pieces of hardware, OK?

Q

A Most of the memories used on most microcomputers are organized so that each memory location stores eight bits, and somewhere along the line, IBM (in their infinite wisdom) came up with the term **byte** to describe eight bits.

Q 43 In the ads, when it says that a computer comes with 2K bytes of RAM, that tells how many memory locations there are?

A Essentially. It tells how many of *what size.*
The **K** there is another piece of quirky terminology. It means 1024. So 2K bytes is 2 x 1024 = 2048 bytes of memory, which is 2048 x 8 = 16 384 bits of storage.

Q 44 1024 is used instead of 1000 because . . .

A . . . because it's 2^{10}, and it's close to 1000 which is usually represented by **k** (for **kilo**).
OK. Now how do you use memory?
To **store a value in memory** means to insert an eight bit pattern into one of the memory locations. To **fetch a value** means to transfer a copy of the pattern in some memory location into the controller. When you store a byte in memory, of course, it wipes out whatever pattern used to be there.

Q 45 How do you specify which particular memory location? I know each one has an address, but . . .

A The **address** is specified as another binary number. The controllers used on the more popular home computers identify specific memory locations by supplying a 16 bit binary value, a **16 bit address**.

*details of binary Q 238-256

Q 46   But that's twice as big as the value that can be stored in a memory location!

A   There's no denying that. Does that bother you for some reason?

Q 47   I'm trying to think back. You said that the program is stored in memory. And one of the instructions you listed tested some value to see if it was zero, and if it was, said something about taking the next instruction from a specific place in memory . . .

A   I see what you're getting at. If an instruction has to refer to a spot in memory, and it takes 16 bits to specify a memory adress, and only eight bits fit in one memory location, then . . .

Q 48   Then how can the instruction itself fit in memory? (See figure 6)

A   I didn't say that each instruction in a program would fit in a single byte, did I? Sorry if I gave you that impression. No. Some of the basic machine instructions take up several bytes. Some take only one, some take two, instructions that include a reference to a specific spot in memory take three.

A 49   Doesn't that make things more complicated?

A   Yes.

Q 50   Then why do it?

A   It results in a more efficient use of memory. As far as I know, the first wide-scale use of **byte-oriented memory** and **variable length instructions** was on the old IBM 1401's. But microprocessor design seems to have been more influenced by the IBM 360 series (which is also a byte-oriented, variable instruction length design). But we're getting off the track again.

Q 51   You seemed to think I'd see something funny in the words RAM and ROM, I believe.

A   Oh yeh. **RAM** stands for **Random-access memory,** supposedly. **Random access** means that no matter what memory location you want to get at (choose one at random), once you specify the address, it takes the same length of time to get the value there. There are other kinds of memories for which that's not the case, for instance, if you store values on a cassette tape, you can get the values stored at the front of the tape faster than you can get the ones stored farther in on the tape. On a tape, you have **sequential access.**
       So here's the funny thing. RAM is random access memory, and so is ROM! When people say ROM, they really mean **random access memory that the program can take**

Memory is organized into a number of **locations**.
Each location has an **address**.

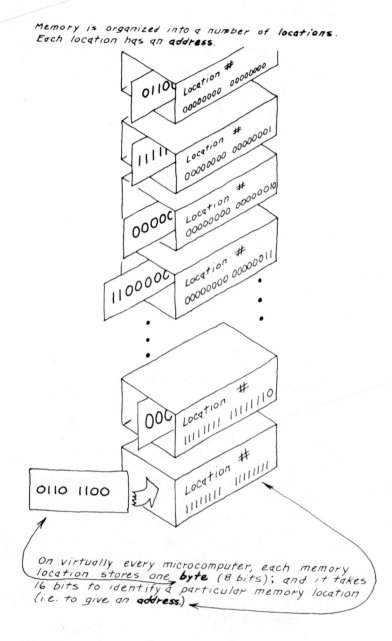

On virtually every microcomputer, each memory
location stores one **byte** (8 bits); and it takes
16 bits to identify a particular memory location
(i.e. to give an **address**.)

Figure 6

values from, but not store anything in. RAM means
random access memory that the program can both read
from and write into.

Q 52   I see. So how did the abbreviations come into being, then?

A   It's a historical thing. Read-only memories came into
popular use a lot later than RAM. I guess since you can't
pronounce RWM (for **read/write memory**), we're stuck
with RAM.

Q 53   Somewhere I came across the term **write-only memory**.

A   It's a joke.

Q 54   Why would you want ROM if your program can't store
things in it?

A   OK. For a long time, the main memory in computers was
core memory. It was made out of ferrite cores, little donut
shaped pieces of magnetic material, one core per bit. You
still hear some people call memory "core" out of habit.

Now core memory has some nice features and some bad
features compared to the newer semiconductor memories
(i.e. the RAM and ROM we've been talking about). The
nicest feature is that no power is needed to maintain the
magnetic field in the cores, so if you turn off the power,
nothing gets lost. When you turn it back on the next day
or the next week, you can just pick up where you left
off. The smaller, less costly semiconductor RAMs we have
now lose the information stored in them if the power is
shut off. (In a few years, RAMs will almost certainly be
available which don't suffer from this drawback.)

[Editor's note: RAM chips are available right now which require so
little power to maintain the information stored in them that flashlight
batteries suffice.]

ROMs, on the other hand, act like core memory in that
shutting off the power doesn't disturb what's stored in
them. So if there are programs you use all the time, you'll
be a lot better off in the long run to have them stored
in ROM so you don't have to wait around to read them
in from tape (or worse, re-enter them by hand) every time
you want to use your system. Make sense?

Q 55   Except for one thing. How do you put these programs
in ROM to begin with?

A   No doubt you've come across weird acronyms like PROM,
EROM, EPROM in the magazines?

Q 56   No doubt.

A   When I said you can't store values into read-only memory,
I meant that in normal operation, your program can't cause
values to be stored there.

With some ROMs, you figure out exactly what you want

stored, and send that off to a company which uses special equipment to (permanently) insert it into the locations on the ROM chips they sell. With other types you can do it yourself by applying the proper voltages for the right length of time to permanently store values by (effectively) blowing fuses at each location that's to store a 1. You can also buy PROM programmer circuits which allow you to store and re-store values in PROM chips (PROM = **programmable read-only memory**), but it takes thousands of times longer than it does to store values in RAM.

There are a lot more details, but I think you know enough now to be able to figure out what the ads are talking about.

Q 57   Maybe one more question about different kinds of memory circuits?

A   Fire away.

Q 58   The difference between **static** and **dynamic** memory? At first I thought that was just another way to describe ROM and RAM.

A   Oh. Because **static** sounds like the values are stored statically or something. No, **static** and **dynamic** memories are both types of RAM and both lose whatever is in them when the power is cut. Another way to say it is that RAM memories are **volatile** and ROM is **nonvolatile**. Dynamic RAMs are so volatile that if left to themselves, they'd lose what they were storing after a few milliseconds, even with the power still on! So that doesn't happen, special circuitry that **refreshes** the memory about once every two milliseconds must be provided.

Q 59   Sounds a lot more complicated. I suppose it's cheaper to make dynamic RAMs?

A   So far. Also, the circuit for each bit of storage is simpler, so the chip manufacturers can squeeze more memory on a single chip when it's dynamic.

What do the i/o devices do, and how do they do it?

Q 60   All right. Let's get back to Figure 5. In the box marked i/o devices, you have two boxes that say **i/o interface**. First of all, what's an **interface**?

A   **Interface** is a very general concept. Any time one system, one process, interacts with another, there's a potential problem. What if the outputs of the first process aren't legitimate inputs to the second?

You could think of a (human) translator as an interface between two people who don't speak the same language. The translator accepts a statement in the first person's

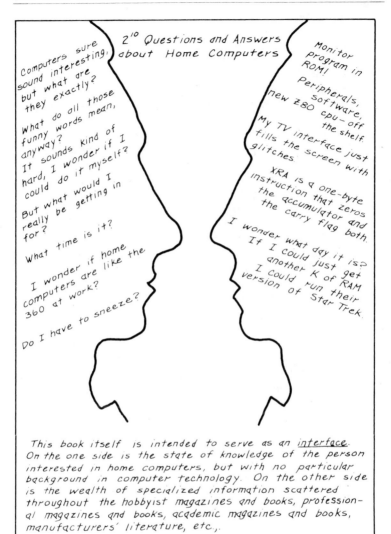

Computers sure sound interesting, but what are they exactly?

What do all those funny words mean, anyway?

It sounds kind of hard, I wonder if I could do it myself?

But what would I really be getting in for?

What time is it?

I wonder if home computers are like the 360 at work?

Do I have to sneeze?

2^{10} Questions and Answers about Home Computers

Monitor program in ROM!

Peripherals, software, new Z80 cpu — off the shelf.

My TV interface just fills the screen with glitches.

XRA is a one-byte instruction that zeros the accumulator and the carry flag both.

I wonder what day it is? If I could just get another K of RAM I could run their version of Star Trek.

This book itself is intended to serve as an *interface*. On the one side is the state of knowledge of the person interested in home computers, but with no particular background in computer technology. On the other side is the wealth of specialized information scattered throughout the hobbyist magazines and books, professional magazines and books, academic magazines and books, manufacturers' literature, etc.,

Figure 7

language and produces an equivalent output which the second person can understand. (See figure 7)

Q 61   Could you say that a pencil is an interface between your hand and a piece of paper?

A   Why not? The word **interface** is used in all sorts of situations. Sometimes programmers write programs that they call interfaces when they have two programs already written, and want to use the two in conjunction, but the first program's outputs aren't in quite the right form for the second program to use. But more to the point here, **interface** refers to hardware which is used to hook some sort of peripheral device to a computer system.

Q 62   **Peripheral** means i/o device?

A   Basically. Something other than the controller, memory, or the stuff which directly supports them (like the power supply). Yeh, it means i/o device.

Q 63   All right. So you show a tape recorder hooked to an i/o interface there. [Figure 5] What does the interface do in that case?

A   Well, there's two problems it has to solve. First of all, the controller (typically) expects an eight bit value (one byte) from the i/o device at a time, just as it accepts one byte at a time from memory. But with the recording scheme used on virtually all tape recorders hooked to home computers, the value is spread out on the tape one bit at a time. The tape recorder reads it one bit at a time as the tape passes under the head.

Q 64   So? Obviously, the controller has to wait until all eight bits have been read.

A   That's not as simple as it sounds. The 8080 microprocessor (the most popular at this point) can do over 6000 additions in the time it takes the typical hobbyist tape recorder to read one byte, and no two cassette tape recorders run at exactly the same speed, so the controller has no way of knowing how long to wait.

Q 65   What do *additions* have to do with anything? Oh. You just used that as an example of how fast the controller is.

A   Yeh.

Q 66   All right. So you need some kind of interface to, what . . . read one bit at a time until it has eight of them, and then what?

A   Well, then it has to put out some sort of signal that the controller can sense that tells that a byte is ready. When the value is ready, the controller can read it in one chunk.

Q 67   And everybody's happy.

A   Almost. Once the controller has the data value, it has to send a signal back to the interface to inform it of the fact that it can forget the last value and set about assembling the next one from the tape.

Q 68   But the tape's running all this while? Or does it go in spurts?

A   The tape keeps running — but there's plenty of time. It's a little hard to imagine at first, but you'll get used to it.

The processes inside a computer, the purely electronic operations, happen tremendously faster than anything that involves mechanical movement.

Let's take an example. Let's use the same assumptions as before, but slow everything down equally so that it now takes the micro-processor *one second to perform an addition*.

Then it would take the tape recorder 137 hours to read in this sentence. Quite a speed differential, huh?

Q   Wow.

[Editor's note: Upon request, A supplied this justification for his statement, which may interest some readers.

"The DAD (Double precision ADd, or 16-bit add) instruction takes 10 clock cycles on the 8080. Each clock cycle takes something like .5 microseconds. So each addition takes 5 microseconds. I assumed that the tape recorder scheme runs at 300 baud [see Q 606 for a definition of **baud**] and uses 10 bits per character (7 bits per ASCII character; plus parity, start and stop bits). That gives

$$\frac{1 \text{ addition}}{5 \times 10^{-6} \text{ seconds}} \quad x \quad \frac{10 \text{ bits per character}}{300 \text{ bits per second}} \quad = \quad 6667 \frac{\text{additions}}{\text{character}}$$

But for fun, we're assuming that everything in the universe has slowed down so that each addition takes one whole second. There are 74 characters in the sentence (counting blanks, of course), so that gives

$$\frac{1 \text{ second}}{\text{addition}} \quad x \quad 6.667 \times 10^{3} \frac{\text{additions}}{\text{character}} \quad x \quad 74 \text{ characters} \times \frac{1 \text{ minute}}{60 \text{ seconds}} \times$$

$$x \quad \frac{1 \text{ hour}}{60 \text{ minutes}} \quad = \quad 137 \text{ hours.]}$$

A   In Figure 5, I also showed an interface for the terminal. It makes a similar sort of translation. Of course, when someone is typing in values, the timing problem is even worse, because who types at a constant speed?

Q 69   I know *I* don't . . . But the same sort of thing would work here too, right? The interface waits until the byte is ready, tells the controller, so on?

A   I'd like to just say "yes", and go on, but I suppose I should tell you a few more details.

You might think that the easiest way to build a keyboard would be so that when you hit a key, that directly results in a byte (identifying the key you hit) being sent down eight wires (one bit per wire) to the interface which then

30,00,0,00.0   *3 million yrs*

10,000,000,000,000

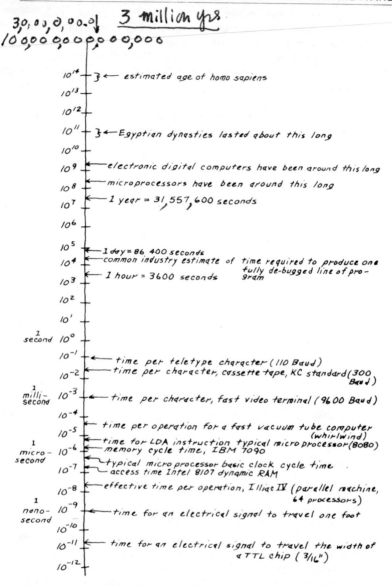

10^{14} ⊃ ← estimated age of homo sapiens

10^{13}

10^{12}

10^{11} ⊃ ← Egyptian dynasties lasted about this long

10^{10}

10^9 ← electronic digital computers have been around this long

10^8 ← microprocessors have been around this long

10^7 ← 1 year = 31,557,600 seconds

10^6

10^5 ← 1 day = 86,400 seconds

10^4 ← common industry estimate of time required to produce one fully de-bugged line of pro-gram

10^3 ← 1 hour = 3600 seconds

10^2

10^1

1 second 10^0

10^{-1} ← time per teletype character (110 Baud)

10^{-2} ← time per character, cassette tape, KC standard (300 Baud)

1 milli-second 10^{-3} ← time per character, fast video terminal (9600 Baud)

10^{-4}

10^{-5} ← time per operation for a fast vacuum tube computer (whirlwind)

1 micro-second 10^{-6} ← time for LDA instruction typical micro processor (8080) memory cycle time, IBM 7090

10^{-7} ← typical micro processor basic clock cycle time. access time Intel 8107 dynamic RAM

10^{-8} ← effective time per operation, Illiac IV (parallel machine, 64 processors)

1 nano-second 10^{-9} ← time for an electrical signal to travel one foot

10^{-10}

10^{-11} ← time for an electrical signal to travel the width of a TTL chip (3/16")

10^{-12}

Table 2   Time Table

informs the controller that it's got a new value, etc. Then
when you hit the next key, a different pattern gets sent
down the wires, and so on. But . . . [Editor's note: It is
not at all clear what A is thinking of here. It is quite common
to interface keyboards to microcomputers in exactly this
manner. The serial interfacing technique he explains below
is also used, and is the usual method to interface to
complete terminals; but he seems to have forgotten that
in many home computer applications, keyboards are pur-
chased separately and connected through parallel interfaces.]

Q 70   Wait. Before you go on. I know you said there's plenty
of time for the controller to respond before you can hit
the next key, but what *if?*

A   What if the controller doesn't get around to processing
the first character before you hit the second key?

Q   Yes.

A   It depends on the details. On some interfaces, everything
but the most recent character gets lost, on others, everything but the first. But you'll be able to tell if the terminal
is running in the full duplex mode.

Q 71   Maybe I'm sorry I asked. What's the **full duplex mode?**

A   Whoa . . . there *are* a lot of specialized terms in all this,
aren't there? OK. **Duplex** itself means two-way transmission. If you operate a terminal in the **half-duplex mode,**
then when you strike a key, the resulting signal goes two
places. It goes to the interface in the microcomputer, of
course, and it also goes to the equipment within the
terminal that displays or prints the character you hit. In
the **full-duplex mode,** when you strike a key, it sends
the appropriate signal down the wire to the interface. Then,
after the controller has plucked the character (the byte
representing the character) out of the interface, it immediately sends a copy of the character back out to the terminal
(that's called **echoing** the character) at which point the
terminal displays or prints it. So, to answer your question,
if for some reason, the controller doesn't get around to
processing one character before the next comes in, if you
were running in the full-duplex mode, you could tell that
something was wrong because you'd see only one character printed even though you'd hit two keys.

Q 72   I see. So if you were in the half-duplex mode you wouldn't
know anything was wrong . . . because the character
would appear on the screen or whatever even if the
controller didn't get it. So why would you ever want a
terminal that worked in the half-duplex mode? Oh . . . it

must be . . .

A   . . . cheaper.

Let's see. I was about to explain that instead of characters being transmitted to the interface all at once like you might think, actually they're usually spread out over time, and sent one bit at a time, over one wire (well, one wire plus a ground connection). That's why interfaces that are sold for terminals are called **serial interfaces.** The data comes in serially or **sequentially.**

Q 73   Why, exactly?

A   Historically, the Teletype was the most widely used terminal, so virtually all computers came equipped with interfaces to Teletypes. And Teletypes, I suspect, were originally designed to work as automated telegraph systems, so they operate serially. At first, video terminals were sold as replacements for Teletypes (you still hear to term **glass Teletype**) so they were built to have the same electrical characteristics as Teletypes. Also, there are industry-wide standards on serial data communications, but let's not go into this too far at this point, OK? It's not something that you have to be concerned about in much detail unless you're planning to build an interface yourself. (See figure 8)

Q 74   All right. I'll save the questions I still have for later. Why don't you finish going over Figure 5?

The controller and what's in it

A   OK. The last box is the one that says **controller.** That includes a microprocessor, and any necessary support circuitry.

Q 75   Like a power supply?

Q   No, the **power supply** isn't considered when people talk about the functional subparts of a computer, just like no one bothers to mention the box **(**or **chassis)** that holds the physical components. All of the parts we've talked about require power.

Q 76   Well then?

A   Oh, most microprocessors need extra circuitry to provide timing signals (called a **clock,** or **clocking pulses,** etc.). The microprocessor's internal workings have to be coordinated to work properly, and the task of providing the necessary synchronization signals is usually left to extra circuitry.

Q 77   What kind of inner workings does a microprocessor have? What needs to be coordinated?

A   OK. I guess this is a good time to start into that.

peripherals Table 5 near Q606

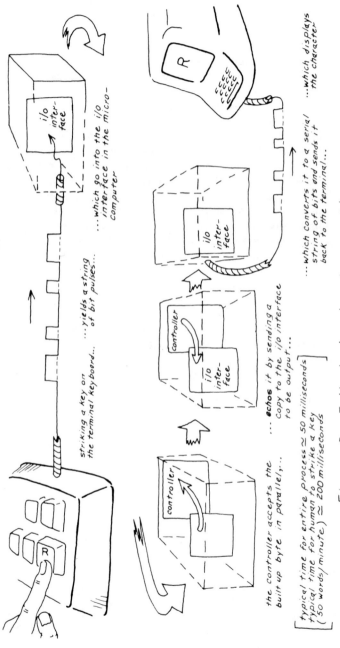

striking a key on
the terminal keyboard...

...yields a string
of bit pulses...

...which go into the i/o
interface in the micro-
computer

the controller accepts the
built up byte in parallel;...

...echos it by sending a
copy to the i/o interface
to be output...

...which converts it to a serial
string of bits and sends it
back to the terminal...

...which displays
the character

typical time for entire process ≅ 50 milliseconds
typical time for human to strike a key
(50 words/minute) ≅ 200 milliseconds

Figure 8 Full duplex input operation

Let's think it through. You remember the sorts of things the controller does in a computer system, so let's see if we can figure out what has to be in it.

Q 78 The main thing I remember is just that it carries out commands . . . it carries out the program.

A OK. If it's going to get commands from memory, it must have some way of telling what memory address to go to for the next instruction, right?

Q 79 Something to keep track of where it is in the program? Is that what you mean?

A Exactly. So we'll need some place to store addresses, that is, 16-bit values. That place is called the **program counter.** For some reason, memory locations that are in the controller itself are called **registers,** so the program counter is a 16-bit register. Now. When the controller receives the next part of the program from memory, it has to save it somewhere while it "figures out" which instruction it got. So there's another register called the **instruction register** that stores the command the controller is currently working on.

Since the controller has to **decode** ("figure out") commands, it needs circuitry to do that and to generate the appropriate signals to carry out the command. That circuitry is usually lumped under the title **instruction decoder and control unit.** So far we have

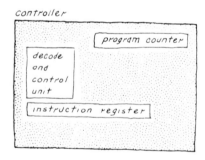

Q 80 The instruction register has to have at least 24 bits in it, right?

A No, where'd you get that idea? On byte oriented machines, it stores one byte . . . 8 bits.

Q 81 Then I'm still confused about something. You said that some instructions are more than one byte long, right? You said that some instructions have to include memory addresses.

A   Oh. I see what you're getting at. I guess I wasn't very clear about that. Instructions can be one, two, or three bytes in length, all right, but the first byte is always enough to specify the type of instruction. The first byte contains what's called the **op code,** that is, a pattern of 1's and 0's that serves as a code for the command that's to be performed. So the instruction register only needs to be big enough to store that. The other parts of multi-byte instructions, which give the rest of the instruction, are stored in other parts of the controller. For instance, addresses are brought into the controller and stored in a 16-bit register called the **address buffer.** Since that register is used in other ways too, you don't usually think of it as being part of the instruction register.

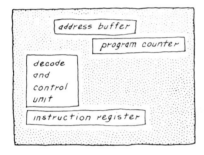

OK?

Q   Think so.

A   Another thing the controller has to do is carry out arithmetic operations, so we need some kind of **arithmetic unit,** and associated with that, we need another register to store the results the arithmetic unit comes up with. That register is called the **accumulator.**

Q 82   Why wouldn't the controller just store the result back in memory?

A   Two reasons. First, it's likely that succeeding instructions are going to operate on the result you just got, so it saves time to have the result in the controller already.

Second, if you wanted the result stored in memory, you'd have to give the address of where you wanted it to go as part of the arithmetic operation instruction, right?

Q 83   So?

A   If the instruction includes the address of one of the values that to be used in the computation in the instruction, and you include the address of where to store the result as well, you'd have an instruction that's five bytes long. Starts to get unwieldly, overly complicated. Maybe the real answer is "it's just not done that way".

Q   Let me brood over that for a while.

A   Gladly. Anyway, now our controller looks like this

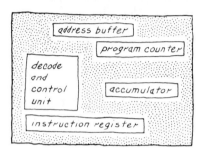

Another thing we need is a way for the control unit to tell something about the value that's currently in the accumulator. Since there are instructions that do different things depending on whether a result is zero, negative, positive, and so on, there's another register called the **condition code register** (or, alternatively, the **status flag register**)* which stores information about the most recent result.

status flags Q 618

Q 84 How long is this going to go on?

A   Just one more thing. All microprocessors provide a few more registers right on the chip. Some of them are used for specialized ways of accessing memory (**index registers,** * **stack pointer registers**). Some of them are there for the programmer to use as he or she sees fit.

Q 85 Do those have special names like everything else seems to?

A   Oh, not really. On the 8080 microprocessor, they're called **general purpose registers,** on the 6800 the extra register takes the form of another **accumulator.** But those details won't concern us until we talk about specific chips. Oh. Sometimes you see general purpose registers called **data counters,** in analogy to the program counter, but that

index register Q 654

8080 organization Figure 59; Q 614
6800 organization Figure 60; Q 624
Z-80 Figure 61

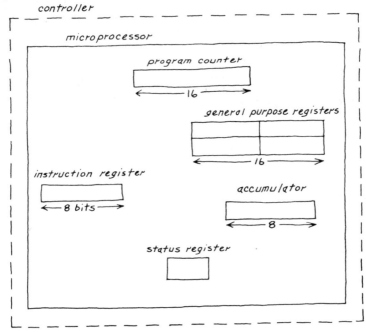

Figure 9 Registers are storage locations within the controller itself.

doesn't seem reasonable to me, since that's just one of the things you can use them for.

Q 86   Would this be a good time to say some more about how the controller actually gets value from memory?

How are the parts of the conceptual computer tied together?

A   OK. Let me start by re-drawing Figure 5, because I deliberately left out some things. In the original sketch, I didn't show any interconnections between the three major functional parts, and obviously, there have to be some.
The most common scheme nowadays is to tie the various parts of a computer system together using sets of wires called **busses**.
There are usually three different busses in microcomputers, a **data bus**, an **address bus**, and a **control bus**, so I'll re-draw the thing that way. (See figure 10)

A 87   Happen to know where the word **bus** came from?

A   Let me think a minute. The idea of a bus is that it provides a common means of communication to a number of different components. Ever since I can remember, the big copper bars that you tie all the ground connections to on big electrical equipment have been called **bus bars** . . . I suppose it might be from that.

Q 88   I'll bet it's from the Latin word ''omnibus'' that means ''for all''.

A   Jeez! Where did you pick that up?

Q   I took Latin in high school.

A   Huh. I took typing instead.
       Anyway, here's the idea [Figure 10].

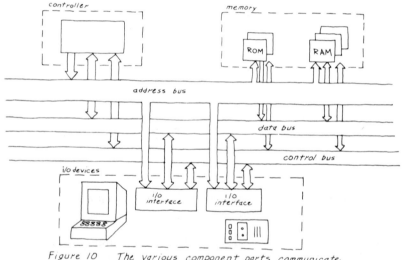

Figure 10   The various component parts communicate through busses.

I've drawn them in a sort of formal way, but they're basically just a bunch of wires.

Q 89   And you what . . . You use the three busses differently, for different things.

A   Right. You'll notice that I drew some of the arrows with two heads. That's to show that signals can be transmitted in both directions. (Such a bus is said to be **bi-directional**.) For instance, values on the data bus can be sent *into* RAM (when the controller wants to store a byte in memory), or they can be brought *from* RAM onto the data bus, and then into the controller (when the controller wants to read from memory). Since the data bus is transmitting in one byte chunks, it consists of eight wires (plus ground), and it's said to be **eight bits wide.** (As before, I'm assuming we're talking about a byte oriented system.) I'm sure you can guess how "wide" the address bus is going to be.

Q 90   I guess it's 16 bits wide. But I have a couple of questions. You drew the busses "open-ended". That's . . .

A   That's to show one of the nice features of a bus organization. If you get more memory at a later date, or add other interfaces, you can just hang it on the busses without having to mess around with the parts you have already. Within limits, of course.

Q 91   My other question was why you show the address bus going to the i/o interfaces. Addresses just specify memory locations, don't they?

A   No, actually, the address lines can be used to select a particular i/o device.
There's two ways i/o instructions are handled in microprocessors. On some microprocessors, there are **explicit input and output instructions** which include a **device number** (or **device code**) as part of the instruction.

Q 92   I'm getting tired of you always qualifying everything. Why don't you name some of them?

A   What do you mean? Why didn't you tell me earlier? What do you want? For me to name the specific instructions?

Q 93   No, name some of the microprocessors.

A   OK, but I'm not sure what use . . . oh well. Let's see. For instance, the Fairchild F-8, the Zilog Z-80, and the Intel 8080 all have explicit i/o instructions.
So when a microprocessor like the 8080 is carrying out an i/o instruction, the device code (I think Intel calls it an **i/o port specification**) is placed on the address bus. So there won't be any confusion, the controller also sends a signal (through the control bus) that signifies that the value on the address lines is to be treated as a device code and . . .

Q 94   "confusion"?

A   Let me finish . . . and not as a memory address.

Q   Ah.

A   OK. Now there's another way of doing i/o which can be used on the microprocessors I just mentioned as well as on ones which don't have explicit i/o instructions.

Q 95   Such as?

A   You want more names.
OK, uh, the Motorola 6800, the National Semiconductor

PACE, and the Mostek 6502 are all microprocessors that don't have explicit i/o instructions. (Oh, I might say that all of the ones I've mentioned are byte oriented except the PACE, which is organized around 16 bit words.)

Here's the idea. Instead of reserving all of the available addresses to refer to memory, you hook things up so that some addresses access i/o interfaces. Then the processor can refer to specific i/o devices in the same way it refers to specific memory locations.

Q 96   But there must be some difference.

A   You, as a programmer, obviously have to know which is which, but it doesn't make any difference as far as the controller is concerned.

Q 97   Why not?

A   Let me give you an example of how busses serve as communications pathways between the controller and the other components. That should give a feeling for what I'm talking about.

I'm sure that since you've read the ads in the magazines you bought, you know that there are all sorts of different kinds of RAM chips available, different sizes, different technologies, different numbers of pins on the chips, and more to the present point, different speeds.

Q   True.

A   Some of the less expensive RAM chips, in fact, run slower than the microprocessors you might want to use them with.

Q 98   Meaning that . . .

A   Although the controller issues the same signals to fetch a value from memory, different memory chips take more or less time to respond, so something has to give somewhere. Otherwise the controller might just go on it's merry way, assuming it received a value from memory when in fact the RAM hasn't had enough time to retrieve the desired value and place it on the data bus.

What's done in that case is to add some additional circuitry to the board holding the RAM chips, and use the control bus to communicate to the controller that it's going to have to wait a while. If a memory location on that board is accessed, that additional circuitry sends a signal (on one of the lines in the control bus, typically called the **READY line**) which stops all activity in the controller long enough for the memory to produce the desired value. Then it changes the READY signal back to its normal state, and the controller starts up again, exactly where it left off, none the wiser that anything has happened. As far as the

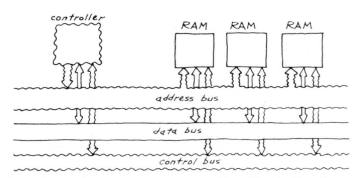

1. Controller initiates a memory read operation. It puts the address on the address bus and signals through the control bus that this is a memory operation (not i/o) and that this is a **read** (not a **write**)

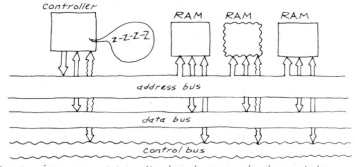

2. The RAM card containing the desired memory location initiates the read operation and signals the controller to wait.

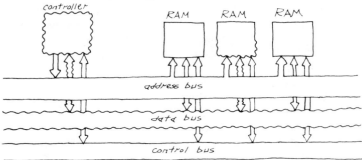

3. The data is finally available on the data bus, the WAIT signal is removed, and the controller carries on.

Figure 11   Sequence of events: getting a value from a RAM that's slower than the microprocessor. Devices that are active are drawn with wiggly lines.

controller is concerned (and the programmer, for that matter), it requested a value from memory, got the result through the data bus, and is ready to go on to the next command.

Q 99 How does the RAM know whether it's supposed to be retrieving a value or storing one?

A You're on your toes today. I did leave that out. The controller has to provide a signal (on yet another line in the control bus) to communicate that to the RAM.

Q 100 I see how it works . . . But it seems kind of, well, wasteful.

A Wasteful?

Q It seems extreme to turn the controller completely off . . . couldn't it be doing something else until the memory responds?

A But the controller can't do anything but carry out instructions in a program, and it has to get each instruction from memory, so you don't have any choice. [Editor's note: This answer is correct as far as it goes. For complete precision it would be necessary to distinguish between **synchronous** and **asynchronous** bus organizations. A seems to have avoided bringing this issue up here; see Q 484-487.]

A few basic buzz words

There's two things we could do now. I think we ought to go over some general ideas about software, but I see that you've got a lot of questions jotted down there. We could cover some of them so you don't get overwhelmed with unanswered questions.

Q 101 Let me ask you some of these. Some of them are pretty general.

A Then let's get to them now.

Q 102 Here's one. In fact, I think it's the first question I asked, and you never really answered it.

A What are we doing here?

Q 103 No, that's not it (but let me write *that* one down).
What does **state** mean, and why are computers made up of **two-state elements**?

A OK. **State** is a really general concept . . . it means **condition** or **status**. In its technical sense, state means something a little stronger — if you tell me the state of a system, then you've told me all I need to know to figure out the future behavior of the system. Remember our Prognosticator?

Q   Yes.

A   OK. Since what the Prognosticator does is completely determined by the position (or we can use the word **state** here too) of the three switches, I can tell you the Prognosticator's state by telling you how the three switches are set. Using the "0 for open, 1 for thrown" notation we used before, I could say "The Prognosticator is in state 011", and you could figure out what it would do.

Q 104 Slow down. Things are getting a little convoluted. When you said we could use the word **state** to refer to each switch . . .

A   Right. All you need to know about a switch is whether it's open or closed. You don't need to know what brand it is, what color it is, what time of day it is . . . So you can describe the state of a switch by telling me either 0 or 1. The switch has two possible states. That's one thing.

Then, since the behavior of the Prognosticator is determined by the settings of the three switches, the state of the Prognosticator as a *whole* can be given in terms of the states of the individual parts, the switches. Each of the switches has two possible states, so the Prognosticator must have eight possible states, ranging from 000 to 001 up to 111.

To carry it a bit further, and to use **state** in a less technical, but still related sense, I could say that the Prognosticator's "prediction" about a specific candidate affects my **state of mind.**

Q 105 Wait . . . I see what you're talking about, but there's one thing. Just knowing the setting of the three switches won't be enough to tell you what the Prognosticator will do if the battery is dead, or the light bulb is burnt out, or . . .

A   True enough. But then the rules of operation of the parts would have changed. You'd have a different system. But you're making a good point — what needs to be counted as part of the state depends on what you're trying to do, what aspects of the system you care about.

When we say that a computer is made up of **two-state elements,** we mean that to figure out what will happen next, all we need to know (in addition to the rules of operation) is which of the two possible states each element is in. Of course, in any but the most primitive computers, there are so many elements that describing the computer's operation that way gets really awkward. But it *is* possible to figure out what a computer is going to do, given the

state of each subpart. We don't need to know what the
elements are made of. They could be coins (head or tails),
relays (open or closed), electrical circuits (high or low
voltage), or iron bars (magnetized one way or the other).
On the other hand, if we want to know how *fast* a computer
is going to do the next thing, or how much it *weighs,*
or how *big* it is, we *do* need to know something about
what the elements are made of.

Let's see. What was your other question back there?

Q 106 Why *two*-state elements? Why couldn't the elements have
ten states, or a hundred?

A   They could. It's just easier to build reliable electronics that
have only two different states. That way, little variations
in the constituent parts, or changes in temperature have
less chance of causing erroneous results. As long as you
can take as many two-state elements as you want, you
can make as many different overall states, as many distinctions as you need, so it's not a limiting factor.

Q 107 Somehow I don't think I'm following what you're saying
. . . It just seems harder to make things out of binary
numbers . . . I mean, I'm used to thinking in terms of
powers of ten, not two. After all I have ten fingers.

A   Yes, but you have *two* arms, and you're used to thinking
in binary (two-valued) distinctions like left/right, up/
down, yes/no, hello/goodbye, heaven/hell, female/
male, true/false, on and on . . . Anyway, if you really don't
want to learn the details of binary numbers and how
two state elements work, you don't have to use computers.
You can buy already assembled equipment, and use a
higher-level programming language. Then you can do all
your numerical problems in decimal.

Q 108 Here's another question . . . well, it's more of a complaint,
I guess. Why do computer people use so much jargon?
It seems like half the battle is figuring out all the specialized
words.

A   Oh, I don't think computer people use much more jargon
than most other special interest groups. Have you ever
tried to understand a surfer who was describing the wave
conditions? Or asked an art critic what it was that she
liked about a particular painting? Or overheard two carpen-
ters talking about a job?

It's just natural that concepts that are used a lot will tend
to be given short names, so that people in the know can
communicate quickly and efficiently.

Of course, there's another side to it — highly specialized
languages can also be used to exclude outsiders, to prove

that you're a member of the cult, to hide your lack of real understanding. People who really know what they're doing don't have to speak in code, because they're not afraid to have someone understand them.

Did I tell you about the malfunction I had in my **solar dehydration system?**

Q 109 Wait . . . you mean your . . . SDS?

A Right! (My clothesline broke.)

Q 110 Since you keep bringing it up, what's a **system?**

A Oh boy. Let's see. **System** is a very general word used to describe anything that has subparts, whose overall characteristics arise from the interaction of its constituent parts. More, when you call something a system, you mean that it can be understood in isolation from the rest of the universe, that its interaction with the environment can be described simply (as **input** and **output**). Now, when you use this idea to talk about computers, you're on pretty safe ground, because the component parts of computers are *designed* to work that way. It would be horrible if you couldn't treat each subpart more or less independently, if adding on one more chunk of memory meant that you had to go back and rewire everything else. Instead, we are told by the manufacturer what type of inputs the new subunit needs, and what sorts of output it will provide, and our troubles are lessened.

When people try to apply "systems thinking" to natural phenomena, though, things can get very complicated very fast, because the effects caused by one subpart may depend on so many aspects of so many other subparts that you don't gain very much by trying to break things into subparts to begin with. That means that although using the word might make sense, it may not be very useful. Sometimes it's used just because it sounds modern. I saw a truck recently that said "WEATHER SYSTEMS" on its side in huge red letters. If you read the fine print, you discovered that it was a company that installed furnaces.

You'll gradually come to see what people mean when they use the word **system.** It doesn't mean anything magic. Usually it just refers to something whose behavior can be conveniently specified in terms of how outputs (effects you can measure) relate to inputs.

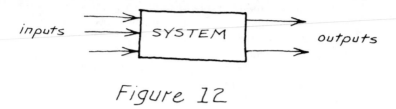

Figure 12

Q 111 . . . and when you started I got the feeling that you weren't
going to be able to think of anything to say. Oh well.
So a computer is a system because it has a lot of parts
that act together. All right. But then what's an **operating
system?** I've seen that in several places, but it doesn't
seem to refer to any kind of equipment.

A   Well, a system doesn't have to be made up of physical
equipment. A group of related beliefs is sometimes called
a "belief system", for example.
Programs can be thought of as systems, especially when
they are organized as a number of interacting subpro-
grams. An **operating system** is a program (or group of
programs) which helps the user to interact with the computer, to help operate it. It makes it easier to enter, run,
or alter programs, so on.
Just to make things more confusing, people often refer
to a particular computer plus its peripherals plus its software as **the system.**

Q 112 As in "you can't beat the system"?

A   Heh. Not exactly. In fact, that's part of the fun of having
a home computer. If you don't like the system you've got,
you can change it.
Anyway, I get the feeling that if people keep using the
word so broadly, pretty soon it won't mean anything at
all. Maybe in twenty years we'll think back fondly to the
good old days when everything was so simple, when
people thought everything was a system.

Q 113 I've got another question written down here . . . oh. Back
in Table 1, you have the term **systems program.**

A   Well, an **operating system** is an example of a **systems
program.**

Q 114 Can you describe that more systematically?

A   It *is* a mess, isn't it . . . The **system** in **systems program**
refers to the whole thing — computer, terminals, software.
So a **systems program** is a program that does something
that helps you use the overall computer system. For

example, you might have a program that takes characters you type on the terminal, converts them into a memory address, and then prints the contents of that address back out on the terminal.

The **system** in **operating system** refers to the program itself.

Q 115 Let's drop it, all right? The word **system** is starting to just sound like a hissing noise.

A   It *is* a buzz word, that's for sure.

Q 116 A **buzz word**?

A   Yeh. A **buzz word** is a word that doesn't convey much besides the fact that the person using it knows one of the "in" words. Sometimes you run across people who seem to speak in solid buzz words. It can get pretty funny. How about "The system availability status is non-viable."

Q 117 Which means.

A   "The computer, she don't work."

The term **buzz word** seems really appropriate. When you hear a buzz word once too often, instead of having a sense of meaning in your head, you just have a dull buzz, like you drank one too many beers on a sunny afternoon. [Is **buzz word** a buzz word?]

What hardware do I need?

Q 118 Looking through the ads, it seems like terminals cost more than the microcomputers themselves.

A   Well, you can buy a keyboard plus circuitry that lets you use the keyboard for input and your TV set for output for about $150-$250*. Sometimes you can find ancient Teletypes for less than that, but you'd better be prepared to do some circuit design and repair work yourself in that case.

Q 119 But you do need something like that. Right? You said that using the switches on the computer itself is too restricted.

A   If it has switches at all. Yeh, if you're going to do any amount of programming at all, you're going to have to get some kind of terminal.

Of course, some people are just interested in learning how to design things with microprocessors, and they can get away with a lot less hardware.

Back in the old days you had a slim chance of doing without decent i/o devices, but . . .

* peripherals Table 5

a sample of representative products Figure 58

Q 120 What do you mean?

A   Well, I guess you know that some of the early machines
          were made out of electric relays? Whole big boxes of them.
          Well, what do I mean *early*? Did you ever see inside a
          pin-ball machine? They're special purpose relay com-
          puters. Anyway, what I was getting at was that I knew
          some people who used to trouble-shoot relay machines
          by listening to how they were clicking!

Q 121 Come on.

A   No, really. These were special purpose machines that were
          used to control big lathes. These guys would run a program
          they were familiar with, stand with their ear to the cabinet,
          and swear they could tell where the trouble was. They
          were usually right, too.

Q 122 How long have you been fooling around with computers?

A   A while.
          Then there were the vacuum tube machines. If you could
          stand the heat, you could actually walk up to a specific
          memory location and use a voltmeter to tell what was
          stored there. And now if you pry the top off a RAM chip,
          you can't even see the individual circuit components with
          the proverbial naked eye.

Q 123 That's all very interesting, but let's get back to the topic.
          There are so many different microprocessors, microcom-
          puter kits, microcomputer ''systems'', so on, for sale, I
          feel lost. You keep talking about all of them at once. Can
          you give me some kind of guidelines or some idea about
          how I'd go about picking one?

A   Hmmm. Well (surprise) first of all, it depends on what
          you want to *do* with computers. Here's a chart I made
          up that should help.
          I guess in a way, the hobby computer, home computer
          field has a lot in common with the first days of Hi-Fi and
          stereo. It's obvious that the time is ripe, there are an
          incredible number of people who are interested, but things
          haven't settled down yet.*
          To get started in home computing right now without
          spending a lot of money ($ 2000, say), you have to have
          some of the old pioneer spirit. I'd guess that in a few
          years, things will be a lot easier for the beginner. But right
          now, you'd better not be afraid to learn a little digital
          electronics to get your kit working the way the manufac-
          turer tells you it will.
          Actually, things are a lot better than in early days of Hi-Fi.
          Computers have been used in industry and research for

          * specifics on two kits Q 548-604

Table 3

type of systems	hardware	for instance	price range (late 1976)	range of applications
single chip	microprocessor	Motorola M6800, Intel 8080, Zilog Z-80, RCA COS/MAC, Fairchild F8, Mostek 6502, Signetics 2650, Texas Instruments 9900, National Semiconductor PACE, etc.	$10 ~ $100	tie tack, conversation piece
microcomputer / trainer	(typically) one board; microprocessor; approx. 1K memory; hex key-board, or switches mounted on board	KIM-1, ELF, MIKE, AMT 2650, Intel SDK-80, Mostek Survival, RCA Microtutor, etc., plus power supply	$50 ~ $400	learn about microprocessor design and hardware; prototype circuits; can be used for control applications
basic microcomputer	chassis, power supply, microprocessor, 2-4K memory, i/o interface; if this front panel then switches and lights. If not, then ROM.	Altair 680, Altair 8800, SWTPC 6800, Imsai 8080, Apple, Baby!, Venus F-8, the digital group Z-80, OSI, Sphere, Poly 88, Astral 2000, etc.	$400 (kit) $1200 / $600 $2000 (assembled)	starter system for home computer; program in machine assembly language; can run Tiny Basic; develop small programs; use for complex control applications
home computer	basic microcomputer plus memory plus i/o, memory & i/o available from kit manufacturers plus	Processor Technology, Cromenco, MIKRA-D, MIKOS, Micro-Term, Bodboart, Percom Data, etc., etc.	basic micro plus $500 ~ $1000	all above plus program in Basic, extended Basic; design and write major programs; share programs; communicate with friends through cassette tape; wide range of elaborate games; etc.
super-charged home computer	home computer plus more memory, hard copy output device	hard copy output available from Teletype, modified Selectric, Centronics, MPI, etc.	above plus $350 ~ $3000	all above plus design and develop very large programs (as programs get larger and larger, you start to go crazy without hard-copy listings to pour over)
small business computer	above plus mass storage device	floppy disc, bubble memory, CCD memory, ultra high density tape (at this date only the first is widely available)	above plus $500 ~ $3000	all above plus extensive record keeping (tens of thousands of records and up), large file maintenance

well over a quarter of a century, so it's not as if all this was starting from scratch. You can be fairly certain that anything you buy now will be usable and useful for quite a while, once you get it running. And there are quite a few people with backgrounds in computers all over the country who can help you keep your equipment running in exchange for a chance to play around with it.

Q 124 Your first entry there. What do you mean — if you have a microprocessor chip you can use it as a ''tie tack''?

A   Heh. Just that a microprocessor all by itself simply can't do anything. Not only do you need the right kinds of power supplies, and not only do you need memory, and not only do you need some kind of i/o, but you need something to put it in, and additional circuitry like clock generators, so on. We've already gone over that.

Q 125 Is that why the prices you have listed take such big jumps? Of course. Let me ask this: how much lower are prices going to go?

A   I suppose you're referring to the fact that prices for the chips keep coming down. The Intel 8080 was around $300 a copy not too many years ago, and now you see the same thing for around $15. It seems to be a fact of life in the electronics industry that prices keep dropping for the basic parts. Right now, the only piece of electronics that's a major factor in home computer prices is memory, and memory prices are going to keep coming down. *But I really don't think that the cost of a complete microcomputer* (kit or assembled) *is going to come down.*

Q 126 What?

A   You need the raw materials to build the case out of, you need switches, plugs, wires . . . the cost of those things is increasing. Then there's all the non-hardware costs like design costs, labor of various kinds, writing the instruction manuals, and repair costs on units under warranty. As time goes on, the cost of the digital electronics becomes a less and less significant part of the overall cost. That's already the case in stereo equipment. A $500 stereo receiver may have $40 worth of electronics in it. The biggest cost item is the fancy case with the knobs and dials. The rest of the selling price gets eaten up by the things I mentioned, plus advertising and profit.
Which is all a long-winded way of saying that even if digital electronics does keep getting cheaper and cheaper, I don't think the price of a basic kit is going to be much lower than now.

Q 127 You qualified that. You said "basic" kit.

A   The cost of memory boards from the manufacturers is
         definitely going to come down, because there the electron-
         ics make up a sizable fraction of the current cost.
         [Editor's note: At the Mini/Micro Computer Conference
         and Exposition (Oct. 19-21, 1976, San Francisco) there
         was a session entitled "The Computer Hobbyist" in which
         the panelists (Dr. Adam Osborne of Osborne Associates,
         E. H. Currie of MITS, Paul Terrell of the Byte Shop chain,
         and Jim Warren — editor of Dr. Dobb's Journal) speculated
         on the shape of things to come. The panelists, Currie and
         Terrell especially, held that in the near future the prices
         of complete home computer systems *will* drop radically.
         Terrell believes that the entry of large companies such
         as Heathkit into the field will mean that huge quantities
         of home computers will be sold, bringing economies of
         scale as yet unrealized in the industry. Currie held that
         "if you can sell TVs for $80", there is no reason mass
         produced home computers should cost more than 3 or
         4 times that in the long run.
         When informed of these predictions, A made these
         responses.
         "They're in a position to know."
         "I can't believe the market for home computers (as we
         know them now) is as big as the market for televisions."
         and "I'll believe it when I see it."]

Is it all too complicated for me to understand?

Q 128 I'm starting to get the feeling, though, that things move
         too fast for me to keep up. That I'd have to be a computer
         professional, or work on it all the time to have any idea
         what's going on. It seems like every magazine I've got
         has a story or ad announcing some new chip or new kind
         of memory.

A   It all depends on what you look at. If you focus on specific
         technologies, specific products and prices (this month chip
         x is $19.95, next month $16.95, next month $9.95),
         then it looks like the computer world is a hurricane in
         search of a place to hit shore. And of course, that's what
         the manufacturers concentrate on — they'd like you to
         believe that your current equipment is outmoded so you'll
         buy something new from them. Every few months.
         But if you look a little bit beneath the surface, you'll see
         that the basic principles, the basic ideas, change very
         slowly. The machine designs from thirty years ago don't

really look that out of date. It's just the packaging.

Q 129 Say that again. I don't quite see what you're saying.

A Computers may be thousands of times smaller, cheaper, and faster today, but they still work pretty much the same. The ways that the controller interacts with memory and i/o, the fact that both programs and data are stored in memory, the basic ingredients in programming, change very slowly. Once you understand the basics, you'll be in pretty good shape to understand most any system you come across. It may take you quite a bit of work, learning the details, so you can get the most out of a specific system, but (how else can I say it?) the basic ideas are virtually identical from system to system.

Q 130 What. Are the ''basic principles'' etched in a tablet somewhere?

A

Q 131 All right. Where do I learn the things you're talking about?

A I'll be trying to emphasize them as we go, of course, but the way to learn them thoroughly is by playing around with different computers. As you find out what works and what doesn't on your own machine, as you read about other computers, and talk with your friends about theirs, as you look at other people's programs as well as write your own, you'll pick up an understanding of the principles on your own. And you'll never hear surf music again.

Q What??

A Computers have a . . .

Q Wait. What was that about ''surf music''?

A Oh nothing. Computers . . .

Q Don't just brush me off, tell me what you meant!

A Don't get so excited. It's just something from an old Jimi Hendrix song. I don't know what made me think of it, it just seemed to fit in with what I was saying.

Q Maybe we've gone on too long for the first day. I think you're flipping out.

A No, I think we should make a first pass over everything today so we can concentrate on the specifics after today. As I was saying, computers have a reputation for being hard to understand, for being alien and confusing. You've got to remember that *people* design and build and use computers. If a particular design turns out to be unbearably complex, it'll die out, because people won't want to use the machine. Or not enough people will be able to figure out how to use it.

Q 132 Well, they seem pretty complicated to me.

A   I'm not denying that there's a lot to learn. Computers are a lot more complicated than an iron or a toaster. I think home computers are about as complicated as a car. And like a car, you can relate to them in a lot of different ways. You can just learn how to drive, and take all your repair work to a mechanic. You can just learn how to program and run your microcomputer, and pay somebody else to fix it. Now that I think of it, it seems like a pretty reasonable analogy. Obviously there are a lot of differences, and cars (new cars at least) cost a lot more than home computers, but there are a lot of similarities.

I can imagine this scene: A home computer hobbyist looks over the shoulder of his neighbor who's re-working the fuel system on her Super Stock dragster and says "Wow! That's really complicated. I could never do that." And the next day, the car nut is looking over the computer hobbyist's shoulder as he finishes wiring his new RAM board kit, and says, "Wow! That's really complicated. I could never do that." And they'd both be wrong!

Q 133 You're starting to get carried away.
       I've got to get you off this.

A   Tell you what. We seem to have wiped out most of the questions you had written down. Why don't we get on with what we were doing?

Q 134 What we were doing? You see some pattern to what we've been doing?

A   Sure! We're starting out with general concepts and ideas. We made a first pass through hardware ideas, and now it's time to go over some general ideas about software. Or would you rather talk about sex?

Q 135 What??

A   Just kidding, just kidding.

What's programming all about?

Q 136 Software is just programs, right?

A   Yeh, I suppose, but there's two different things I think we should touch on. First, what's involved in writing your own programs, and second, what kinds of programs might you want to buy along with your home computer (i.e. what sorts of programs are usually available).

Q 137 Do you need to know a lot of math to program?

A   Where would you get an idea like that?

Q 138 I don't know.

A   You don't have to know much mathematics, certainly

The car/computer analogy

> A microcomputer is roughly comparable to a car in complexity.

> A medium sized commercial computer is roughly comparable to a private plane in complexity.

> A super-computer is roughly comparable to a jet airliner in complexity.

these are about as complex as these

Ways of relating to your car	Ways of relating to your home computer
Riding in a car, "back seat" driving	Watching someone run a computer, and making remarks over their shoulder
Driving a car	Running other people's programs (e.g. using a game program)
Planning and taking a long trip	Designing and running your own program in a higher-level language
Tuning up a car, doing minor trouble shooting	Trouble shooting minor hardware problems; programming in assembly language
Installing speed equipment (e.g. headers, new rear end)	Building a computer from a kit, installing more memory,...
Designing a new type of ignition system	Designing and building a component (e.g. an i/o interface)
Designing and building a new type of engine	Designing and building a complete computer

[EDITOR'S NOTE : A has recently requested that the following appear with Table 4.

"After I did this Table, I discovered that it wasn't a new idea at all. There's a remarkably similar comparison between home computers and cars in The Best of Creative Computing, Vol. 1 (on page 142). What goes around, goes around."]

Table 4

nothing beyond what you get in junior high school. You'll probably wind up learning some as you get farther and farther into programming. You do need some ability to deal with abstract ideas. I mean, you can't *touch* an algorithm like you can a microprocessor chip.

Q 139 An algorithm is . . .

A   An **algorithm** is a statement of a solution to a problem.
         A list of the steps necessary to do some task. (There's
         an analogy to cooking. The controller is the cook, the
         data is the food, an algorithm is a recipe . . .) When you're
         programming, you start with some problem and then work
         to discover an algorithm that solves the problem. Then,
         you encode the solution in some computer language to
         form a program.

Q 140 There's a difference between an **algorithm** and a **program**?

A   Right. A **program** is a sequence of instructions for the
         controller. The way the word **algorithm** is usually used,
         it means a sequence of instructions (not necessarily in
         any specific computer language) that's *guaranteed* to solve
         some specific problem in a finite number of steps. **Finite**
         just means not infinite.

Q 141 Not infinite. But no one is going to write a program that's
         infinitely long. That's ridiculous to even consider.

A   Ah ha. But that's one of the really amazing things about
         programming. Although the program may be short itself,
         it might take an infinite number of steps to carry it out!
         Here. Let me give you an example. I found this sequence
         of instructions on the label of a bottle of shampoo:
         1 wet hair
         2 apply shampoo
         3 lather
         4 rinse
         5 repeat

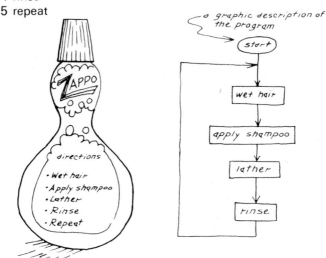

Figure 13   A household program

See anything funny about it?

Q 142 I suppose if you wanted to be picky, you could say that instruction 5 should be "repeat once".

A   Well, when you write programs, you can be sure the machine is going to be "picky".
       If you really followed the instructions, you'd wash your hair forever, right?

Q   I suppose.

A   So there's an example of a "program" that's only 5 instructions long, but requires an infinite number of steps to complete. It's really easy to write computer programs that do the same.

Q 143 Why would you do that?

A   Well, usually, you don't do it deliberately, but it's not hard to make a mistake that'll cause it.

Q 144 And your program goes on forever when you run it?

A   Actually, of course, something will stop it eventually. The sun will go nova in a few million years, a nuclear war will destroy the computer, or, more likely, you'll get bored and flip a switch (or type something on the terminal) to stop the program.

Q 145 This is getting hard to imagine.

A   Let me outline some of the main ideas, and then give you some small examples of programs.
       The shampoo example should give you an idea of how you can write small programs that do a lot of work when they run. The thing is to do a big task piece by piece, having the program re-use groups of instructions over and over. There are two main ways to do that. One is the **loop**. The shampoo program has a **loop** in it. It also happens to be an example of an **infinite loop**.
       Here's an outline of a program that has a more reasonable kind of loop. Can you tell what it does?

       infinite loop: please look at the note near Q 228

```
             store Ø in memory location COUNT
             store Ø in memory location TOTAL
  ┌→LOOP:    add the value of COUNT to the value of TOTAL
  │          store the result in TOTAL
  │          add one to COUNT
  │          if the value of COUNT is less than 10, repeat from
  └              "LOOP", otherwise,
             stop
```

Figure 14 Verbal description of an algorithm

Q 146 Explain a little about what's going on.

A   OK. First of all, instead of giving actual memory addresses (16 bit binary values, remember), I've given names to memory locations. It's a lot easier to think in terms of names that have something to do with what you're using the memory locations for (like COUNT and TOTAL) than it is to use the actual addresses. All languages except raw machine language let you do that.

Q 147 They *let* you do that? What do you mean?

A   You use names for memory locations, and the program that interprets or translates your program into machine language figures out the actual addresses for you. Oh. Maybe I haven't said that computers (that is, the actual hardware) can't run programs that are expressed in anything but machine language, so when you program in anything but machine language, you need another program to carry out the translation for you.

Anyway, the first statement says to store the value 0 in the memory location we're calling COUNT. We can depict that by drawing a box to represent the memory location and writing the value 0 in it. By following through the whole program, writing down what would happen if the machine were to run it, we'll be able to figure out what the program does.

Q 148 Why not just run the program to see what it does?

A   Well, we could see what the *result* was that way, but what we're trying to do is understand how the program *gets* the result, what each step in the program does and how all the steps fit together. What we're doing, writing down each value that's produced as we go through the program, is one of the things you do when you're trying to figure out why a program you're working on doesn't work right. Some people call it "playing computer".

Q 149 Some people call it that. What do *you* call it?

A   I don't call it anything. I just do it.

So far we've got

COUNT   [0]

Q 150 All right, I get the idea. The next statement [in Figure 14] says to store a 0 in TOTAL.

COUNT   [0]

TOTAL   [0]

A   OK. Notice that the next statement has a name in front of it (namely, LOOP). That's so other statements can refer to this point in the program. We'll ignore that for the moment. The statement itself tells us to add together the values stored in COUNT and TOTAL. What do you get?

Q 151 Zero, of course, so what?

A   Hmmm. Maybe I wrote the program a little wrong. Let's go on. It says to store the result in TOTAL.
     Since storing a value wipes out any old value in the memory location, I'll erase the old value and write in the new one.

Q 152 Frankly, I don't feel very enlightened so far.

A   The next instruction says to add one to COUNT. In machine language, that corresponds to bringing the value from memory location COUNT into the controller, adding one to it, and then storing the result back in COUNT. Mark that in.

Q 153 We don't have a drawing for the controller.

A   That's OK. Just figure out what value will now be in COUNT and put it there, erasing whatever was there before.

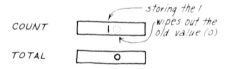

     OK. Now the next instruction says to test the value of COUNT and see if it's less than 10. Is it?

Q 154 Of course it is. It's 1. Can't you see it?

A   Look. If you're not going to get in the mood to do this, we can stop and go on to something else.

Q 155 It just seems silly.

A   We're trying to simulate all the things the controller has to go through to carry out the program. The value of COUNT is stored away in memory, and the controller has to get it from memory and test it. It can't just glance over its shoulder and see it.

Q   All right, all right.

A   OK. The test succeeded, so we do what the statement says, namely, repeat from ''LOOP''. So I'll move my finger back up there, and it says to add the value of COUNT to the value stored in TOTAL.

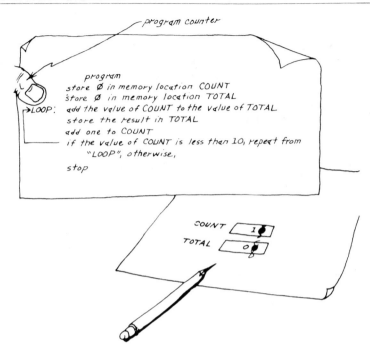

Figure 15 Playing computer

Q 156 That gives 1.
A   Now store that value in TOTAL.

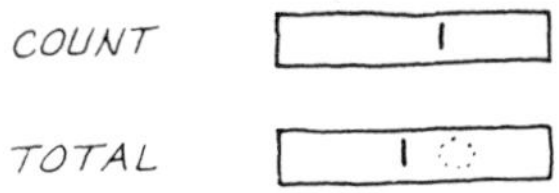

COUNT   [I   ]

TOTAL   [I   ]

Next [still following the program in Figure 14] we add
one to COUNT. That gives 2. Now we test COUNT to
see if it's less than ten. It is, so back we go. Why don't
you keep going for a while?

Q 157 All right. For a while. I add the values of COUNT and
TOTAL and . . .

[Editor's note: Hopefully, the idea is clear. Q and A
continued following the program to its completion — the
middle section of the transcript has been removed on the
grounds that it would be boring to read.]
So now we have

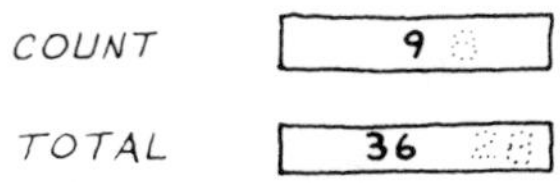

COUNT   [9   ]

TOTAL   [36   ]

Phew.

A   We're almost done. I trust you've picked up what the program is doing?

Q 158 I guess. COUNT has gone from 0 up to 9 in steps of one so far, and TOTAL is keeping track of, uh, what? Itself plus COUNT, or something.

A   Well, it's a little simpler than that. TOTAL, so far, is just the sum of the values that COUNT has had, namely 0,1,2,3,4,5,6,7,8.
Finish it off and we'll have a closer look.

Q 159 Let's see. I'm at LOOP. I add 36 and 9 and store it in TOTAL. All right. Then I add one to COUNT, and that gives

COUNT	10
TOTAL	45

Now what? COUNT isn't less than ten anymore, so. . . The program says ''otherwise stop.'' All right. I stop.

A   OK. Let me write out the program in another form, and let's go over it.

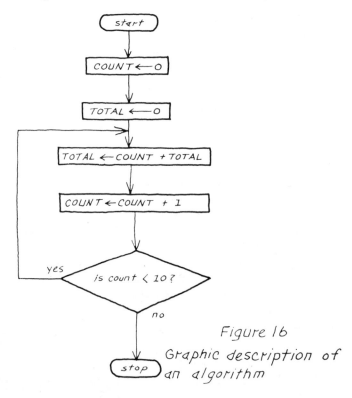

Figure 16
Graphic description of an algorithm

This [Figure 16] is called a **flowchart.** It's a graphic (or pictorial) representation of a program.

Instead of having names like "LOOP" on statements, it has arrows (**flowlines**) that show you where the program goes next. OK? see that they're the same?

Q 160 The arrows in the boxes mean the same thing as **store,** or something?

A   Oh. Right. The expression

TOTAL←TOTAL+COUNT

means "get the values of TOTAL and COUNT from memory, add them together, and store the result in memory location TOTAL."

Q 161 And some of the boxes are different shapes. I suppose that means something too?

A   Right. I'm using the standard flowchart symbols. The **oval** shape is used for places where the program starts or stops. The **rectangle** is used to indicate some kind of computation that results in values being changed. The **diamond** is used to indicate tests.

OK? Just follow through it a bit, and you'll see that it's the same program.

Q 162 Yes, it's the same. . .and it *does* sum up the numbers from 0 to 9. Just out of curiosity, why did you pick 0 to 9?

A   Heh. I originally meant to go from 1 to 10, but I blew it when I wrote the program out.

Why don't we change the program so it counts from 1 to 10. What would you do?

Q 163 First of all, I'd change the first statement to store a 1 in COUNT instead of O.

A   OK. And of course we still want to start TOTAL off at zero because before we've added in any terms, the sum is zero.

Q 164 And then, I guess all we have to do is change the test . . . change the 10 in it to an 11.

A   Yeh. That would work. Just for fun, let's write down a bunch of different ways you could change it.

You might . . .

Q 165 Wait. Is one of them the best way to do it? How would you decide which one to use?

A   Which ever seems clearer to you. If this was one part of a larger program, there might be some other consideration that would suggest one over another, but usually there are a number of reasonable ways to do any given problem.

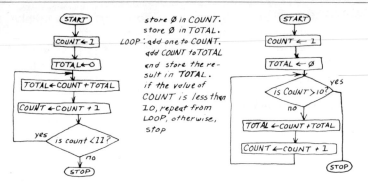

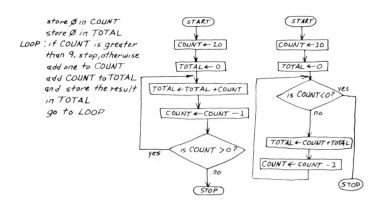

Figure 17 Each algorithm does the same thing,
namely, computes 1+2+3+4+5+6+7+8+9+10
and leaves the result in memory location TOTAL

Q 166 These flowcharts. Would you actually draw them out when you were working on a program?

A Yeh, either **flowcharts** or **verbal descriptions** (or both) of what the program is to do, step by step. Then, once you're sure you know what you're doing, that is, it all makes sense, you translate your flowcharts or verbal descriptions into whatever computer language you happen to be using.

Q 167 Show me an example.

A   OK. But first, let me finish what I was saying earlier. I
        said that a loop is a way to get a lot of work out of a
        few statements (for instance, in the program we just went
        through, each of the statements in the loop got carried
        out 10 times, each time making a contribution to the final
        answer).
        The other basic method for getting more power from fewer
        statements is the use of **subroutines.** A **subroutine** is
        a sequence of statements that perform some useful task
        and which can be called on to do that task a number
        of different times from different places in other programs.

Q 168 That's a little abstract.

A   OK. Suppose you were writing a program to draw a graph
        on the TV screen. At a lot of different places in your
        program, you'd want to send some specific character out
        to the TV screen and have it placed at some specific point.
        For example, you'd have to draw the axes, you'd have
        another part of your program put labels on the axes, you'd
        have another part that made the marks corresponding to
        the values you were graphing. At each point, you'd need
        some sequence of statements that caused a character to
        be sent to the right interface, and to be displayed at the
        proper position on the screen. Instead of repeating those
        statements each time, you could write them once, as a
        subroutine, and then **call** the subroutine when you need
        it.

Q 169 But can't you give me a real example, not just words . . .?

A   When we get into software in detail, sure. [Editor's note:
        This material occurs in Day 6 in Volume 2: Software.]
        Right now we're trying to get an overview. OK? Let me
        show you a little about each of the languages you're likely
        to come across when you tangle with a home computer.

What does raw machine language look like?

Q 170 There's **machine language,** right?

A   Right. Each microprocessor has its own machine language.
        A **machine language program** is a sequence of instruc-
        tions to the controller, expressed as a pattern of 1's and
        0's. Let's do an example. Let's write the machine language
        version of the part of the program we went through. The

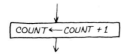

first thing we have to do is bring a value from a specific place in memory into the controller. Since the instruction has to give a memory address, it has to be three bytes long. One byte to specify the instruction (namely, "get a value and stick it in the accumulator"), and two bytes to specify the address.

On the 6800 microprocessor, we can use the **load accumulator instruction**. The first byte for the LDA A (LoaD Accumulator A) instruction (i.e. the op code) is 10110110.*

6800 op codes: Appendix — 6800 instruction set

Q 171 Accumulator *A*?

A   I think I mentioned in passing [Q85, also see Figure 60] that the 6800 has two accumulators? They're called A and B. I just arbitrarily decided to use accumulator A here.

Q 172 How would you decide if you were really writing a whole program?

A   In the context of a program, there may be factors which would affect your choice. For instance, if accumulator A is holding a value you want to use again, then you could leave it alone and use accumulator B for some intermediate computation.

Q 173 What if you had several values you were going to use again in the program?

A   You'd store them in RAM until you needed them.

Let's use accumulator A, and assume that we've decided to use memory location 00000000 00100000 to store the value we're calling COUNT. (I just picked that arbitrarily too.)

Then the instruction which brings the value stored in COUNT from memory into the controller would consist of these three bytes

```
first byte of instruction→ 1 0 1 1 0 1 1 0 ← op code for LDA A
2ⁿᵈ byte ──────────────→ 0 0 0 0 0 0 0 0 ← first (leftmost) 8 bits of
3ʳᵈ byte ──────────────→ 0 0 1 0 0 0 0 0 ⌐ memory address
                                        └ last (rightmost) 8 bits of
                                          memory address
```

To add one to that value, we could use the **increment register instruction** (**increment** means to increase by one). We want to add one to whatever's in accumulator A. That takes just one byte:

```
first and ──→ 0 1 0 0 1 1 0 0 ← op code for INC A
only byte of
instruction
```

And finally, we need to store the new value back in memory, so we can use the **store accumulator instruction**

1ST byte ——→10110111 ←— op code for STA A
2nd byte ——→00000000 ← first byte of memory address
3rd byte ——→00100000 ← second byte of memory address

So the part of our machine language program that corresponds to the step COUNT←COUNT + 1 would be these seven bytes:

10110110
00000000
00100000
01001100
10110111
00000000
00100000

I should mention that just as we come up with quite a few different ways to write the whole program, there are a number of different ways we could have translated COUNT←COUNT + 1 into machine language. But this one will do as an example.

Q 174 That's kind of hard to look at for very long.
After a while, do you memorize all the op codes?

A   Personally, I don't think that's a very good idea. If you really have to program in raw machine language, you'll make a lot fewer mistakes if you write your programs out in something like assembly language (which we'll get to next) and then look up the op code for each instruction at the last step . . . as you enter the program into the machine.

Q 175 But if you *do* program in machine language, after a while wouldn't you just naturally start remembering them? And it would save time if you didn't have to look them up.

A   Yeh . . . what I'm really trying to say is that it's self-defeating to learn to *think* in machine language (or any other computer language, for that matter). There's a large number of pragmatic reasons that it's bad. Here's one: if you get locked into the machine language for your particular computer, it'll make it harder for you to understand programs written for other machines, or in other languages. And looking over other people's programs (in the magazines, in books, your friends' programs, etc.) is one of the best ways to get ideas and learn techniques — to pick up things you can use in your own programs.

Q 176 All right, how would you do it in **assembly language**?
What *is* assembly language?

A   Before we get into that, why don't I write out the same
three instructions in another microprocessor's machine
language. You'll see that the general idea is the same,
but the details differ. Let's do the same operation on an
8080 microprocessor.

First, we want to load the accumulator from memory.
There's only one accumulator on the 8080, so we don't
have to worry about which one to use. The op code is
00111010, which you can see is a different bit pattern
than on the 6800. Here's another difference: on the 8080,
you put the second byte of the memory address first, so
the entire instruction is

```
first byte of instruction→ 0 0 1 1 1 0 1 0 ← op code for load accumulator
2ⁿᵈ byte ──────────→ 0 0 1 0 0 0 0 0 ⎱ command
3ʳᵈ byte ──────────→ 0 0 0 0 0 0 0 0 ⎰ last (rightmost) 8 bits of
                                        memory address
                                      ⎩ first (leftmost) 8 bits of
                                        memory address
```

8080 op codes: Appendix — 8080 Instruction Set

Q 177 Why's that?

A   I really don't know why the designers chose it that way
. . . On the 8080, the op code for the **increment accumulator instruction** is 00111100, and the whole thing
would be these seven bytes

```
0 0 1 1 1 0 1 0 ← op code for LDA
0 0 1 0 0 0 0 0
0 0 0 0 0 0 0 0
0 0 1 1 1 1 0 0 ← INR A op code
0 0 1 1 0 0 1 0 ← STA op code
0 0 1 0 0 0 0 0
0 0 0 0 0 0 0 0
```

What's assembly language like?

An **assembly language program** consists of some number
of lines, each of which contains either a machine instruction mnemonic or a command to the assembler. The
assembler is the program which takes your assembly
language program and converts it into pure machine
language.

Q 178 Wait a sec. What's a **mnemonic**? [pronounced ''knee-
mah-nik''.]

A   A **mnemonic word** is one chosen to remind you of something.

Q 179 Remind you of what?

A   Well, the mnemonic for the load accumulator instruction is LDA. When you see it, it makes you think of LoaD Accumulator. OK? Now. The big advantage of assembly language over raw machine language is that instead of having to look up bit patterns and entering them into the machine, you type in short words which are abbreviations of the operation you want the controller to perform (i.e. you get to use the mnemonics instead of the op codes themselves).

Instead of writing 00111010, like we did for the load accumulator instruction on the 8080, we'd just write LDA. You still have to have a detailed understanding of what each machine instruction does, though, because the mnemonics are in a one-to-one correspondence with the actual machine instructions.

Another major advantage of using assembly language is that you don't have to worry about where each instruction and each piece of data goes in memory. You can make up a name for each memory location you want to use, and use that name to refer to that location without worrying about its actual address.

Q 180 You still have to know the language for each different microprocessor.

Oh. I see. LDA is just easier to remember than the actual op code, but it means the same thing.

A   Right. Each different microprocessor has a different assembly language, because you're basically still programming in the specific machine language of that microprocessor.

Let's write out the assembly language version of the 8080 machine language instructions I just wrote down.

In assembly language, there are several things that can go on each line. The first thing is a **name** (optional) that you can use to refer to that spot in your program. The second thing (mandatory) is a **mnemonic** for some operation. Next come the **operands** (if any), and finally, you can write a **comment**. A **comment** is a statement in English that says something about what's going on at that point in the program. It's ignored by the machine, but it's of real value to the programmer.

```
    LDA        COUNT ; we've just added
                       another term to TOTAL, so


    INR        A       ; add one to COUNT.

    STA        COUNT
   ↑           ↑          ↑          ↑
names (also   mnemonics operands  comments
called labels) for machine
would go here instructions
```

Q 181 Just to be sure I'm following, why don't you go over it? And what's the A doing there in the second line?

A The program (fragment) reads "LoaD the Accumulator from memory location COUNT. Then, INcrement one of the Registers, namely the one called A (the Accumulator). Then STore the Accumulator's contents in memory location COUNT."

[Editor's note: assembly language programming is covered much more extensively in Q 707 — 792, in the last five days. Here A's purpose is simply to show Q what assembly language statements look like.]

I should mention one more thing. Once you pick a specific microprocessor, the instruction set (that is, the machine commands) are fixed, so 00111010 means "load accumulator" on any 8080 based system.

Q 182 Of course.

A But there may be a number of different assemblers available for a given microprocessor, and some of the *mnemonics* may vary from assembler to assembler. Some assemblers offer more options, and there are other little variations, too. For intance, some assemblers don't require the semicolon that I put in front of comments.

Q 183 So it depends on what assembler you've got. Where do you get an assembler, anyway?

A You can buy assembler programs from a number of different sources. Most likely, if you buy a complete microcomputer kit, some software, probably including an assembler, will come with it.

Q 184 Why would anybody use raw machine language? It looks easier to program in assembly language.

A Well, the assembler takes space in memory. If you have only a tiny chunk of memory, you may not have room to run an assembler. Also, you need some kind of terminal to enter the assembly language program. Oh. And some of the less popular chips may not have an assembler available for them yet, and you've got to start somewhere.

Q 185 I have to admit, I still don't really have much of an idea of how to write a program.

And higher-level languages?

Well, we're going pretty fast. I just wanted you to get a general feeling for what's involved, and we can go over some complete programs when we start going into the details of software.

Why don't we keep rolling though, and talk about a **higher-level language.**

Q 186 I've come across that term quite a bit in the magazines. Apparently there are quite a few of them?

A Right, but not many are widely available for home computers (yet). First of all the idea.

Both machine language and assembly language are concerned with intimate details of the specific microprocessor you're working with. And neither is particularly easy for humans to use. Since specific computers come and go, but problems that you want to write programs to solve stay around, it would be nice to have a language that will run on a wide number of different machines. And, while you're at it, it would be nice to have a language that's more convenient for humans to use. The so-called **higher-level languages** are attempts to fill those needs.

Q 187 Why do you say "so-called"?

A Because no higher-level language has come along that completely fits the first criterion, let alone the second. The first commercially available higher-level language was Fortran II, which was released in 1958. Since then, a steady stream of higher-level languages have come and gone. Some of the more popular are COBOL, Algol, Fortran IV, PL/I, and Basic. Of those, only Basic is widely available on home computers.

Q 188 Why's that? And is it a lot simpler than the others?

A In some ways it's simpler. It was originally designed to be easy to learn. It has a number of features that make it really well suited to home computers. For one thing, the program (called an **interpreter**) which translates statements in Basic into machine instructions is relatively small, so it can fit in the small memories most home computers have. For another, it's an **interactive** language.

Q 189 As opposed to?

A As opposed to an **assembled** or **compiled** language. When you write an assembly language program, or when you write a program in a compiler language like Fortran or COBOL, what you do is this: you prepare your entire program, then run it into the assembler or compiler program. If there are no illegal statements in your program (i.e. you haven't misinterpreted some little detail in the manual, and haven't made any typing mistakes), then the assembler or compiler produces a machine language translation of your program which you then load into the machine and run. If you *have* made errors, then you'll get output informing you of that fact. Once you figure out what the error messages mean and what to do to fix the errors, you make the necessary changes to your program, run it back into the assembler or compiler, watch for more error messages, and so on. With an interactive language like Basic, the process is more pleasant. You enter a line at a time, and if there's an error in what you just entered, you get an error message right away. You can correct a line just by re-typing it — you don't have to reenter the whole program.

Q 190 If I see what you're saying, I don't understand why anyone would want to do it any other way.

A There's a penalty. Basic keeps each of the statements you enter in the same form you entered it, and when it's running your program, it goes from statement to statement, converting each into the appropriate machine language commands and carrying them out. If it comes to the same statement in your program 1000 times (as it may if you have a big loop in your program), it has to convert the statement into machine language 1000 times. On the other hand, an assembler or compiler converts your statements into machine language only once.

So programs written in Basic run much more slowly than the equivalent statements written in other languages.

But for most small programs, that doesn't matter, because you save more time in the program preparation phase than you lose when the program's running. Overall, Basic seems like a pretty good language for home computers.

Q 191 You said that Basic was a higher-level language. That means that you can run the same program on different computers, right?

A If everything were perfect, it would . . .

But each manufacturer provides a slightly different form of Basic, so often you do have to make minor changes to get a Basic program to work on another person's computer.

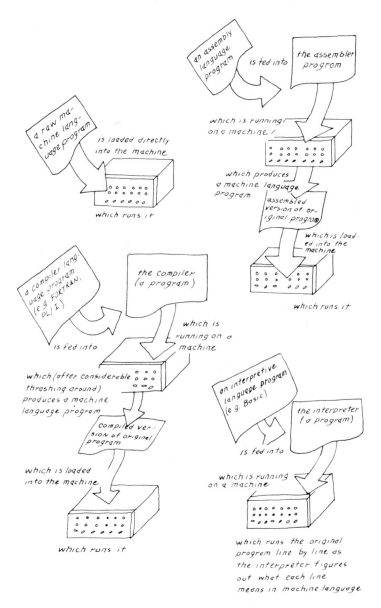

Figure 18 The steps involved in running
different kinds of languages

Q 192 All right. Show me some Basic.

A   OK.

First of all, each statement in Basic corresponds to a *number* of machine instructions, unlike assembly language programs in which each line corresponds to exactly one instruction. So there's a lot bigger variety from statement to statement than in assembly language.

In Basic, each statement has a **line number** (a decimal number), and when the program is run, the statements are carried out in order of their line numbers. That's another difference. In assembly language, the statements have to be entered in the order you want them carried out. In Basic, if you forget a line, you can add it in later with no problem — you just give it the appropriate number. There are about a dozen different types of statements, ranging from . . . well, wait a minute.

Tell you what. The flowcharts we wrote out before are so close to being Basic already, that I'll just go ahead and write down a complete program in Basic.

```
10 REM : PROGRAM TO SUM THE FIRST TEN NUMBERS.

20 LET  C = 1      We called this COUNT before, but Basic doesn't
30 LET  T = O      allow names that long.
40 LET  T = T + C      We called this TOTAL before.
50  (LET  C = C + 1)
60    IF  C < 11  THEN  40      This corresponds to
70 END                         [COUNT ← COUNT + 1]

                              in the flow chart
```

Q 193 The first line is like a comment, I suppose . . . but what does REM mean?

A   REM stands for REMark, which is what comments are called in Basic. Most of the statement types are identified by a three letter mnemonic, and I suppose they were afraid to use COM for COMment.

Q 194 Afraid?

A   Oh, I'm just being silly. I was thinking COM might stand for COMmunist . . .

You can probably tell what LET statements do. And you can also tell that each LET statement gets interpreted as a number of machine instructions, right?

Q 195 I guess it does what you were doing before in machine language. Brings values from memory . . .

A   Right. For example, statement 40 means "bring the value stored in memory cell T into the controller, add the value of memory cell C to it, and store the result in T."

Q 196 Statement 60 isn't completely obvious, or is it . . . the THEN 40 means to do statement 40 next?

A   Right. It says "if the value stored in C is less than 11, then go to statement 40. Otherwise, just go on to the next statement, as usual." And of course, that's exactly what our flowchart says to do. If C is less than 11, we want to keep looping, and otherwise we're through.

Q 197 Is there some reason you didn't line all the statements up?

A   Yeh. One thing to keep in mind is that it's awfully easy to get confused and make mistakes when you're writing programs, and any little tricks you can think up to keep things more organized will probably be worth it. I make it a habit to indent all the statements in a loop (after the first). Statement 40 starts the loop, and 50 and 60 are in it. It makes the loops easy to spot when you're looking over the program.

Let me ask you a question. Suppose you were sitting at the terminal, had entered the program, had corrected all your typing errors,. . .

Q 198 How did you know I can't type very well?

A   I didn't. It's just that most everybody makes mistakes typing in programs.

Anyway, and then you ran the program. . .

Q 199 How do you do that?

A   Oh. In Basic, all you have to do is type RUN. So suppose you did that. What would you see then?

Q 200 I don't know. How should *I* know?

A   Unfortunately, the way I wrote the program, you wouldn't see anything, except a message telling you that the program had stopped. I forgot to stick in an output statement to inform us of the answer the program gets.

Let's see. After the loop is through, we'd like to know what the total is, i.e., what value is stored in memory cell T. So we want another statement in between statements 60 and 70. Fortunately, that's easy to do in Basic. We'd just type in

65   PRINT "TOTAL=",T

and run the program.

Q 201 The TOTAL=T part does what, exactly?

A   OK. A PRINT statement sends output to the terminal. Anything in quote marks gets sent exactly as it appears, and anything else gets evaluated. So statement 65 would send TOTAL= to the terminal, followed by the value currently stored in T.

```
LIST ←— Typing this causes the whole program to be listed (in order)
10 REM : PROGRAM TO SUM THE FIRST TEN NUMBERS.
20 LET  C = 1
30 LET  T = 0
40 LET  T = T + C
50 LET  C = C + 1
60  IF C < 11 THEN 40
65 PRINT "TOTAL=", T ←— Here's the statement we added.
70 END

READY ←— The system is through LISTing, and is READY
RUN          for our next command.
 TOTAL =    55 ←— Line 65 PRINTed this

 READY
  — Our next command is to RUN the program.
```

Any more questions? I think we've seen enough for a first pass.

Q 202 Guess not.

A OK. Why don't we go over what sorts of programs you're likely to get with a home computer.

What general sorts of programs do all computer systems have?

Q 203 I'll play your silly game: what kinds of programs will I get?

A The most important types of programs are **systems programs,** that is, programs that will let you interact with your machine without having to worry about all the little details and quirks of your system. You don't want to have to keep re-inventing the wheel, as it were.

Q 204 You've mentioned systems programs before. What exactly are they?

A The most basic piece of software is the **bootstrap loader.**

Q 205 I've come across the term. I thought it was some kind of joke.

A Well, it's sort of a mythical name. A reference to the imaginary process of "picking yourself up by your boot-straps". Actually, of course, you can't pick yourself up by pulling on the little strap at the back of your boots — you use the strap to pull your boots on. That's what a bootstrap loader is for.

Q 206 To pull your boots on.

A To get started. Remember — a computer can't do anything unless there's a program in memory for the controller to carry out. So, for instance, if you've written a program and you want it to be loaded into memory as you type it on your keyboard, there has to be a program in the machine already. A program that takes characters from the keyboard and stores them in successive memory locations. That's what a bootstrap loader can do.

Q 207   To enter a program, you've already had to enter a program.

A   Right. The bootstrap loader.

There's two ways to get the bootstrap loader itself into the machine. On machines that have front panels, you can load the program (of course it has to be a raw machine language program) by flipping the appropriate switches. Since that's an error-prone, slow, basically obnoxious way to enter programs, the bootstrap loader will tend to be very simple, have few instructions in it (say, 30 instructions at the *very* most), won't do any error checking, but it'll get the job done.

The other option is to have a ROM chip which has the loader on it. In that case, since you don't have to enter it by hand, it can be more elaborate. You start the loader running by flipping a switch (maybe even the on-off switch).

In either case, getting the bootstrap loader in the machine is the first thing you do when you turn on the power and get ready to use the machine. Then you forget about it.

Q 208   If you don't have a ROM chip with a loader on it, do you have to write it yourself?

A   No. Every manufacturer provides a listing of a bootstrap loader. Since the people who designed the machine need a bootstrap loader themselves, and since they know the machine inside and out, they'll come up with a good one. In fact, going over the loader provided by the manufacturer is a good way to pick up tips about programming your machine in machine language.

Q 209   So you get the bootstrap loader running and then what? You start typing in instructions?

A   Usually, you'll read in another program supplied by the manufacturer. Either from paper tape (if you happen to have a Teletype with paper tape equipment) or from cassette tape. The next most commonly supplied program is a **monitor.**

Q   . . . and a Merrimac . . .

A   What?

Q   Nothing. Go on.

A   A **monitor** is a program that accepts commands from the user. The commands let you do things like:

1   print out the contents of a specific memory location (or register)

2   store a value (specified as part of the command) in a specific memory location or register

3   load a program from tape or keyboard into memory

4   output a block of memory to tape (for storing programs you've entered and de-bugged)

6 start running a program that you've loaded

By using the monitor, you can enter a machine language program, run it, and, if you're having trouble with the program, you can inspect parts of it, make changes, so on.

If you didn't have a monitor, you'd have to do all those things using the switches, which, as I seem to keep saying, is more error-prone and much slower.

Q 210 So you use it when you're writing a program.

A   You can use it for the final stages of writing a program, that is, for entering the individual machine instructions, and for de-bugging the program. Right. Oh. I should say that you use it for entering machine language programs only. We'll use other systems programs for assembly language or higher-level languages. Also, a major (probably *the* major) use of the monitor is to read in other systems programs.

And finally, you can use parts of the monitor to do things for other programs you write.

Q 211 You lost me there. In fact, it's getting . . . confusing.

A   Yeh. It'll make a lot more sense when we get around to doing it. Let me try to sketch out the general idea . . . [Figure 19].

Q 212 Well, that helps a little.

What were you saying about using parts of the monitor to do things for other programs?

A   Oh.

Well, since the monitor program accepts inputs from the keyboard and any tape devices you may have, it has subroutines that carry out the necessary details of the i/o operations. If you write a machine language program that processes things you type in at the keyboard, instead of re-writing the i/o statement involved, you can just have your program call the subroutine in the monitor program.

Q 213 Are all monitors pretty much the same?

A   No, there's a wide variation in monitor programs. They all do the same sort of program loading tasks, but on some large machines, the monitor program becomes a sort of "overseer," which keeps track of everything that goes on, including who has used how much machine time and other accounting information. On big computer systems, the

Using the bootstrap loader, read in
the monitor

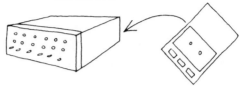

using the monitor, read in the text editor

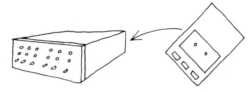

using the text editor, enter assembly language program

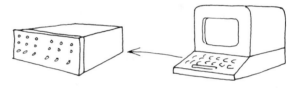

store the program on tape

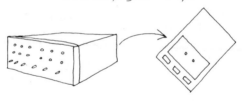

read in the assembler

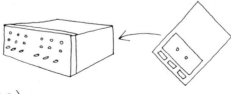

(page 1 of 2)

Figure 19 Using systems programs: monitor,
text editor, two pass assembler

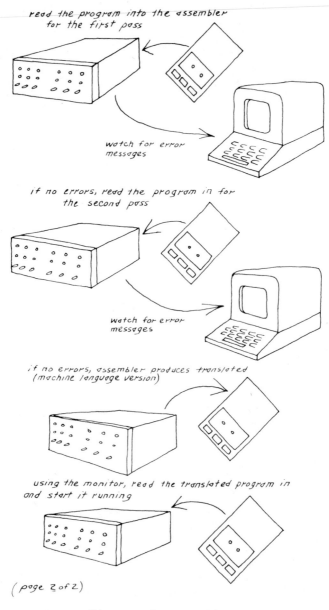

read the program into the assembler
for the first pass

watch for error
messages

if no errors, read the program in for
the second pass

watch for error
messages

if no errors, assembler produces translated
(machine language version)

using the monitor, read the translated program in
and start it running

(page 2 of 2)

Figure 19 —continued—

terms **monitor** and **operating system** refer to the same thing.

Q 214 All right. But there are also programs that let you do assembly language and Basic. Those are in addition to the programs you've talked about so far, right?

A   Those are additional programs. Right. An **assembler** for assembly language and an **interpreter** for Basic. But there's another program that's often provided by the manufacturers, a **text editor.**

Q 215 For preparing manuscripts?

A   You can certainly use it for that, but it's primary use is in preparing assembly language programs. An assembly language program has to be entered in order (unlike a Basic program which can be entered in any order because the line numbers can be used to sort it out). That means that if you have an assembly language program that has an error in it, and you've got to add a new line in the middle, you have to re-type the whole thing unless you have some kind of editing facility. What a **text editor** does is accept a body of text (either from tape or the keyboard), and then alter it on command.

Q 216 Alter it on command . . .

A   Yeh. You type a command into the text editor program, and then it makes the desired change to the text. Like "delete line such and such," or "insert a new line here," and so on. When you've finished making alterations, you can have the text editor write the altered text out to tape. If you're working on an assembly language program, then you can take the tape from the text editor and run it into the assembler.

Q 217 Could you use it to do form letters?

A   I suppose so. You'd keep the basic letter on tape, read it into the text editor program, use the text editor commands to insert the proper name and address, and then have the finished letter printed out on a hard copy terminal. Sure, you could do that with it.

Q 218 All right. So far you've said that I'll need a bootstrap loader, a monitor, a text editor, and what . . . an assembler and an interpreter, was it?

A   Right. An **assembler** is a program that translates assembly language programs into machine language, and there . . .

Q 219 You've already said that several times. You must think it's really important.

A   No, I'm just trying to remember where we are . . . It's been an awfully long day. Assemblers are usually classified by the number of **passes** they make. That is, the number of times you have to read your program into them before the translated version comes out.

Q 220 Wait a minute. Why on earth would you have to read a program in more than once?

A   Most assemblers are **two-pass assemblers.** Let me see if I can make this sound reasonable.

First, is it obvious that a machine language program is a lot shorter (requires fewer bytes to store) than the equivalent assembly language program?

Q 221 No, it's definitely *not* obvious. You said yourself that there's a one-to-one correspondence between lines in the program and machine instructions. And some of the machine instructions are more than one byte long.

A   You sound like you think you've got me on this one.

Q 222 Well?

A   Let's consider what's involved in storing one of the lines in the program fragment we saw before. [Q 180] Can you find the notes we made?

A   Here.

A   OK. Look at this line

LDA COUNT ;we've just added another term to TOTAL, so

How many bytes will it take to store that line?

Q 223 How should I know?

A   How about if I remind you that it takes one byte to store a character?

Q 224 *Remind* me? You haven't told me that yet . . . **Character** means a letter?

A   **Character** means whatever you can find on a keyboard. Letters, numbers, special symbols like ''#$%&'()*+, so on. All you can ''really'' store in memory is binary patterns, so you assign each character a binary pattern. The standard way characters are represented uses up a byte of memory per character. So how many characters are there in the line there?*

Q 225 ''LDA'' is three, ''COUNT'' is five more . . . looks like 44 in all.

A   Look again.

Q 226 Did I count wrong? What difference does it make? *You* count them.

A   What I'm getting at is that you forgot the **blanks.** They're characters too. You have to hit something on the keyboard

*character code: Appendix — ASCII character set

to get a blank. You also forgot that you have to hit a **carriage return** or something like that at the end of the line. Counting those, there's 66 characters in the line, I think, so it takes 66 bytes of memory to store the line while the assembler works it over.

How many bytes does the machine instruction take? The one that the assembler will put out for this line.

Q 227   Now wait a minute. This has gone on long enough. I'm supposed to be the one asking the questions, and if I remember right, you're supposed to be telling me why an assembler has to make two passes through the program it's working on.

A   Calm down! I'm answering your question. I guess I'll answer *my* question too. The 66 characters in the line get translated to three bytes. The LDA op code takes one byte, and then you need two bytes for the address of COUNT. What I'm trying to get at is that the assembly language program can be thirty or forty or fifty times as big as the final machine language version. That means to be useful, your assembler has to be able to translate programs that are too large to fit in memory all at once in their original (assembly language) form. You need a way of translating the program ''on the fly''.

Q 228   All right. I'll believe that. But it still doesn't say why you need two passes.

infinite loop (cont'd) please see the note near Q 145

A   Patience, patience. We're almost there.

Now suppose the assembler gets the line we've been talking about:

LDA COUNT ; we've just added another term to TOTAL, so

In order to figure out what machine instruction the line corresponds to, it not only has to look up LDA and stick its op code (00111010) in the translated version of the program, it also has to know what memory address the name COUNT corresponds to. The only way it can know that is to have come upon the statement that defines COUNT. But that statement can be at the very end of the program, who knows how far away from the line it's working on at the moment. So, on the first pass, the assembler finds all the names like COUNT, and figures out what address they'll correspond to in the translated version of the program. Then on the second pass, it can produce the finished machine code.

Q   You win that round.

A   We do seem to get into battles sometimes, don't we . . .
        Maybe we've been at it too long for the first day. We're
        almost through.

Q   That's good. I'm running out of . . .

A   The last piece of systems software that's likely to be
        available with a home computer is a **Basic interpreter.**
        As I mentioned before, Basic is a pretty good language
        for home computing. The Basic system is a monitor, text
        editor, and language processor all rolled into one. Once
        you get the Basic interpreter running on your machine
        you've got quite a tool at your fingertips.
        You can use it as a calculator. You can run other people's
        programs. You can enter your own program a little bit
        at a time, checking to see that what you've entered so
        far works the way you want it to. You can change programs
        that you've entered, adding and deleting lines with ease.
        Really a useful tool.

Q 229   You said that each manufacturer provides a slightly dif-
        ferent version of Basic. Is one better than another?

A   Each person or group that writes a Basic interpreter puts
        in features that they believe will make their version of Basic
        better than others.
        The most extreme example I can think of is a version called
        Basic-Plus. It was originally developed by DEC (the people
        who make the LSI-11 micro), but I believe you can buy
        a Basic-Plus interpreter that runs on 8080 based systems
        from Imsai. The Basic-Plus manual describes page after
        page of special features.
        Basic-Plus starts with Basic, but includes features from
        a number of other languages.

Q 230   It must be really good.

A   It's great if you don't ever want to share your programs
        with people who don't have Basic-Plus.
        If you do intend to write your programs so they'll work
        on a wide range of systems, you can't use the special
        features that give Basic-Plus its advantages.

Q 231   Does most everybody use some form of Basic?

A   Well, I've been emphasizing the good points about Basic.
        There are some drawbacks too. It takes a lot more memory
        and a lot more computer time to program in Basic as
        opposed to doing the same thing in assembly language.
        (But then again, the time it takes *you* to prepare a program
        and get it working is a lot less using Basic.) And Basic
        isn't very good for really big problems. It lacks a number
        of features that the bigger higher-level languages like
        Fortran, PL/I, or Algol have. One of the most annoying

things is how limited you are in your choice of memory cell names. In the program we did before, I really would have rather called the memory cells COUNT and TOTAL instead of C and T, but Basic won't allow names to be that long.

Q 232 You use just one letter in Basic? There's just 26 possible names?

A Either one letter or a single letter and a digit, so there's $26 \times 11 = 286$ to choose from: A,A0,A1,A2, . . . Z9. There are enough different ones available, but it's really important to choose memory cell names that remind you of what's going on. Of what each memory cell is being used to store in your program.

You can't have everything, and if longer names were allowed, the interpreter would take up even more memory space. It's liveable, and, as I seem to keep saying, overall, Basic seems to be a good language for home computers.

Q 233 What about a language like Fortran?

A If you get hold of a Fortran compiler for your microcomputer, you use it in a similar way to using an assembler. You prepare a complete program, run it into the compiler, it gives you error messages, you fix the program and run the whole thing in again. When you finally have a program that doesn't have any obvious errors in it, the compiler gives you a machine language program that's equivalent to your Fortran program, and you load that into your machine and run it.

Q 234 Why did you say "any obvious errors"?

A Well, it's one thing to make sure that every line in your program is a legal statement in the language (that's all an assembler or compiler can tell you, and that's all the Basic interpreter can check for as you type in each line). It's another thing to be sure that the program actually does what you want.

See what I mean?

Q 235 Sort of.

A Suppose that I'd accidentally mistyped one of the numbers when I was entering the program. Suppose I'd typed line 20 like this

20 LET C = 2

That's a perfectly legal Basic statement, it just happens to foul up the program. As far as the Basic interpreter is concerned, it's a valid program. But the answer would be wrong.

Q 236 I see what you mean. How do you make sure your program is right?

A Ultimately, you *can't* be sure, and every large program is almost guaranteed to have something wrong with it, even after you've knocked yourself out running test cases and checking everything you can think of.

Q 237 Then where do people get the idea that computers don't make mistakes?

A I really don't know . . . somebody must have hired a good ad agency somewhere along the line.

[Editor's note: This ends the initial overview of home computing. The next four days of conversation cover hardware aspects in more detail, starting with an introduction to the special notations (binary, octal, and hexadecimal numbers, logic equations, logic elements) used in computing.]

DAY 2: NUMBERS, LOGIC, AND BUILDING BLOCKS NUMBER SYSTEMS

Q 238 I keep coming across different kinds of numbers. You've mentioned several yourself.

A OK. There are four different number systems that get used quite a bit. **Decimal, binary, octal**, and **hexadecimal.** Probably you've seen them a little in school.

Q I don't think so.

A You must be older than I thought. Didn't you get any "new math?"

Q No. Our parents complained about it too much.

A Oh well. It's not really as complicated as it may seem at first.

All the number systems I mentioned are kinds of **positional** number systems. The value a particular symbol represents depends on its **position** in the whole number. Let's start in **decimal**. The "3" symbol in the number 13 means three, but the "3" in 327 means three *hundred*. Right?

Q Sure.

A OK. Why does the "3" in 327 mean three hundred?

Q 239 I don't know. It's in the hundreds column, so that means there's three hundreds in the number . . . something like that.

A Right. Each successive column, as you move left, represents the next power of ten.

Q 240 That sounds vaguely familiar.

A The **units column** tells how many units or 10^0's there are in the number, the **tens column** tells how many tens or 10^1's there are in it, the **hundreds column** tells how many 10^2's there are, and so on.

$$327 = 3 \times 10^2 + 2 \times 10^1 + 7 \times 10^0 = 300 + 20 + 7 = 327$$

Q 241 So?

A   So the analogous thing happens with the other number systems. In **decimal (also called base 10)**, there are 10 different symbols,

0 1 2 3 4 5 6 7 8 9

and each column in a number is associated with a different power of 10.
In **binary (base 2)**, there are 2 different symbols,

0 1

and each column is associated with a different power of 2.
In **octal (base 8)**, there are 8 different symbols,

0 1 2 3 4 5 6 7

and each column is associated with a different power of 8.
In **hexadecimal (base 16)**, there are 16 different symbols

0 1 2 3 4 5 6 7 8 9 A B C D E F

and each column is associated with a power of 16.

Q 242 But why so many different ones? And why just *those*?

A   Well, computer people use **decimal** because everybody is comfortable with it. They use **binary** because that's the number system computers are organized around. They use **octal** and **hexadecimal** because they provide a more convenient way for people to deal with binary numbers. Let's start by taking some binary, octal, and hexadecimal numbers and converting them into their decimal equivalents.

[Editor's note: In what follows, subscripts are used to denote the base of a particular representation of a number. Thus in

110_2

the subscript indicates that the number is expressed in binary. Similarly,

110_8

is a number expressed in octal.
The two numbers are different, even though the symbols 110 are
the same, because the subscripts show the bases to differ.

$$110_2 = 6_{10}$$
$$110_8 = 72_{10}$$

The subscripts will be omitted when there is no danger of confusion.
All computations used to transform from one representation to another
are done using decimal arithmetic.]

binary to decimal	octal to decimal	hexadecimal to decimal
$10_2 = 1 \times 2^1 + 0 \times 2^0 = 2 + 0 = 2_{10}$	$10_8 = 1 \times 8^1 + 0 \times 8^0 = 8 + 0 = 8_{10}$	$10_{16} = 1 \times 16^1 + 0 \times 16^0 = 16 + 0 = 16_{10}$
$1010_2 = 1 \times 2^3 + 0 \times 2^2 + 1 \times 2^1 + 0 \times 2^0 = 8 + 0 + 2 + 0 = 10_{10}$	$12_8 = 1 \times 8^1 + 2 \times 8^0 = 8 + 2 = 10_{10}$	$A_{16} = 10 \times 16^0 = 10_{10}$
		A is the next hexadecimal digit after 9_{16}

Is it starting to make sense? See the Pattern?

Q 243 Yes, but it's sort of bewildering . . . do one more example.

A   OK. What do you want?

Q 244 Convert, oh, 100100_2 to decimal.

A   OK. Here's the way I'd do it without trying to be neat
like before. I'll just draw lines through the digits so we
can tell what column we're on, and then write down the
power of two that each column corresponds to. If a column
has a 1 in it, I'll write that value down. If a column has
a 0 in it, I'll ignore it. Then we'll add up the values we
wrote down, and be done.

$$32 \quad \text{from } 2^5 \text{ column}$$
$$\underline{\quad 4 \quad} \quad \text{from } 2^2 \text{ column}$$
$$36_{10} \quad \text{column}$$

Ready to go the other way?

Q 245 From decimal to binary? All right.

A   I'll show you a formal way to do it first, and then a quicky
           way that's easier (for me at least) when you're dealing
           with small numbers.
           Let's start with a decimal number, oh, say 19. Let me
           see if I can make this sound reasonable . . . We want
           to convert 19_{10} to a binary representation, that is, we want
           to wind up with a number of the form
           $vwxyz_2$
           where each of v,w,x,y, and z is either 0 or 1. Now what,
           for example, does the digit z (the digit in the 2^0 column)
           mean?

Q 246   Wait a minute here . . . don't get so anxious. What in
           the world are you doing? Don't spring any fancy math
           on me this early in the morning. What are you using those
           letters for, again?

A   You don't like the way I'm doing it, huh?
           Here. Let me try again.
           We want to convert 19_{10} to binary. That means we want
           to figure out how to fill in the boxes here

           $$19_{10} = \square\,\square\,\square\,\square\,\square_2$$

           Right? We want to put either a 0 or a 1 in each box so
           that the binary number we wind up with is equivalent
           to 19_{10}.

Q 247   Oh. All right. I see what you're doing . . . now what?

A   OK. What does the rightmost box represent?

Q 248   It tells how many 2^0's there are. Is that what you mean?

A   Exactly. Now $2^0 = 1$, and 1 is an odd number, right?

Q 249   That's true, even in the morning. So what?

A   All the other powers of two are even numbers, right?
           Like $2^1 = 2$, $2^2 = 4$, $2^3 = 8$, so on.

Q 250   That's true too . . . oh . . . maybe I'm starting to see what
           you're getting at. Since 19 is odd. . .

A   . . . the rightmost digit of the binary representation must
           be 1. There's no other digit that can contribute an odd
           value to the total. Since 19 is odd, we already know that
           the binary version must look like this

           $$19_{10} = \square\,\square\,\square\,\square\,\boxed{1}_2$$

           for a table of the powers of 2, 8, and 16, see Appendix-Powers
           OK?
           Now let me give you a formal way (i.e. a way that's easy
           to program) to do it.
           To tell if a number is odd or even, just divide it by 2

and see what the remainder is. If there's no remainder, the number you started with was even. If the remainder is 1, then 2 doesn't go into it evenly, and so it was odd. That means that the rightmost digit of the binary representation is just the remainder when you divide the original number by 2.

$19 \div 2 = 9$ remainder 1, so again we see that the rightmost digit must be 1.

Q 251 All right, but now what?

A   The same pattern holds for all the other digits. We take the result of the last division (9 in this case), divide it by 2 and see what the remainder is. If the remainder is 0, there's an even number of $2''$s, so the next to rightmost digit must be 0 in the binary representation. If the remainder is 1, the next to rightmost digit must be a 1.
In our case, $9 \div 2 = 4$ remainder 1, so now we have

$$19_{10} = \square\ \square\square\ \square\ \boxed{1}\ \boxed{1}_2$$

Here's the overall scheme: repeatedly divide the decimal number by 2, writing down the remainders from right to left as you go.
When you have zero left, you're done.

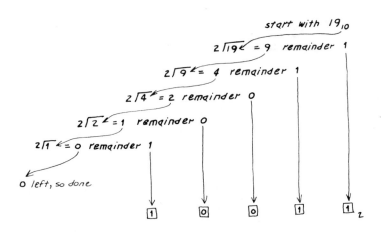

So $19_{10} = 10011_2$

Q 252 Are you sure that's right?

Let's check it to make sure I did all the divisions right.

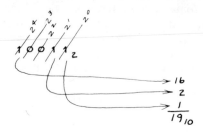

Fortunately, the same scheme works for converting decimal numbers to any base — you just keep dividing by the base, and writing down the remainders from right to left as you go. For example, let's convert 19_{10} to octal (base 8).

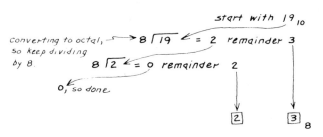

So $19_{10} = 23_8$. Going back to check, we get

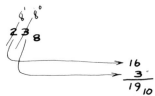

Q 253 That doesn't seem too awful. But didn't you say there was another way to do it?

A   Oh, right. It's a sort of a seat of the pants method. Its one drawback is that you have to know some of the powers of two for it to save any time over the method I just showed you. But it's handy for converting small decimal numbers to binary.

Give me a number to convert to binary.

Q 254 How about 17_{10}?

A   That's an easy one. First, you find
      the largest power of two that's
      not larger than the number. Right
      away I can see that 16 fits. Since
      16 is 2^4, I know that the 2^4
      column in the final binary version
      will have a 1 in it.

17_{10} = ☐1 ☐? ☐? ☐? ☐? $_2$

Then I take the 16 out of the
number (subtract it out), and that
leaves 1_{10} left to account for. But
that's easy. 2^0 is 1, so the 2^0
column has a 1 in it, and all the
others must be zero. So 17_{10} =
10001_2.

Give me another one that's
harder.

a few powers of 2	
0	1
1	2
2	4
3	8
4	16
5	32
6	64
7	128
8	256
9	512
10	1024

Q 255 How about 29_{10}?

A   OK. 32 is too big, so 16 must be the largest power of
      2 that fits. So, like last time, the 2^4 column will have
      a 1 in it.

29_{10} = ☐1 ☐? ☐? ☐? ☐? $_2$

Ok. We took care of the 16, so we have 29-16 = 13 left
to play with. Now I just keep doing the same thing.
8 fits into 13, so the 2^3 column has a 1 in it.

☐1 ☐1 ☐? ☐? ☐? $_2$

Now we're left with 13-8 = 5. Well, obviously 4 fits into
5, so the 2^2 column has a 1 in it.

☐1 ☐1 ☐1 ☐? ☐? $_2$

And now we're left with 5-4 = 1, and that's 2^0, so the
whole thing is

29_{10} = ☐1 ☐1 ☐1 ☐0 ☐1 $_2$ = 11101_2

See how it works?

Q 256 Yes, but I'll have to learn the powers of two before I can
      do it.

A   That's not really very hard. The first few are easy to
      remember. If you memorize a couple of the others, you

can figure the rest out when you need them. It's easy to remember that 2^6 is 64 because 64 starts with a 6. And $2^{10} = 1024$ is easy to remember because 1024 starts with 10. Of course, it's not imperative that you memorize them at all. You can look them up in a table if you happen to need them. And of course, if you just want to program in Basic, you don't need to know about binary . . .

Let's see. I still haven't told you why octal and hexadecimal are more convenient ways of dealing with binary numbers.

Q 257 True.

A   In particular, it's really easy to go from binary to octal and vice versa. And it's easy to go from binary to hexadecimal and vice versa. Maybe you can get a hint from the fact that both 8 (the base in octal) and 16 (the base in hexadecimal) are powers of two.

Q 258 And maybe not. So what?

A   OK. How about the fact that there are exactly 8 different three-bit binary numbers (and 8 is two to the *three*). And there are exactly 16 different four-bit binary numbers (and 16 is two to the *four*)?

3-bit binary numbers	octal digits	4-bit binary	hexadecimal digits
000	0	0000	0
001	1	0001	1
010	2	0010	2
011	3	0011	3
100	4	0100	4
101	5	0101	5
110	6	0110	6
111	7	0111	7
		1000	8
		1001	9
		1010	A
		1011	B
		1100	C
		1101	D
		1110	E
		1111	F

Q 259 I still don't see what the big deal is.

A   Let's start with **octal to binary.** It works out that each octal digit corresponds to three binary digits, and to convert an octal value to binary, all you have to do is convert each digit in place. One at a time. Like this.

Suppose we want to convert 51_8 to binary. 5_8 is 101 in binary (as you can see from what I wrote out above). So the leftmost three bits of the binary version are going to be 101. Now all we have left is the 1_8, and the binary equivalent is 001, so $51_8 = 101001_2$.

To go back, that is, to go from **binary to octal,** you just reverse the process. You take the rightmost three bits, figure out what octal digit they correspond to, write it down, then take the next three bits, and so on.

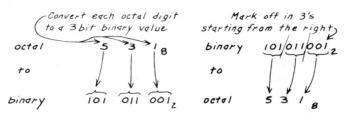

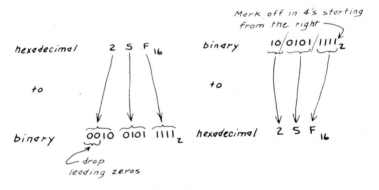

Q 260 I see. I suppose after a while you can do it in your head.

A Right.

Going between **binary and hexadecimal** is the same idea, except you go four bits at a time instead of three.

The big advantage to using octal or hex instead of binary is that binary numbers are much harder for humans to remember and use without making mistakes. But if you *have* to have a number in its binary form, like if you're flipping switches on your computer, you can convert it to binary in your head about as fast as you can flip the switches.

It's easy to remember $FD06_{16}$, but it's murder to try to remember 1111110100000110_2.

Q 261 When would you use octal as opposed to hexadecimal?

A Personal taste, I suppose. Hexadecimal wasn't used much until IBM swamped the market with byte-oriented machines (360's) in the middle sixties. Hex is convenient to use on byte-oriented equipment because one byte stores two hexadecimal digits, exactly. 00_{16} is a byte of all zeros, and FF_{16} is a byte of all ones.

Q 262 You said most of the microprocessors are byte-oriented, so I guess most everybody uses hexadecimal on them?

A   What? Everybody be consistent? Heavens no! A lot of people feel more comfortable using octal. In fact, one of the most common schemes for writing memory addresses (which are 16 bits long in binary) is a hybrid octal scheme. You come across it in a lot of assembly language listings. It's called **split octal,** or sometimes **page-offset** or **page-address.** OK. Each memory address takes up two bytes, right?

Q 263   Yes. Let me see if I'm following you so far. That would be four hexadecimal digits, right? Two for each byte.

A   That's right.

Now in the **split octal** scheme, you write an octal number for each of the bytes *separately,* and leave a space between them (or put a slash between them).

Q 264   I get the feeling you think there's something weird about that.

A   Well, there *is* something a little weird about it. What's the biggest three digit octal number?

Q 265   Let me think . . . the largest octal digit is 7, so I guess it would be 777_8.

A   And what binary number does that correspond to?

Q 266   All right, where's the chart? 7 in octal is 111 in binary, so it must be 111111111. Nine 1's.

A   OK. And how many bits are there in a byte? Eight, right? So three octal digits are a little too much (a little more than you need) to describe one byte.

The byte that's all ones, 11111111, corresponds to 377 in octal.

See why?

Q 267   3 in octal is 011_2 . . . so 377 is eight 1's. All right.

A   Sometimes that causes some strange looking things. For example, look what happens when you go one memory address past 000/377.

binary	decimal	hexadecimal	split octal
00000000 11111110	254	00FE	000/376
00000000 11111111	255	00FF	000/377
00000001 00000000	256	0100	001/000
00000001 00000001	257	0101	001/001

See what I mean? In pure octal, the next number after 377 is 400, but since 400_8 is 100000000_2 (a 1 followed by eight 0's, nine bits in all), it won't fit in one byte, so you write 001/000.

Q 268   I think I see what you're talking about, but my head is spinning from all the numbers. And I had to think a while to see that 377_8 plus 1 should be 400 in octal . . .

Why don't you go over addition?

A   OK. Adding is pretty easy once you get the hang of it. If you get overwhelmed trying to add two octal or hexadecimal numbers, probably the best thing to do is to convert them to binary (that's easy), add them in binary (that's easy because there are so few possibilities), and then convert the result back to octal or hex (that's easy). Better yet, write a computer program to do it and forget about doing it yourself.

Q 269 Go on. Why's it so easy to add in binary?

A   Well, you go one column at a time, from right to left, just like normal, but in binary, there are only six different situations possible in each column. Either there are no 1's in the column, or there's one 1 and one 0, or there are two 1's. Right?

Q 270 Right, but that's three possibilities, not six.

A   And for each of those cases, either there's a **carry** from the previous column or else there's not. There you are.

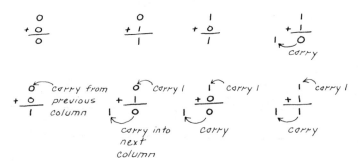

So, for example

$$
\begin{array}{r} 101101 \\ +\ 10001 \\ \hline 111110 \end{array}
\qquad
\begin{array}{r} 1011111 \\ +\ \ \ \ \ \ 1 \\ \hline 1100000 \end{array}
\qquad
\begin{array}{r} 10000010 \\ +\ \ \ \ \ \ 111 \\ \hline 10001001 \end{array}
$$

Try a few yourself. It'll be easy after a while.

Q 271 All right. Now how about in octal?

A   I have to admit, I'm not real good at thinking in octal. If I was, when I was adding, oh say, 7_8 and 2_8 together, I'd immediately think 11_8, but instead what I do is say "Hmmm. 7 + 2 is 9_{10} but that's not an octal digit, so I have a carry into the next column. The carry takes away eight, so I have 1 left in this column, and the carry makes 1 in the next column, so the answer is 11_8." Kind of awkward, but it works.

That's what I go through in hex, too. Here's a couple of examples.

adding in octal

$$2\,0\,3\,7\,7_8$$
$$+\quad 5\,5\,0\,1_8$$

$0 \leftarrow (7+1)=8_{10}= (0 \text{ carry } 1)_8$

$0 \leftarrow (7+0+\text{carry})=8_{10}=(0\text{ carry }1)_8$

$1 \leftarrow (3+5+\text{carry})=9_{10}=(1\text{ carry }1)_8$

$6 \leftarrow (0+5+\text{carry})=6_{10}=6_8$

$\underline{2}$

$$2\,6\,1\,0\,0_8$$

adding in hexadecimal

$$A\,2\,0_{16}$$
$$+\quad 9\,B\,6_{16}$$

6

$D \leftarrow (2+B)_{16}=(2+11)_{10}=$
$\qquad\qquad\quad 13_{10}=D_{16}$

$1\;3 \leftarrow$

$\underline{\qquad\qquad} \quad (A+9)_{16}=$

$1\;3\;D\;6_{16} \quad (10+9)_{10}=19_{10}=$
$\qquad\qquad\qquad (3 \text{ carry } 1)_{16}$

Unless you're working with machine language, you won't have much need to do any involved arithmetic in octal or hexadecimal.

Q 272 How about subtracting and multiplying and dividing?

A   Well, binary multiplication is easy conceptually . . .
Just lay it out like you do in decimal long multiplication, and 0 times anything is zero, and 1 times anything is the thing itself, so, for instance

$$\begin{array}{rl}
1101 & (13_{10}) \\
\underline{\times\quad 10} & \underline{\times\,(2_{10})} \\
0 & \\
\underline{1101\quad} & \\
11010 & \overline{(26_{10})}
\end{array}
\qquad\qquad
\begin{array}{rl}
11000 & (24_{10}) \\
\underline{\times\quad 101} & \underline{\times(\;5_{10})} \\
11000 & \\
0 & \\
\underline{11000\quad\quad} & \\
1111000 & \overline{(120_{10})}
\end{array}$$

Subtraction is going to require a lot of explanation, and I'm not going to be able to give you just one answer, since how you do it depends on how you represent negative numbers.

What is two's complement all about?

Q 273 How you *represent* negative numbers? What are you talking about?

A   Oh, I'm sorry, I just sort of jumped ahead of myself there. If *you* want to subtract in binary, it's simple.

$$1\ 1\ 0\ 1$$
$$-\ \ 1\ 1\ 0$$

$1 \longleftarrow 1-0=1,\ obviously$

$1 \longleftarrow 0-1=1\ borrow\ 1$

$1 \longleftarrow borrow\ makes\ this\ 0-1=1\ borrow\ 1$

$0 \longleftarrow borrow\ from\ last\ column\ gives\ 0-0=0$

$0\ 1\ 1\ 1_2$

What I was thinking of was how it's done on the computer. Why don't we go into that a bit.

See, here's the problem. To write "minus three" in binary, we can write -11_2, and everything is fine. The question is, how do you represent the minus sign when all you've got to store the value is a pattern of 0's and 1's?

Q 274 Oh . . . to store the value in a memory location, it's got to be all 0's and 1's . . . right. I can see that you can't put a "+" or "-" in directly, but couldn't you use one of the bits in the memory location to indicate whether the number is positive or negative?

A Yes! In fact, the scheme I think you've just thought of is called **sign-magnitude**, and it's one of the three main schemes that have been used in computers.

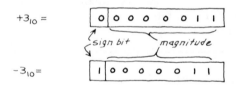

$$Figure\ 20\ \ \ Sign\text{-}magnitude$$
$$representation\ of\ numbers$$

Suppose we let the leftmost bit in a byte be 1 to indicate that the number is negative, and let it be 0 to indicate that the number is positive.

So 00000001 represents $+1$, and 10000001 represents -1. Then what's the biggest number you can store?

Q 275 Uhmm, it would be 01111111, whatever that is . . .

A It's $=127_{10}$

Q 276 Wow . . . that's pretty small.

A In most cases, we'll have to use more than one byte to store a number, but let's stick to one byte to keep things simpler. If we did use more than one, we'd let the leftmost bit of the leftmost byte be the sign bit.

OK. A strange thing happens with the number zero when you use the sign-magnitude representation. There are two different zeros. $+0 = 00000000$ and $-0 = 10000000$, but that's not too much trouble. There's another reason that the sign-magnitude scheme is hardly ever used in computers.

Q 277 And that is?

A   Let's look at an example. How would you compute $(+1) + (-1)$?

Q 278 What are you getting at?

A   Well, you can't just add them whole, can you? Look

$$\begin{array}{r} 0 0 0 0 0 0 0 1 \longleftarrow +1 \\ + \ 1 0 0 0 0 0 0 1 \longleftarrow -1 \\ \hline 1 0 0 0 0 0 1 0 \qquad -2 \quad oops! \end{array}$$

What you have to do in this case, is *subtract* the magnitude parts of the numbers. But there's another case. Suppose you want to subtract two from minus five. The result should be minus seven, right? We represent two as 00000010, and minus five would be 10000101. In this case, we have to strip away the sign bits, *add* the magnitudes, and then put the sign of the larger number on the result to get 10000111. To tell what operations to perform, you have to test both sign bits.

Q 279 So what? If that's what you have to do, so what?

A   What if I told you that there was a way to represent numbers so that you didn't have to test any sign bits, and so that you always add and never have to subtract?

Q 280 I'd think you were crazy, but if it were true, I can see that it would make building a computer easier.

A   In fact, there are two different schemes that do that, although they both do require one additional operation that we didn't need before, called **complementing**. But that's easy to do, so overall, there's a large savings in the effort required.

The two methods are called **one's complement** and **two's complement**.

Q 281 Never heard of them.

Say, if these things are so great, why don't people use them in everyday life?

A   Ah. Computer numbers have a special property that makes the complement schemes work, namely, they are limited in size. Once you tell me how many bits your program uses to store a number, I can tell you how many different numbers your program can represent. Often it's surprisingly few. For instance, if you use one byte to store a number, then there can be only $2^8 = 256$ different numbers. Obviously, the numbers we use in everyday life *don't* have that property — there's no limit to how big a number can be. Take a look at the national debt sometime.

Q 282 I still don't see . . .

A   Let me show you the basis of the method, and then I'll show you how **two's complement** works. (It's the most commonly used scheme.) Here's the idea. Since the number of bits that we can use to store a number is limited (we're taking 8 bits for simplicity), the numbers "wrap around". If I start somewhere, and keep adding 1, the result won't keep getting larger forever — after a while it'll come back to zero and repeat the cycle.

Q 283 What on earth are you talking about?

A   Calm down, OK?
         I'll show you. Let's start with 00000000. Now add 1.

Q   That's not too hard. 00000001.

A   OK. Now add 1 again.

Q   00000010

A   And again.

Q   00000011. Now come on. I'm not going to do this all day.

A   OK..You'll agree that eventually if we keep adding 1, we'll get to 11111111.

Q 284 Yes, but it would take a while.

A   Not really all that long. Just 255 times, but that's irrelevant. Eventually we *will* get there. Now add 1 to that.

Q 285 All right . . . 0 carry 1, 0 carry 1, . . . , I get 100000000. So what?

A   Ah. But you cheated. You've written down a 9 bit number, and we only have 8 bits to store our numbers in. Better throw away that last carry.
         Then what do you have?

Q 286 Just throw it away? That would give 00000000.

A   Now add one again.

Q   00000001.
         Now that you see how that works, all we have to do is figure out how to use it to help us represent both positive and negative numbers.

Q 287 "All we have to do." Sometimes you sound like a college professor.

A   I'll choose to ignore that.
         Just like before, we'll use the leftmost bit to tell whether a value is positive or negative, and we'll use the usual

binary notation for the positive numbers, so 00000001
is 1, 00000010 is 2, 00000011 is 3, and so on up
to 01111111 which is +127.
Now all we have left to do is figure out what patterns
correspond to the negative numbers.

Q 288 What *patterns?*

A   Right. We've already established that if the leftmost bit
       is a 1, the number is negative, but remember the trouble
       we got into when we made negative numbers by just taking
       the positive number and changing the leftmost bit to a
       1. What we want is . . .

Q 289 Now wait a minute. You're talking like we can choose
       what the numbers are.

A   Well of *course* we can. One byte gives us 256 different
       binary patterns to play with, and we can assign numbers
       to patterns in any way we want. Of course, we're trying
       to find the most *convenient* way, so that writing programs
       (and building the hardware) using our number repre-
       sentation will be easy.

Q 290 But the way you're doing it is the way it's done in the
       things I'd buy, right? I hope?

A   Sure. I'm just trying to make that way sound reasonable.
       In English, the word **complement** means (at least accord-
       ing to my dictionary) ''one of two mutually completing
       parts''. We could say that +1 is the complement of -1
       because when you add them together, you get zero. Same
       with +2 and -2, +3 and -3, . . .

Q 291 So? Those aren't in binary.

A   We want to choose our representation of negative numbers
       so when we add our binary pattern for +1 to our binary
       pattern for -1 we get zero as the result.
       We've already chosen 00000001 to represent +1. What
       happens if you add that to 11111111?

Q 292 Let me see . . . That's 0 carry 1, 0 carry 1, . . ., I get
       100000000.

A   You did it again. That's a 9 bit result, and we've only
       got 8 bits to store it in. Throw away the last carry, and
       you get 00000000.
       So 00000001 and 11111111 are **complements**, and
       we can let 11111111 be our binary representation for
       -1.

Q 293 But how did you come up with that?
       What if you started with, oh, +5? How would you find
       the complement of 5?

A   Here's a way to think about it. When we added the
       representations of +1 and -1 together, we got

100000000 (and then, of course, threw away the 9th bit). So, to find the complement of a number, we can just subtract that number from 100000000. Note that that's 2^8. In general, if you're using n bits to store numbers, you can find the complement of a number by subtracting it from 2^n. So, to find the two's complement of 5, first we need the binary representation of 5. That's 00000101. Then, we subtract that from 2^8.

```
 100000000
-00000101
 11111011
```

So we can let 11111011 represent -5.

Q 294 Hey! I just remembered — you said this was a way to do arithmetic without ever having to subtract. And you just did a subtraction.

A   I also said that this was a way to *think* about forming the complement. The practical way to do it (and the way it's done in computers) takes two simple steps, neither of which involves subtraction. But before I show you that, let me write down some numbers and their complements so you can pick up the pattern. Stare at these for a while.

decimal value	binary representation	two's complement	decimal value of the complement
0	00000000	00000000	0
+1	00000001	11111111	-1
+2	00000010	11111110	-2
+3	00000011	11111101	-3
+4	00000100	11111100	-4
+5	00000101	11111011	-5
.	.	.	.
.	.	.	.
.	.	.	.
+126	01111110	10000010	-126
+127	01111111	10000001	-127

[Editor's note: The careful reader will have noticed that one binary pattern has not been assigned a decimal value. Most systems treat this pattern (10000000_2) as -128, so using one byte (and two's complement) all the numbers from -128 up to +127 can be represented. All the numbers from -32 768 to +32 767 can be represented in two bytes.]

Q 295 All right. I see a pattern.
      Now how do you figure out the complement without doing any subtractions?

A   OK. It takes two simple steps. First you change all the 0's in the original binary pattern to 1's and vice versa.

Then you add 1. Here's an example. Let me form the two's complement of +5. We start with the binary representation of 5, namely 00000101, then "flip" all the bits to get 11111010. Then we add 1, to get 11111011, which is the same as before, of course.

Q 296 What do you mean *of course* it's the same as before?

A   Want me to show you why, or do you just want to take my word for it?

Q 297 Show me.

A   Boy. you never let up, do you? Maybe I should cut off your coffee supply.

Q   Come on.

A   Let's see. Before, to form the complement of a number, we subtracted it from 2^8, right? So it won't make any difference if we subtract the number from one less than 2^8 and then add one later, will it?

Q 298 You want to take the number from 2^8-1 and then add 1 later.

       No, that should be the same.

A   Right. If we want to complement x, we can either take 2^8-x, or we can take $(2^8-1) - x + 1$, and we'll get the same thing. In the practical way of taking the complement, we first invert all the bits in x and then add 1. So, if I can prove that inverting all the bits in x is the same as subtracting x from 2^8-1, then I'll have proved that the two techniques get the same answer, right?

Q 299 True . . .

A   OK. What's 2^8-1? It's 11111111. Eight 1's. Imagine subtracting some binary number from 11111111. You start at the right. If the rightmost digit is 0, then in the rightmost column of the result we have 1 with no borrow. Right? In that column we have 1 minus 0, so we get 1 with no borrow.
       On the other hand, if the rightmost digit of x is a 1, then in that column we have 1 minus 1, which is 0 with no borrow. No matter what the rightmost digit of x is, it gets "flipped", and there's no borrow, so there's no effect on the next column. The next column works exactly the same. If there's a 0 in that digit, it appears as a 1 in the result and vice versa. Since it works for each column, it's true for the entire number.

Q 300 That's funny. It seems . . . odd . . . that they'd be the same. But I'm convinced.
       [To "undo" the complement operation, take the complement again. Just as $-(-x) = x$, so does **complement(complement(x)) = x.**]

A   OK. Let's do some examples so you can see how easy
        adding and subtracting is using two's complement arith-
        metic. You never have to worry about the sign of the result,
        that's all taken care of. If you want to add two numbers,
        you just go ahead and add them. If you want to subtract
        x from *y*, you complement *x* and add that to *y*.
        Here's some examples.
        problem: add 3 and -2

            00000011   3
          + 11111110   + (two's complement of 2)
            00000001   1

        problem: add 3 and -4

            00000011   3
          + 11111100   + (two's complement of 4)
            11111111   (two's complement of 1)

        problem: 7 minus 5

            00000111   7
          + 11111011   + (two's complement of 5)
            00000010   2

        See how it works?

Q 301   I see *that* it works.

A   It's not hard to see why it works. Let's go over some of
        the ''problems'' and see what's going on, OK? Let's take
        adding 3 and -2. To do that, we added the binary repre-
        sentation of 3 to the two's complement of 2. So, in
        decimal, what we did was $3 + (2^8 - 2)$, which is $2^8 +$
        1. Since we're restricted to 8 bit values, the 2^8 doesn't
        appear, and we're left with 1.
        In the next problem, we added 3 and -4, or $3 + (2^8 -$
        4), which is $2^8 - 1$. But that's the two's complements of
        1, so we got -1. Presto.

Q 302   Amazing. And I suppose that using two's complements
        makes multiplying and dividing easier too?

A   Eh, heh heh. No, it doesn't.

Q 303   How is it done, then?

A   Multiplication and division are actually very complex
        operations. We take them for granted because they are
        drilled into us at an early age.
        Let's concentrate on multiplication. On the problems in-
        volved in multiplying two's complement values. For
        starters, you have the problem that if you multiply two
        8 bit values, you can get a result that won't fit in 8 bits.

Q 304   Wait . . . Oh, I see. If you multiply two *single* digit decimal
        numbers, like 8 times 9, the answer is *two* digits long.

Is that it?

A   Exactly.

Then you have the problem of multiplying negative numbers. If both numbers are positive, you can interpret multiplication as repeated addition, but what if you have, say, 45 times -3? It doesn't mean "add 45 to itself -3 times", it means "subtract 45 from itself 3 times", or alternatively, "complement 45 and add that to itself 3 times".

Then there's the problem with . . .

Q 305   Enough, enough. I don't care about all the problems. There must be a way to do it. Why don't you just tell me how it's done by microprocessors.

A   If you mean by the hardware, that's easy. It's not.

Q 306   It's not? There's no **multiply** instruction?

A   If you want to multiply two numbers together, you have to write a program to do it.

Here's a crude way to do it. I'll give it to you in the form of a flowchart.

Q 307   It looks pretty involved, all right. How about an example?

A   OK. Suppose we want to multiply 00000110 (i.e. 6_{10}) by 11111101 (-3_{10}).

Let's follow through the flowchart. The variable x will take the value 11111101 since it's the smaller of the two, and y will be 00000110.

Next, we test to see if x is negative, and it is, so we complement both x and y. That way, instead of trying to add 6 to itself -3 times, we add -6 to itself 3 times.

Tell you what. Let's act out what the controller would do in following this algorithm. Draw a memory cell for each of the variables so we can follow what's going on.

Q 308   Yes sir.

[Editor's note: At this point, Q and A carried on at length, acting out the operation of the multiplication algorithm running with the data $m = 00000110$ and $n = 11111101$. This portion of their conversation has been deleted for the following reasons:

1 this day's conversation was to cover the representation of numbers, so the details of interpreting flowcharts are hardly relevant here.

2 this particular multiplication algorithm (Figure 21) is wasteful of execution time. A more practical algorithm is given in Figures 79 and 80 (near Q 757) in the last five days.

3 nearly a third of the transcript consists of petty bickering over who is to play controller and who the memory in their simulation.

Comments on the algorithm:
The statement "$x \leftarrow$ smaller of m and n" is somewhat ambiguous, as is the one following it. The point is that since the algorithm adds together x copies of y, the process will take less time if x is the smaller of the two numbers. The problem is in how the "smaller"

Multiply m by n
using repeated
addition.
Product is returned
in z.

Values may be positive
or negative (two's
complement representa-
tion).

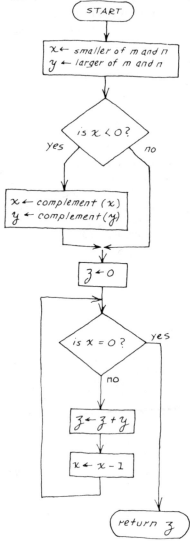

Figure 21. A crude multiplication
         algorithm

relationship is interpreted. Is -30 "smaller" than 2? Perhaps a more
rigorous way to state it would be

$x \leftarrow$ whichever of m and n is closer to 0

The algorithm works by starting z off at 0 and then adding in exactly
x copies of the value y. At the termination of the loop, z contains
the product of m and n.]

Q 309 I just remembered a question I had a while back. You talked about the **leftmost** bit of a binary number. Is that the same thing as the **least significant bit**? I came across that term in one of the articles I read.

A   The **leftmost bit** is the **most significant bit**. The **rightmost bit** is the **least significant bit**.

The **least significant bit** is the one that tells how many 2^0's are in the number. Since the 2^0 part is the smallest part of the number, if somebody told you everything about the number except that bit, you'd still know pretty well what the number was. If someone told you all the bits in a byte except the most significant bit, however, you'd have much less idea what the whole number was. It's the same reason the bits to the right are called **low-order** bits and the ones to the left are **high-order** bits.

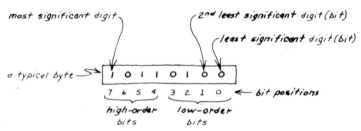

Figure 22   Notation

Q 310 Why are there so many different words for the same things?
A   I don't know. But they're not confusing, are they?
Q 311 I guess not . . .
A   Oh! I just thought of another thing. There's another way of representing numbers on computers that you come across sometimes, called **binary coded decimal**. It's just what it says. You start with a decimal number and code each of the digits separately. That is, there's a binary code for each of the digits, namely

decimal digit	binary code
0	0000
1	0001
2	0010
3	0011
4	0100
5	0101
6	0110
7	0111
8	1000
9	1001

1010 ⎫
1011 ⎪
1100 ⎪
1101 ⎬ unused patterns
1110 ⎪
1111 ⎭

For example, the BCD representation of 725_{10} would be 0111 0010 0101.

See how it goes?

Q 312 Yes. When do you use it?

A   I, personally, don't use it at all.

Some people like to use it because it's easier to see what's going on if you're used to thinking in decimal. It has the advantage that it's easier to convert from decimal to BCD than it is to convert from decimal to binary.

It has the disadvantage that it wastes memory. Using one byte, you can store two BCD digits, so you can store one of a hundred BCD values in one byte. Using binary you can store one of 256 different values in one byte.

BCD is perfect for a situation in which the user wants to think in decimal, and there are only a few values to store at one time, because then you save memory space overall.

Q 313 You lost me there.

A   OK. Suppose you were writing a program to run a cash register in a supermarket. If you decide to store prices in binary, when the clerk punches in a value, your program has to build up a binary value out of the decimal digits as they come in. If you store prices in BCD, all your program has to do is store the digits, two per memory location. So obviously, the program will be shorter if you use BCD.

Q 314 And faster, too, right?

A   But that's not a consideration. No matter *what* scheme
         you use, any microprocessor can do the job much faster
         than anyone can hit the keys on the cash register . . .
         Anyway, you get the idea? You save memory because
         converting the keystrokes into stored values (and back
         again) is easier, but you waste a little memory because
         BCD digits don't use up all the possible combinations of
         4 bits. Since a cash register doesn't have to store very
         many values (current item, running total for current cus-
         tomer, running total of taxable goods for current customer,
         running totals for the whole day), you get away with less
         memory overall. And if you can save a few bytes on every
         cash register in every supermarket in the Free World, . . .

Q 316   Say! As long as you're talking about supermarkets and
         coding things . . .

A   Yes?

Q 316   Do you happen to know how those bars on boxes of food
         work?

A   I suppose, but what does that have to do with what we're
         talking about?

Q 319   That's one of my great ideas! To use those things to keep
         track of my groceries.

A   No kidding.

Q 318   I'll bet you're being reluctant because you don't know
         how they work.

A   Look. There's not very much to tell. It says what's encoded
         in the bars right across the bottom.
         Let me run out to the kitchen and see if I can find some.

                 •

                 •

                 •

         OK. Here's a couple of cans of soup. They have the large
         size symbol on them. The digit out to the left tells which
         code is being used. The leftmost five digits along the
         bottom are used to identify the manufacturer and the
         rightmost five identify the product. The . . .

Q 319   Wait a minute. You mean it doesn't tell the price?

A   No, the store . . .

Q 320   Then why's it called a Universal Price Code?

A   It's not! It's called a **Universal Product Code**. Does that
         cause problems for your idea?
         If they had the price on the symbol, then the store wouldn't
         have any option in what to charge. The way it works is
         this: the checkout clerk runs an optical scanner over the
         bars, the pattern of light and dark is converted to a number
         which the computer uses to look up that product, find

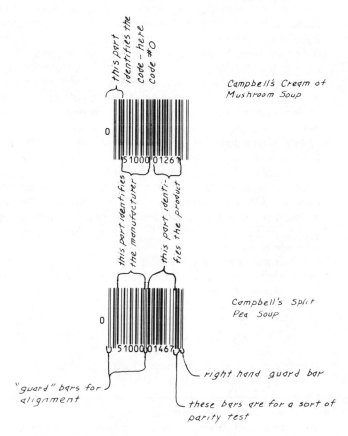

this part identifies the code - here code #0

Campbell's Cream of Mushroom Soup

0

5 1000 01261

this part identifies the manufacturer

this part identifies the product

Campbell's Split Pea Soup

0

5 1000 01467

"guard" bars for alignment

right hand guard bar

these bars are for a sort of parity test

Figure 23   UPC symbols

Since the code and the manufacturer are the same in both symbols, the left halves of the symbols are identical. UPC stands for Universal <u>Product</u> Code. The <u>price</u> of the product is stored elsewhere.

its price and a description of it which it sends back to the cash register to be printed. All, supposedly, in the blink of an eye.

Q 321 Why did you say *supposedly*? I thought . . .

A   If everything works right, it *is* really fast. But as I was saying it, I was suddenly struck by the image of a huge line at the checkout counters, backed up almost into the frozen foods section, with people passing the word back that "the computer is down", and groaning . . .

Q 322 Can you read the bars themselves?

A   I can tell you how they're encoded. There are several neat ideas in these things. Each of the numbers is represented by a seven bit pattern of light and dark bars. The dark bars represent 1, the light ones 0. The numbers on the right half of the pattern use a different code from the ones to the left so the circuitry reading the thing can tell whether the symbol is being read from right to left or from left to right. Another nice feature is the high degree of redundancy.

Q 323 That's a *nice* feature? You just got through saying that BCD was that it wasted memory . . . isn't that a form of redundancy? Or am I missing something?

A   That's a form of redundancy, all right, but we've got two radically different situations here. When the controller and memory are interacting, we don't worry about error creeping in, and any redundancy in storing values in memory represents waste.

On the other hand, when you're trying to translate a visual pattern into a machine usable form, you *do* have to worry about errors. If there's a smudge on the label, or the clerk misses part of the symbol, or you're in a strange lighting situation, you want the system to be able to tell something has gone wrong instead of accepting an incorrect code.

If there are 7 bars for each digit, how many possible patterns are there?*
parity codes Q 523

Q 324 I'd guess 2^7, but I'm not sure why.

A   Well, take each bar at a time. The first one can be either light or dark, so that's 2. For each of those, the second bar can be light or dark, so that's 2 times 2. And for each of those 4 possiblities, the third bar can be light or dark, so that's 2 times 2 times 2. So overall, there must be 2^7 possible patterns of 7 light or dark bars. Remembering that 2^6 is 64, that makes $2^7 = 128$.

So we have 128 possible patterns. Since we want to encode the decimal digits in two different ways (one for the left part of the UPC symbol, and one for the right), there are 20 different legitimate patterns, and 128-20=108 illegal ones. The hope is that with that much redundancy, a smudge will change a legal pattern into an illegal one instead of another legal (but wrong) one. So the machine just checks to see if each pattern it gets is legal. If so, it goes ahead assuming everything is OK. If not, it signals the clerk that something's amiss, and the clerk passes the scanner over the symbol again. Get the idea?

[Editor's note: Perhaps this discussion of UPC symbols seems irrelevant. Much of it has been retained because there have been recent attempts to use a version of these bar codes to communicate a wide range of materials, including program listings. This seems promising because the cost of the scanners required for reading such codes should be very low, and the speed with which programs can be read compares favorably with cassette tape systems.]

Boolean algebra — logic equations

Q 325 I've been looking over some of the circuit diagrams in one of the magazines and I'm having trouble figuring out what the notation means. The words with bars over them, and plus signs in between them. Obviously it tells something about what's going on in the circuit, but what exactly?

A   Ah. That's a good thing to go over now. It's called **Boolean algebra,** and it's a notation for **two-valued logic.** It's used in a lot of different aspects of computing. If you're going to get into the nitty-gritty of hardware, it's especially good to know.

Q 326 All right, but . . .

A   I know, "what *is* it?". I'll tell you, but I can't resist giving you a little history, because the way things truned out fits my biased way of thinking so well.

Q   Groan.

A   If it gets too boring, go make yourself a sandwich and I'll keep talking to the tape recorder.

       When George Boole worked out the details of what we now call **Boolean algebra,** he believed he was uncovering rules about how we think. The title of his book was **An Investigation of the Laws of Thought.** It was published in 1854, by the way. He provided a formal way to determine when two different statements mean the same thing. For instance, the statement "It is raining or I am picking cherries," is the . . .

Q 327 I suppose I shouldn't mention that not only isn't it raining, but you're sitting babbling in your living room, not picking cherries.

A   Right.

Q 328 Right?

A   Right. You shouldn't mention it. It doesn't have anything to do with what I'm trying to say.

       The statement I just made is equivalent to the statement "It is not true that, it isn't raining and I am not picking cherries."

By **equivalent**, I mean that the two sentences will be **true** in exactly the same circumstances, and **false** in exactly the same circumstances.

Q 329 Really?

A   Let's take one possibility. Suppose that I am, in fact, picking cherries, but it's not raining. OK?

Q 330 I guess.

A   OK. Then the first statement is certainly **true**, since it says "It is raining or I am picking cherries," and we're imagining that I'm picking cherries. Now how about the second statement?

Q 331 I can't really understand what it says. It's got too many "not's" in it.

A   Let's go through it slowly. In fact, let me re-write both statements so they look simpler. Instead of writing out "It is raining", let me just use the letter R. And instead of writing out "I am picking cherries", let me write the letter C. So far we have

statement 1: R or C
statement 2: It is not true that (not R and not C)

Agree that those are the same as before?

Q 332 Let me stare at them a while.

A   OK.
Now where were we?
We're assuming that C is **true** (i.e. that I am picking cherries) and that R is **false** (i.e. that it is not raining).
Statement 1 is **true** since C is **true**.
Now let's look at statement 2 piece by piece. Let's start with the part in parentheses. It says "not R and not C". Since we've assumed that C is **true**, then "not C" is **false**, right?

Q 333 Wait. C means "you are picking cherries", so if that's **true**, then it must *not* be **true** that you aren't picking cherries, so "not C" is **false**. Got it.

A   Next, since "not C" is **false**, that means that the entire expression in parentheses must be **false**, since it has the form "X is **true** and Y is **true**", where X is "not R" and Y is "not C". We already know that the Y part is **false**, so we don't even have to bother with the first part to know that the entire expression in parentheses is **false**.

Q 334 This is pretty weird. Are you sure it has anything to do with my question?

A   Since the part in parentheses is **false**, statement 2 as a whole must be **true**. So in this particular case, both statement 1 and 2 are **true**. If we went through all the other possibilities (R is **true** and C is **false**; R is **true** and C is **true**; R is **false** and C is **false**), we'd see that sometimes the overall statements are **true** and sometimes they're **false**, but in any given situation, the two statements are the same. That is, whenever statement 1 is **true**, so is statement 2; and whenever statement 1 is **false**, so is statement 2. They're **equivalent**.

Q 335 My mind is spinning.

A Let me re-write the two statements again. Instead of writing out the word ''or'', let me use a $+$, and instead of writing out ''and'' I'll use a $\cdot$, and instead of writing out ''not'' or ''it is false that'', I'll draw a bar over the term being modified by the negation. Then we'd have

statement 1: $R + C$

statement 2: $\overline{R} \cdot \overline{C}$

Do those look more like the things you've been seeing on the circuit diagrams?

Q 336 Yes! So you actually are answering my question.

A Don't I always?

Q 337 Sometimes I think you go off on a tangent until I forget what I was thinking about to begin with.

A Perfect! That ties right in. One of Boole's purposes in developing his ''algebra'' of the ''laws of thought'' was to keep people from getting confused. If you have trouble doing arithmetic in your head, you get out a pencil and paper and write the numbers down. His hope was that if people were having trouble with the logic of some statement, they could get out a pencil and paper and figure out what was going on using his ''algebra''. Later, some people took the idea to an even more extreme position. They thought that once you figured out all the basic true statements (''two plus two equals four in the decimal number system'', ''water is made up of hydrogen and oxygen'', ''circles are round'', on and on), that by using the rules for manipulating logic expressions, you could deduce all true facts, all possible true statements about the world. A grand scheme, no?

Q 338 I take it it didn't work. What happened?

A Several things. For one, it was proved in the 1930's that the idea won't work even if you just try to do it for numbers.

Q 339 For numbers?

A   Yeh. If you try to deduce all true statements about numbers, you've got problems. Kurt Gödel proved that no
consistent set of axioms can be found that allows you to
deduce all true facts about numbers.

Q 340 **Consistent** means what, exactly?

A   It means that the axioms you start with don't disagree
with each other in any way. Here are three statements
that *aren't* consistent.

statement 1: everybody thinks that politicians are not
honest.
statement 2: everybody thinks their parents are honest.
statement 3: Ralph's mother is a politician.

Q 341 I think you're getting off the topic again.

A   Probably. Let me add one last thing. What I find really
interesting is the sequence of events that's just now
coming to a head. Before Boole, logic was obviously felt
to be an important part of thinking. In fact, in some ways,
he must have felt that he was capturing the most important
part of thinking with his algebra. Then it turned out that
machines could be built which could carry out all the
manipulations that he set down, but faster and better than
humans. Now that those machines are in common use,
popping up at the corner grocery store, in the home, people
are gradually coming to feel that logical thinking is less
important, that the important part of thinking (or ration-
ality) is that part that comes up with the axioms, the values,
the . . .

Q 342 All right, all right. I see what you're getting at. How about
getting to something I can use.

A   Humph. OK, OK. How does this apply to circuits. Since
computer logic (notice the way the word **logic** is now used
to describe digital electronics) is based on two-state components, it's natural to think of one of the states as **true**
and one of them as **false**. From now on, I'll use the terms
true, **1**, and **high** pretty much interchangeably, and the
. . .

Q 343 Why **high**?

A   Because in most computer circuit design (these days), the
high voltage state of the components is called **1**, and the
low voltage state is called **0**.
So, as I was saying, I'll use the terms **false**, **0**, and **low**
interchangeably, too.
In Boolean algebra, there are **variables**, which we'll repre-

sent by writing a letter or phrase, and which correspond to signals in computer circuits (if we're dealing with hardware) or variables in programs (if we're dealing with software).

Q 344 Like the R and C you used before, right?

A   Right. At any point in time, a **signal** or **variable** can be either **true** or **false,** but not both, OK?

Q 345 Sure.

The Boolean operators

A   Now what I'll do is go over all the **logical operators,** show you how they're defined, show you the symbols people use for them and so on.

Q 346 Finally.

A   We've already seen the three basic ones. First, there's **not.** If A is **true,** the **not** A (written $\overline{A}$) is **false,** and vice versa. A really useful way to express that is to write out a **truth table.** A **truth table** is a graphic description of what a logical operator does, showing the output for every possible input.

A	$\overline{A}$
false	true
true	false

or, equivalently

A	$\overline{A}$
0	1
1	0

See how it works?

Q 347 Sure, sure.

A   Oh! I just remembered, there's another way the **not** operator is written sometimes: like this A'. The most common method, though, is the one I showed you — putting a bar over the expression the **not** applies to.

Q 348 How do you read that — ''A prime'' or something?

A   That's an interesting thing. For some reason I won't even pretend to understand, the people who use the two different notations read them differently. People who use the bar notation read $\overline{A}$ as ''not A''. People who use the primes read A' as ''A not''. Of course they mean the same thing. In circuit diagrams, the device that performs the **not** operation is drawn like this

*logic symbol for **not***

Then there's the **and** operation. The expression

A and B

is **true** only if both A **and** B are **true**. Unfortunately, there's not much agreement on the best way to write some of the operators and you'll come across a number of different notations. A **and** B is usually written A·B, but if there's no danger of confusion, sometimes the dot is left out, and it's written AB. Still other ways of writing it are A∧B, and A&B.

Q 349   Why so many?

A   It's just one of those things . . .
        Anyway, here's the truth table for **and**

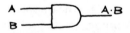

i.e. when A is false and B is true, A·B is false

A·B	B false	true
A false	false	false
true	false	true

or equivalently,

A·B	B 0	1
A 0	0	0
1	0	1

or,

A	B	A · B
0	0	0
0	1	0
1	0	0
1	1	1

And here's the way the circuit component is drawn (usually)

A ———⊐D— A·B
B ———

The third operator we've already talked about is the **or**. It's usually written as a +, as in A+B, but there are other forms for it too, like A∨B, and A∣B.

A+B	B false	true
A false	false	true
true	true	true

Or,

A+B	B 0	1
A 0	0	1
1	1	1

or

A	B	A+B
0	0	0
0	1	1
1	0	1
1	1	1

The **or** operator is inclusive. That is, the expression $A+B$ is **true** if A is **true** or if B is **true** or if both are **true**. It's called **inclusive** because it includes the case in which both terms are **true**.

Q 350   What if you want the other kind of **or** . . . what would you call it, an **exclusive-or**?

A   That's exactly what it's called. You can get it by combining the operators we've seen so far. Let's put that off for a second.*

Here's the logic symbol for the **or**

exclusive-or Q 379

Any questions about what I've done so far?

Q 351   Not that I can think of, except about the exclusive-or.

Using Boolean logic

A   OK. Let's see what happens when we combine some of the operators. Suppose you wanted . . . oh, I know. Remember the Prognosticator that we talked about last time?*

Prognosticator Q 25

Q 352   Vaguely.

A   Let me remind you. The Prognosticator lit the WINNER light if the candidate had a lot of money and either the candidate was a Republican or a Democrat, or a scandal had occurred in the last four years.

Let's write that out in our new notation. I'll write WINNER to represent the state of the WINNER light, MONEY to represent the statement "The candidate has a lot of money," MAJOR to represent "The candidate belongs to either the Republican or Democrat party," and SCANDAL to represent "A scandal has occurred in the last 4 years."

So if I tell you that MAJOR is 1, what does that mean?

Q 353   That means MAJOR IS **true** . . . that means that the candidate belongs to either the Republican or the Democrat Party. Are you going to use **0** and **1** or **true** and **false**?

A   Doesn't matter to me. Well, maybe we should use **0** and **1** so you get used to it. That's what we'll use when we're talking about computer innards.

Anyway, here's the Boolean expression for the Prognosticator.

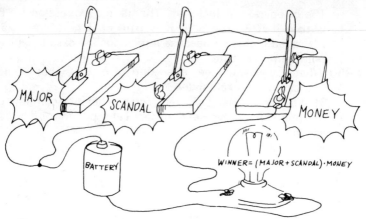

Figure 24 The Prognosticator expressed logically

WINNER = (MAJOR + SCANDAL) • MONEY

Can you draw out a circuit for it?

Q 354 Using the symbols you drew? . . . I'll give it a try. Doesn't seem too hard.

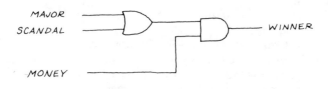

Figure 25

A   Perfect!
        The big advantage to using Boolean algebra is that you can take a logic expression and manipulate it, play around with it until you get it in the most convenient form for building into hardware.

Q 355 What do you mean "manipulate" it?

A   I mean write it in a different but **logically equivalent** form. For example, (MAJOR + SCANDAL) • MONEY is logically equivalent to MAJOR • MONEY + SCANDAL • MONEY.

Q 356 How can you tell for sure that they're equivalent?

A   Two ways. One way is to show that you can transform one expression into the other using the rules of Boolean algebra (which we'll get to in a minute). The other way is to write out the truth table for each expression and show that they're the same. Let's do that.

MAJOR	SCANDAL	MONEY	(MAJOR + SCANDAL)	MAJOR · MONEY	SCANDAL · MONEY	(MAJOR + SCANDAL) · MONEY	MAJOR · MONEY + SCANDAL · MONEY
0	0	0	0	0	0	0	0
0	0	1	0	0	0	0	0
0	1	0	1	0	0	0	0
0	1	1	1	0	1	1	1
1	0	0	1	0	0	0	0
1	0	1	1	1	0	1	1
1	1	0	1	0	0	0	0
1	1	1	1	1	1	1	1

All possible combinations of values of MAJOR, SCANDAL, and MONEY

sub-expressions (written out to make it easier to evaluate the two expressions we're interested in.)

identical for all possible combinations of the 3 variables

Q 357 And that proves they're equivalent?

A   Right. No matter what values the variables MAJOR, SCANDAL, and MONEY have, (MAJOR + SCAN-DAL) · MONEY always has the same value as MAJOR · MONEY + SCANDAL · MONEY. So the two expressions are logically equivalent.

Of course, when you go to build the circuit, there may be differences between the two expressions that matter. For example, the second form requires one more gate than the first.

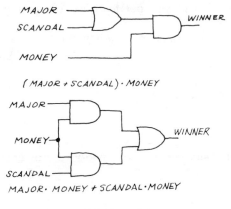

(MAJOR + SCANDAL) · MONEY

MAJOR · MONEY + SCANDAL · MONEY

Figure 26

Q 358 **Gate?**

A   Logic circuit elements are called **gates** sometimes. You can think of an **or** as a gate that lets **1**'s through it . . . I don't really know where the term came from.

"Rules" of logic

Q 359 You mentioned the **rules of Boolean algebra.** What are they?

A   The "rules" of Boolean algebra aren't really "rules" . . . they're just statements about basic equivalent forms. You can figure them all out yourself once you know what the operators do. If any of them look strange, we can prove them by writing out a truth table.

I'll show you the common ones, and I'll write the name they're usually called beside them in case you want to look them up later in a book on logic design.

I'll use **A, B,** and **C** for variables.

Here's the first ones. Basically they say that **and**ing or **or**ing a variable with itself doesn't change anything.

$$A = A + A$$
$$\text{(idempotency)}$$
$$A = A \cdot A$$

Q 360 Why would you ever do that to begin with? I mean, obviously A+A is the same as A. If A is **false,** it's **false;** and if A is **true,** it's **true.**

A   Well, it usually comes up when you're trying to find the simplest way to build some logic expression. If you can manipulate the expression so that something like A+A appears in it, you get to throw everything but the one A away.

I'll give you an example of how you use them in a minute.

$$0 \cdot A = 0$$
$$1 \cdot A = A \qquad \text{(identity and zero elements)}$$
$$0 + A = A$$
$$1 + A = 1$$

Then there are rules involving the **not** operation.

$$\overline{(\overline{A})} = A$$

That is, the **not** of the **not** of something is the same as the thing itself.

$$A + \overline{A} = 1$$
$$A \cdot \overline{A} = 0$$

And of course, order doesn't matter.

$$A + B = B + A$$
$$A \cdot B = B \cdot A$$

Then there are rules involving parentheses.

$$A \cdot (B + C) = A \cdot B + A \cdot C \qquad \text{(distributivity)}$$

Now we come to the real biggie, called **DeMorgan's Theorem.**

Q 361   I suppose someone named DeMorgan discovered it?

A   Sort of. Yeh, he discovered it, but actually it was known in the Middle Ages . . .

Q 362   In the Middle Ages? I thought you told me this stuff was invented in the 1800's. By Boole . . .

A   Parts of logic have been known for a long time. The Greeks did a number of things. Aristotle talks about some aspects of logic . . . maybe you've heard his classic example of a deduction? "All men are mortal, Socrates is a man, therefore Socrates is mortal." What Boole did was bring together a lot of things that were disjoint before, organized them, came up with a good notation, so on.

Q 363   And I thought computers were the most modern things there were . . .

A   Well, there *are* a lot of new things in computer technology, but there's quite a few old ideas too. The ancient Greeks invented a number of algorithms that are used in programs even today . . . Anyway, DeMorgan's Theorem says that to take the **not** of an expression, you take the **not** of each subexpression and change all the operators from **and** to **or** and vice versa. For instance,

$$\overline{A + B} = \overline{A} \cdot \overline{B}$$
$$\text{(DeMorgan's Theorem)}$$
$$\overline{A \cdot B} = \overline{A} + \overline{B}$$

Since this one is so important, let's write out the truth

table to prove it.
Let's take the first form.

A	B	A + B	$\overline{A+B}$	$\overline{A}$	$\overline{B}$	$\overline{A} \cdot \overline{B}$
0	0	0	1	1	1	1
0	1	1	0	1	0	0
1	0	1	0	0	1	0
1	1	1	0	0	0	0

identical for all possible combinations of values of A and B

for a use of DeMorgan's Theorem see Q. 455
These two circuits are logically equivalent, as shown by DeMorgan's Theorem.

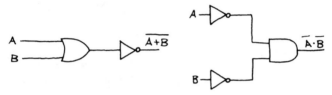

Q. 364 You were going to do some examples . . . or are there more rules?

A   I think we've got all the basic ones. If we come across more complicated situations, we can figure them out as we go. One thing we can do now is take a truth table, and figure out a circuit that will carry it out. Why don't you make up a truth table for some expression that involves two variables.

Q. 365 Just make one up? All right. How about this

A	B	?
0	0	1
0	1	0
1	0	1
1	1	1

A   OK. Now, one way to do this is to write down the expressions for every combination of inputs that makes the output 1, and **or** them all together.

Q. 366 What?

A   Like this. Looking at the truth table, you can see that the output is 1 if A and B are both 0, **or** if A is 1 and B is 0, **or** if A and B are both 1. So I'll just write that down.

$$? = \overline{A} \cdot \overline{B} + A \cdot \overline{B} + A \cdot B$$

See what I did?

Q 367 I think so . . . there's a term for each 1 in the truth table . . .

A   Instead of just going ahead and building the circuit from
the expression we have, let's play around with it and see
if we can make it simpler.

First of all, I notice that two terms have $\overline{B}$ in them, so
let's use the **distributive** rule to factor the $\overline{B}$ out.
That gives

$$? = (\overline{A} + A) \cdot \overline{B} + A \cdot B$$

Q 368 I see . . . and now you can replace the $(\overline{A} + A)$ part by
1, right?

A   Right, and since $1 \cdot \overline{B} = \overline{B}$, we're left with

$$? = \overline{B} + A \cdot B$$

That can still be simplified.

Q 369 Really? How? There aren't any terms in common.

A   You can think about it this way. Let's look at the situations
in which each part of the expression has the value 1.

Q 370 All right. The first term will be 1 whenever B is 0.

A   Right. So, if B is 0, the whole expression is 1. What if
B is 1?

Q 371 If B is 1, then the second term depends on what A is.

A   Try it this way: what if A is 1?

Q 372 If A is 1? If B is 0 . . . oh. No matter what B is, the
whole thing is 1 if A is 1.

A   Right. So what we've said is, if B is 0 or A is 1, the
whole expression is 1.

$$? = \overline{B} + A \cdot B = \overline{B} + A$$

Q 373 Really? It's just that?

A   Yeh. To prove it, you can always draw out the truth table
and see that it's the same as the one we started with.

Q 374 That seemed pretty hard. I'm sure that must be the
simplest you can make that particular truth table, . . . but
how do you know?

A   Actually, there are formal ways to simplify logic expressions. If you get interested in it, you can find it in most
any book on circuit design. [See McCluskey's book in the
Bibliography, for example.]

Anyway, the circuit for your made-up truth table needs
just two elements:

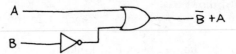

Q 375 Do people who have home computers use Boolean algebra a lot?

A   If they're designing their own circuits, yes. Otherwise, not as much. It helps to know some Boolean algebra if you're trying to trouble-shoot a piece of equipment, or understand a circuit diagram.

Q 376 If I wanted to design a circuit, what I'd do is figure out the truth table for what I wanted to do, and then go through something like what we just did. Right?

A   Sort of.
      Now that we've gone over the basics, I can expose you to the way things are actually done.

Circuit components

For starters, it turns out that you don't need all the operators we've been talking about. You can do anything with just *one* type of operator, either a **nor** or a **nand**.

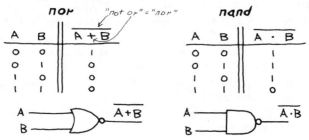

Either of them is a **universal logic element.**

Q 377 You can make *any* logic expression out of them? Is that what you mean?

A   Right.

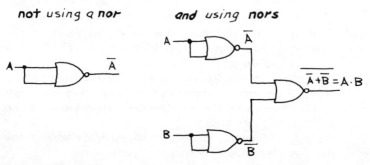

or using **nors**

So, instead of having to have a bunch of different types of circuit components, you just need a supply of **nors** or **nands.** Sometimes circuit diagrams are drawn showing **ands** and **ors** because it's easier to see what's going on, but when you get around to actually building something, usually you use **nors** or **nands.**

Q 378 What other bits of reality have you been hiding from me?

A   Nothing substantial. Let's see. There are a couple of other circuit elements you'll come across. Oh. Remember you wanted to know about the **exclusive-or**?

Q 379 Right.

A   Here's the truth table and logic symbol for the **exclusive-or.** The exclusive-or operator is either ⊕ or V.

exclusive-or

A	B	A ⊕ B
0	0	0
0	1	1
1	0	1
1	1	0

truth table

logic symbol

Q 380 Can you buy **exclusive-ors**?

A   Yes, or you can build them out of **nors** or **nands.** The logic expression for **exclusive-or** is A · B + Ā · B̄ or, equivalently.

$\overline{A \cdot B} + \overline{\overline{A} \cdot \overline{B}}$, so you can do it like this:

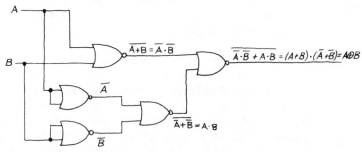

Figure 27 The **exclusive-or** *operation constructed from* **nor** *gates*

When you are actually building a circuit, there are some
more considerations that come into play. The components
come in clumps, like, four **nand** gates on one chip. That
particular item is usually described as a **quad 2-input
nand**. You can also get 4 and 8 input **nands** and **nors**.
The quad 2-input nand chip has two pins for the two inputs
to each **nand,** one pin for the output of each **nand,** and
two pins for power and ground connections, or 14 pins
in all.

Q 381 I presume the pins are marked so you can tell what's what.

A   Well, they're marked so you can figure out what number
each pin is. You have to have the manufacturer's specs
to know what each pin is hooked to inside the chip.
chip markings: Figure 57 near Q 577

Q 382 **Specs** is short for specifications?

A   Yeh. Here's the pin layout for the SN7400 chip, which
is a quad 2-input nand.

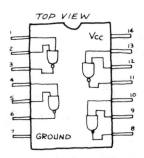

Figure 28   Pin layout on the SN7400
chip – a TTL quad 2-input nand

Q 383 What does the V_{cc} beside pin 14 stand for?

A   It's a term that comes from transistors. It just means the
supply voltage. In digital electronics, V_{cc} is almost always
+5 volts.

Q 384 But what does the **cc** part stand for?

A   C stands for **collector,** which is one of the three parts
of a transistor. **Collector, emitter,** and **base.** I don't really
know why the **c** is doubled . . . maybe so you won't forget
it. The V stands for **voltage,** of course . . .
But what I really want to get across is that the circuitry
used to perform the Boolean operations (**nor, nand, or,
not,** etc.) introduces some additional complexities. Things
that don't enter into the pure, ethereal world of Boolean
logic itself.

Q 385 For example, they require power?

A   Right. And not only does each gate consume power, it has to supply a certain amount of electrical power through its output.

Q 386 I'm not sure what you mean.

A   Suppose a particular gate is giving a **1** as its output. That means that it's holding its output line at a voltage of around three and a half volts. (That's the signal that represents a logical **1**). But that's not the whole story. The output line goes somewhere, serves as input to other devices, and each of those inputs is an electrical load on the line. If there are too many loads on a particular line, the gate may not be able to supply enough power to keep the voltage up to the proper level, and the overall circuit won't work right. The number of places a particular output connects to is called its **fan-out.**[*]

for details of fan-out, etc., see TTL Cookbook (Bibliography)

Q 387 Is that a big problem?

A   In some cases. Most commonly used types of logic elements don't start running into trouble until an output is connected to a dozen or so other chips. After that, you've got to do something to reduce the load on that output.

Q 388 What do you do?

A   Glad you asked. There are several things you can do. You can redesign the circuit. You can use two gates in parallel so they share the load, or you can use a special circuit element called a **driver.**

A **driver** doesn't correspond to any Boolean operator, it just puts out whatever signal it receives. But it's capable of handling a fan-out several times as big as a regular gate.

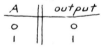

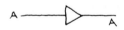

Q 389 The symbol is just like the symbol for a **not**, except for the little circle.

A   Un huh. Maybe I should mention that the little circle means **negation,** and sometimes you see it used in sorts of strange ways in circuit diagrams.

Occasionally you'll see things like this

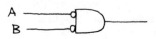

4-29-81

Can you tell me what operation that represents?

Q 390 The circles mean **not** . . . the symbol is the **and** symbol . . . I guess it's $\overline{A} \cdot \overline{B}$.

A Right you are. But what operation is that equivalent to? Use DeMorgan's Theorem. Here. Since taking the **not** of the **not** of something is equivalent to the thing itself, I can re-write it as

$\overline{\overline{A \cdot B}}$

$$\overline{A \cdot B} = \overline{A} + \overline{B}$$
$$\overline{A + B} = \overline{A} \cdot \overline{B}$$

temporarily.

Q 391 Good grief! It looks like a hexagram!

A A hexagram?

Q 392 Like in the *I Ching* . . . never mind.

A Now I'll use DeMorgan's Theorem to convert it to

$\overline{A + B}$

which is the **nor** operation.

Q 393 So it's just another way to draw the **nor** . . .
Are there a lot more components?

A In a sense, yes. Since a microprocessor comes on a single chip, you can think of it as a circuit component. Complicated components like that are drawn as rectangles on circuit diagrams, and the name of the device is written in the rectangle, so you can tell what it is.
Oh. There's another component that has a special symbol. It's one that isn't really a Boolean logic element . . . it's a special kind of driver. A tri-state bus driver. Remember we talked a little about busses last time? And I was saying things like "the i/o interface puts a value on the data bus"?
bus organization Q 473-487

Q 394 Vaguely.

A Well, one way of designing a bus is to use drivers that (essentially) disconnect themselves from the bus unless they are putting a signal on it. That means the drivers have to have *three* possible output states. They can be in the **1** state, or the **0** state, or they can be in a special **tri-state** in which they don't affect the bus at all.

Q 395 Wait a minute. I'm not quite following you. Why do you want the third kind of output again?

A Since there can be quite a few things (i/o interfaces, RAM and ROM memories) on the bus, you don't dare let more than one of them put a signal on the bus at one time — who knows what value the controller would receive?

There are other ways around it, but then you can get into the kind of loading problems we were just talking about. When a tri-state bus driver is in the special, third state, it doesn't put any load on the bus. It looks like an open circuit, electrically. [Editor's note: This subject is covered extensively in later conversations, Q 473-487. Here A's purpose seems merely to introduce Q to the symbol for the tri-state bus driver.]

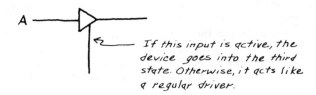

If this input is active, the device goes into the third state. Otherwise, it acts like a regular driver.

Flip-flops/putting components together

Q 396 All right. I've got the idea. I wanted to ask you about another component I came across in one of the magazines. At least, I assume it's a circuit component. A **flip-flop**?

A OK. A **flip-flop** is a form of memory — a one bit memory. You can build a flip-flop out of the components we've already seen, or you can buy chips that have flip-flops on them. There are three or four diferent kinds . . .

Q 397 What are you saying? Do you build memories out of them?

A You use them in circuits which need a small amount of memory. Well, static RAMs are essentially large groups of flip-flops.

Q 398 Go on, explain it.

A I'm just trying to think what kind to go over. I guess I'll pick . . .

Q 399 Come on. What's a **flip-flop**?

A OK. OK. It's a device that has two **stable states.** The state can be changed by particular values of its inputs (so you can make it enter whatever state you want, **0** or **1**), but other combinations of inputs leave the state unchanged (it *stores* its state). One common use of a flip-flop is as a **latch,** which is a circuit that receives a momentary signal and holds it for some other circuitry to deal with at leisure.

Q 400 Can't you be more specific?

A OK. I'll pick the **J-K flip-flop.** It's the most general. It has three inputs, one called **J,** one called **K,** and one called **C.** It has two outputs, called **Q** and **Q̄.**

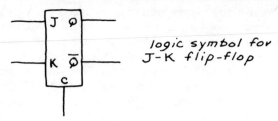

logic symbol for J-K flip-flop

Since, as its name implies, $\overline{Q}$ always has the opposite value of Q, we can concentrate on Q. If you know what value it has, you know the entire state of the flip-flop.

Q 401 What's it there for, then?

A What? $\overline{Q}$? Convenience. If you're designing a circuit and you want the inverse of Q, you can just hook up to the $\overline{Q}$ output instead of running the signal from Q through a **not.**

If the **clock input** (that's what **C** stands for) isn't active, then nothing changes in the flip-flop. For the time being, I'll just cover what happens when the C input *is* active.

Q 402 Do you hook it up to the clock that runs the microprocessor?

A Usually not. It's just a historical thing that the input is called the clock input. Maybe it should be called **enable,** or something like that.

Here's the rules of operation. If both J and K are 0, then Q stays the same. (And, of course, $\overline{Q}$ doesn't change either.)

If both J and K are 1, then Q changes to the opposite value. You can think of it as if Q and $\overline{Q}$ trade their values when J and K are both 1.

There are two more possibilities. If J is 1 and K is 0, then Q becomes 1, and if J is 0 and K is 1, then Q becomes 0, no matter what it was before.

That means we have complete control over Q. We can set it to whatever value we want, and we can also make it stay the same or switch it to the opposite value without having to care what value it had to begin with.

Here's the way the operation is usually shown — it's called a **transition table,** and it's like a truth table, except there's a time dimension thrown in. Q^n means ''the state of Q at time n''.

J^n	K^n	Q^{n+1}
0	0	Q^n
0	1	0
1	0	1
1	1	$\overline{Q}^n$

Boolean expression for the
J-K flip-flop:
$$Q^{n+1} = (J \cdot \overline{Q} + \overline{K} \cdot Q)^n$$

While I'm at it, let me write down a description of the other kinds of flip-flops. You come across them in circuit diagrams fairly often.

D flip-flop

transition table

D^n	Q^n	Q^{n+1}
0	0	0
1	0	1
0	1	0
1	1	1

Comments

if C input is active,
$Q^{n+1} = D^n$
otherwise,
$Q^{n+1} = Q^n$

T flip-flop

transition table

T^n	Q^n	Q^{n+1}
0	0	0
1	0	1
0	1	1
1	1	0

Comments

if C input is active,
T=0 yields no change
in Q
T=1 changes Q to $\overline{Q}$

R-S flip-flop

transition table

R^n	S^n	Q^n	Q^{n+1}
0	0	0	0
0	1	0	1
1	0	0	0
1	1	0	illegal
0	0	1	1
0	1	1	1
1	0	1	0
1	1	1	illegal

Comments

if C input is
active, S is **set**
input, sets Q to
1
R is **reset**,
makes Q=0
You can't set
and reset at the
same time

J-K flip-flop

transition table

J^n	K^n	Q^n	Q^{n+1}
0	0	0	0
0	1	0	0
1	0	0	1
1	1	0	1
0	0	1	1
0	1	1	0
1	0	1	1
1	1	1	0

Comments

J is like **set**
K is like **reset**
if C is active,
J=K=0 causes
no change in Q
J=K=1 changes
Q to $\overline{Q}$

Figure 29 All manner of **flip-flops**

And I can't resist a few more comments. Here's a circuit using **nands** that serves as a **R-S flip-flop**.

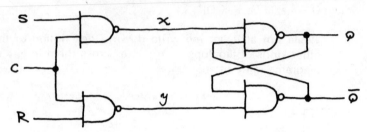

To see how it works, we can use a **timing diagram**.

Q 403 I was going to ask you about them sooner or later. I've run across them, but they seemed a little obscure.

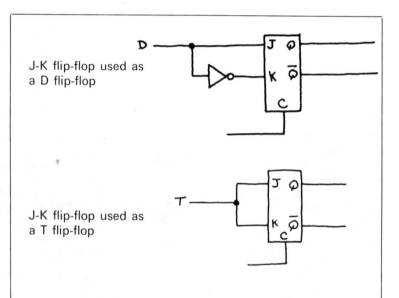

J-K flip-flop used as a D flip-flop

J-K flip-flop used as a T flip-flop

Note: There are a large number of slightly different versions of the J-K flip-flop. For instance, some require the C input to be 1 for anything to happen, some require it to be 0, some require the C input to *change* from 1 to 0 for anything to happen, some have additional inputs (**preset, clear,** etc.) which will force the flip-flop into a specific state regardless of the C input. Read the manufacturer's specs for the particular ones you have.

Figure 30 J-K flip-flops

A   Let's start small, and do a timing diagram for the upper left **nand.** A **timing diagram** shows how signals in a circuit change and interact over time. I'll use one line to show the signal we called S, one for C, and one for the output of the **nand,** which I called x in the diagram.

I'll make up some signals for S and C, and then we can use our knowledge of the **nand** truth table to figure out what x will do. I'll draw some vertical dashed lines to let us line things up. Oh. And I'll assume that the C input is active when it's 1.

Q 404 What's the truth table for **nand** again?

A   Why don't you figure it out while I'm drawing the timing diagram.

Nand stands for **not-and,** so just take the **not** of the **and** truth table.

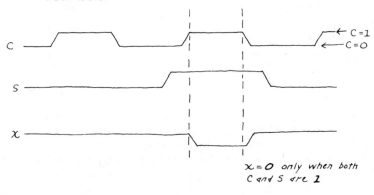

$x = 0$ only when both C and S are 1

*Figure 31 Timing diagram for the R-S flip-flop made out of **nands***

OK. What do you have?

Q 405 Is this right? The output of a **nand** is 1 unless both inputs are 1?

A   Right. So you can see that I've shown x staying at 1 except during the time period when both S and C are 1.

Q 406 You didn't line things up very well.

A   You mean . . . oh. Like the fact that x doesn't drop down into the 0 state until a little after both inputs are 1? That's deliberate. There's a time delay before a logic gate can respond. That's one of the factors that limits how fast a computer can run. You have to leave enough time for the circuit elements to react. I've tried to indicate that by drawing the **edges** (the transitions from 0 to 1 and vice versa) sloped instead of straight up and down. The idea

is that if you stuck an oscilloscope on the inputs and output
of the **nand**, you'd see something like the timing diagram.
Since a logic component can't change state instantaneously, the oscilloscope trace won't jump instantaneously
from the 0 value to the 1.

Another notation you see sometimes is like this:

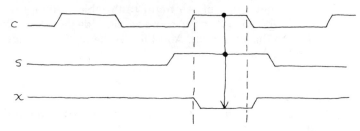

Figure 32   The dots and arrow show that x
        depends on the particular state of C and S

The arrow shows that x's going to 0 is caused by the
states of C and S. On really complicated timing diagrams,
that kind of notation can make it easier to see what's going
on.

Q 407 What good is the diagram, though? I already know how
a **nand** works.

A   But do you see how the circuit for the R-S flip-flop works?
It's not that easy to figure out just using truth tables. Let
me draw out the timing diagram for the whole circuit . . .
in the following situation. Let's assume that Q is 0, and
then, at some point in time, the S input goes high. What's
supposed to happen?

Q 408 Let me look at the transition table [Figure 29]. If S is
1, then Q is supposed to become 1.

A   Right. When the C input is active, S = 1 **sets** the flip-flop,
making Q be 1 and Q̄ = 0. Let's see if we can figure out
how all that happens.
First, let's verify that there really are two different stable
states, corresponding to Q = 1, Q̄ = 0 and Q = 0, Q̄ = 1.
Look at the circuit a minute. As long as the C input is
0, then both x and y are guaranteed to be 1, right?

Q 409 Right. It goes into the **nand** . . . right.

A   OK. Now look in the timing diagram [Figure 33] where
I've marked "stable state Q = 0", and follow around the
circuit.
Since x is 1 and Q̄ is 1, the upper **nand** puts out a 0.
That doesn't cause anything to change, because the 0
from Q makes the lower **nand** put out a 1. Right?

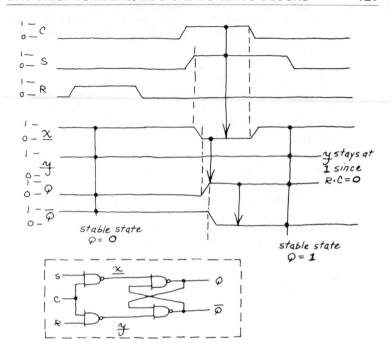

Figure 33 The circuit has two stable states
corresponding to $Q = 0$ and $Q = 1$

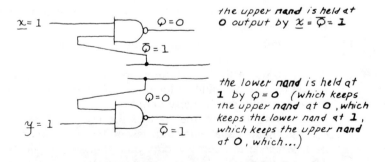

the upper **nand** is held at
0 output by $\underline{x} = \overline{Q} = 1$

the lower **nand** is held at
1 by $Q = 0$ (which keeps
the upper **nand** at **0**, which
keeps the lower **nand** at **1**,
which keeps the upper **nand**
at **0**, which...)

Figure 34 The conditions which combine
to make $Q = 0$, $\overline{Q} = 1$ a stable
situation

Q 410 I _think_ I see what you're getting at. If Q is 0, it makes
       Q̄ be 1 which makes Q stay at 0, which makes Q̄ stay
       1, which . . .

A   Exactly. Maybe that's a good way to describe it.
       OK. Over to the right of the timing diagram, I've marked
       "stable state Q=1", which is the other stable state. It's
       symmetric to the first stable state. Now Q is 1 which makes
       Q̄ be 0 which makes Q stay 1 which . . . as you described
       it before.
       Now the only question is, how do you switch the circuit
       from one stable state to the other? And that's shown in
       the center of the timing diagram. When S and C are both
       1, suppose x suddenly goes to 0. Then no matter _what_
       Q̄ is, Q is going to switch to 1 (because if either input
       to a **nand** is 0, the output is 1). When that happens,
       the lower **nand**'s inputs change from 0, 1 to 1,1 so Q̄
       switches from 1 to 0, and the overall circuit is now in
       the other stable state. It'll stay in that state until the R
       and C inputs are both 1.

Q 411 Phew. That _was_ a little tricky. Are flip-flops always that
       complicated to figure out?

A   No. You usually just think of a flip-flop as a black box,
       without worrying about how it works inside. You think
       in terms of the transition diagram.

Q 412 Is that what you mean by **black box**?

A   Oh, right. **Black box** is an old term from circuit analysis.
       A black box is a circuit that you deal with in terms of
       its inputs and outputs, without knowing the details of
       what's inside.
       Using flip-flops isn't nearly as hard as figuring out how
       that circuit worked. Let me give you an example.
       Suppose we have an i/o device (say, a keyboard) that
       sends in **serial data.**

Q 413 If I remember right, that means the signal comes in one
       bit at a time, right?

A   Right. To make things a little simpler, let's assume that
       we get 8 serial bits, and all the timing problems are solved
       by circuitry we won't worry about.
       So we want to build the part of the i/o interface that
       accepts the 8 serial bits and assembles them into one
       byte, which it puts on the data bus. Remember that the
       data bus is parallel, i.e. it has a wire for each bit and
       brings all 8 bits to the controller at once.
       Here's a circuit which uses J-K flip-flops to convert serial
       bits into a parallel 8-bit pattern.

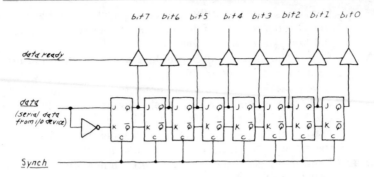

Figure 35 Circuit which converts 8 bits
received serially into one byte in
parallel

Here's how it works. Data enters (from the left of the diagram) one bit at a time from the i/o device. Each time a bit arrives, the line marked **synch** (for **synchronization,** of course) goes high (into the **1** state) for a while. Since the synch line is wired to the C inputs on the flip-flop, it allows the latest bit to enter the first (leftmost) flip-flop. See how that goes?

Q 414 I think so. You've got the first flip-flop wired so it acts like one of the other kinds, don't you?

A Right. It's wired to work like a D flip-flop. If you have D flip-flops lying around, you could use them just as well. I usually just have J-K's since they're the most general and they cost about the same.

Anyway, if a **O** has come in from the i/o device, when the **synch** pulse arrives, Q will become **O,** because the input makes the J input on the flip-flop be **O** and the K be **1.** If the circuit is designed right, namely if the **synch** signal doesn't stay 1 too long, then that's the end of it until the next bit comes.

Q 415 Wait a minute. What do you mean "if the synch signal doesn't stay 1 too long"? [Editor's note: Using flip-flops whose C inputs are enabled by a *transition* from 0 to 1 eliminates this worry.]

A Well, first let's see what we *want* to happen. At the same time a bit arrives at the first flip-flop, the second flip-flop is receiving the current state of the first flip-flop. Right? So when the synch line goes high to allow the incoming bit to enter the first flip-flop, it also enables the second flip-flop. So what happens?

Q 416 Let me see . . . the J input to the second flip-flop comes

from the Q output of the first one, and the K comes from
the Q, so the second flip-flop goes into whatever state
the first one is in.

A   Right. The second flip-flop enters whatever state the first
flip-flop was in *before* the most recent synch pulse. See
how it works? The data bits enter one at a time, and as
each one enters, the previously stored values shift one
position to the right. After all eight bits are in, the **data
ready** signal goes to 1, and the parallel data appears on
the eight lines at the top of the diagram.

Q 417 I still don't quite see how the **synch** pulse affects things,
and I don't understand what the **data ready** line is doing . . .

A   OK, I'll try again.

Maybe the way to answer your first question is to draw
what happens in a specific case.

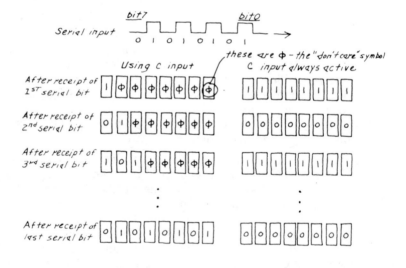

*Figure 36 Action of the circuit. Using the synch
signal on the left, ignoring it on the right*

I've drawn a box for each flip-flop, without bothering to
put in all the interconnections. Inside each box, I've written
the flip-flop's state. Since we don't care what states the
flip-flops were in at the beginning (it's whatever was left
from the last serial to parallel conversion), I've written a
∅ to indicate that. ∅ is the symbol that's usually used
to indicate that you **don't care** what value is there,
although sometimes a *d* is used instead. You can read

$\emptyset$ as the Greek letter "phi", or else think of it as a **1** on top of a **0,** meaning it could be one or the other.

Now do you see what the **synch** signal is for? Why it's hooked to the C inputs of all the flip-flops? If we didn't do that, when the next serial bit comes in, all the flip-flops would go ka-chunk, ka-chunk, ka-chunk into the same state, and we'd lose everything but the last bit.

Q 418 All right. I see that now. But . . .

A   Right. Your other question.

The **data ready** line controls the **tri-state bus drivers** (along the top of the diagram). You certainly don't want the values stored in the flip-flops to affect the data bus until the entire 8 bits are in their proper places. And more, you don't want to place the value on the data bus until the controller is ready to receive it, so other (unshown) circuitry will have to provide the **data ready** signal when the right conditions are met.

Once all 8 serial bits have been received, the flip-flops store them until the **data ready** line releases them in parallel. There are a couple of terms that refer to that sort of situation. The flip-flops can be called a **buffer,** or a **latch.** Either term refers to a circuit that serves as an interface between two subsystems by accepting a value from the first subsystem and holding it until the second subsystem is ready for it. When the C input to a flip-flop is inactive, you say the value stored in the flip-flop is **latched,** because even if the signals at J and K go away or change, Q won't change.

Q 419 My basic feeling is that overall, the circuit isn't that complicated, but there's a tremendous number of little details. And words.

A   I'll agree with that.

We could go on with this example, elaborating it, but I think you've seen enough to get the general idea. We've gone over pretty much today . . . All the way from the very basics of binary numbers, to Boolean algebra, through the circuit components that implement the Boolean operators, to a little bit about how you put those components together to form circuits. Why don't we quit?

DAY 3: DIAGRAMS - GETTING INTO THE HARDWARE

Structure vs. Function

Q 420 You know, I was thinking that if I could really understand all the diagrams I come across in the magazines, I'd be half-way to understanding what's going on.

A That's probably true, but there are so . . .

Q 421 I know — there are so many different kinds of diagrams that you can't say anything in general. I'm way ahead of you this time. I brought along a bunch of diagrams, and I thought you could go over one of each type. How's that sound?

A Fine. Actually there *are* a few things you can say in general. The thing you need to keep straight when you're looking at a diagram is what that specific diagram is actually used for. People who are soldering components on a circuit board need a different sort of diagram from people who are planning a complete computer system from people who are trying to program a particular machine. Each type of diagram represents a different mix of physical reality and functional conceptualization.

Q 422 I'm going to get some coffee. Want some?

A Let me put it this way. Any piece of computer hardware has two aspects to it. It has a **structure,** an actual physical shape, something you can touch. And it has a **function,** that is, it does something that's meaningful to us, some sort of information processing.

A pocket calculator is a device that has a **structure,** it has buttons in certain places, has IC chips mounted in it in specific spots, has wires, etc. It also has a **function,** namely that it adds, subtracts, so on. You can hand me the device, but you *tell* me about the function.

133

Different diagrams represent different mixes of **structural and functional information**.

Q 423 Here's your coffee. Why don't you just explain this diag. . .

A   One kind of diagram may be showing things about a circuit's function, telling the meaning of the inputs and outputs, without much regard for what the circuits are made up of. Another may concentrate on the structure, and show where the circuit components are placed without showing what they do.

Q 424 Why don't you just take this diagram and tell me what you see in it?

Functional block diagram

A   OK. OK.
      This one conveys functional information mostly. It's called a **principles of operation diagram** or a **functional block diagram** of a microprocessor. It shows those parts of the microprocessor design a person needs to know to write programs for it.

Q 425 What does **block diagram** mean?

A   A **block diagram** is a diagram that shows interconnectivities among component parts without showing the internal structure of those parts. Instead, it gives a word or phrase that describes the function of each component. It shows the basic building blocks of the system.
      The diagram you've got there shows the major functional components of the microprocessor and the data flow paths between them. The skinny arrows that stick out of the dotted line show signals that enter or leave the microprocessor chip. To know which pin on the actual chip those signals correspond to, we'll need a different sort of diagram.
      The fat arrows indicate 8 bit wide data paths that are on the chip itself.*

Q 426 How do you know they're 8 bits wide?

A   Well, I'm assuming that because each of the subsystems they connect is shown to have a capacity of 8 bits. By looking at this diagram, we can tell that this particular microcomputer can directly access a memory of $2^{16} =$ 65 536 bytes. There are 16 **address lines** (so 2^{16} different addresses are possible) and there are 8 **data lines** (so each memory location can contain up to 8 bits).
      Of course it has an **instruction register** to hold the current

---

*Major subsystems of a microprocessor Q 77-85

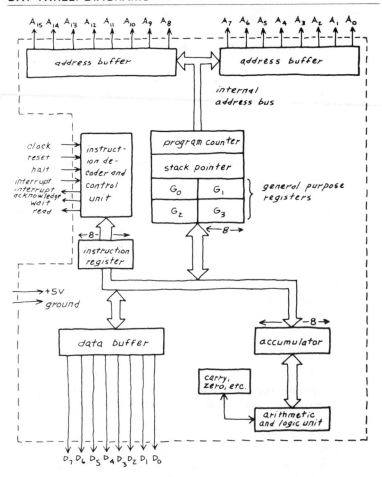

Figure 37 Functional block diagram for a hypothetical 8-bit microprocessor

program instruction, and a **decoder and control subsystem** to figure out what the instruction is and to generate the control signals to carry it out. It has an **accumulator** and an **arithmetic and logic unit (ALU)**, a **program counter**, a **stack pointer register**, and four **general purpose registers**.

We can tell a few more things from the diagram. For instance, some of the instructions probably take longer to execute than others, and . . .

Q 427 Wait. What makes you say that?

A   Well, the whole block of registers is shown connecting to a single **internal data bus.** That means that if more than one byte has to be moved around to carry out an instruction, they'll have to go one byte at a time, so it'll take more than one basic machine cycle.

Q 428 What sorts of instructions would there be?
        details of specific microprocessors Day 5

A   Well, we could sit here all day making reasonable guesses about what instructions a microprocessor with this particular organization would have, but let's not get ridiculous. This kind of diagram isn't used to show that — it's used to show you what registers the thing has and how data values can flow in it. You'll never come across a diagram like this all by itself. It'll be with the manufacturer's description of the basic machine instructions. It gives you a picture to think in terms of as you read what the individual instructions do.

Q 429 And it shows how the microprocessor is wired.

A   Not really. It shows the main functional interconnections. The things that concern you when you're programming in machine language or assembly language. It certainly doesn't show *all* the interconnections.

Q 430 It doesn't.

A   No. Look. The connections that supply power to each component part aren't indicated at all. And the box labeled **instruction decoder and control unit** obviously has to have connections running all over the place . . .

Q 431 If you pried off the top of the chip and looked in with a microscope, would it be laid out like this, at least? I know it would have a lot more detail, but would it be roughly like this?

A   Not necessarily, no. Again — this kind of diagram is concerned almost exclusively with details of function, not the actual physical structure.

The incredible complexity of it all

A   I just happen to have a couple of blow ups of the inside of some chips. Want to see them?

Q 432 Sure.

A   OK. This one shows the inside of an Intel 8080. Pretty wild, huh?

Figure 38: The insides of an Intel 8080 microprocessor chip. Thanks to the Intel Corporation for permission to use this photo.

Q 433 What are the large light colored squares around the edges?

A   That's where the inputs and outputs enter and leave the chip. They weld tiny wires to them, wires that run to the pins you see on the completed chip.

If you wanted to think of this photograph as a diagram, you could say that it's the other extreme from the last one. It's virtually all structural information, whereas the last one was virtually all functional information.

Q 434 Are you saying that you can't figure out how the machine works from the photograph?

A   I would guess that even if you were very familiar with computers and digital electronics, that if someone handed you this photograph, put you in a sealed room with just pencil, paper, and food, and told you you couldn't come out until you had an accurate description of the machine organization . . .

Q   Yes?

A   That you'd never make it out of the room. Just think of how many ways the inputs and outputs could be assigned to pins!

Blow ups like this are fun to look at, though. They're amazingly complex.

Q 435 What's the other one you have?

A A minute. I don't want to give you the idea that someone couldn't tell you what each subpattern you see there does. Certainly every zig and every zag is there for a purpose.

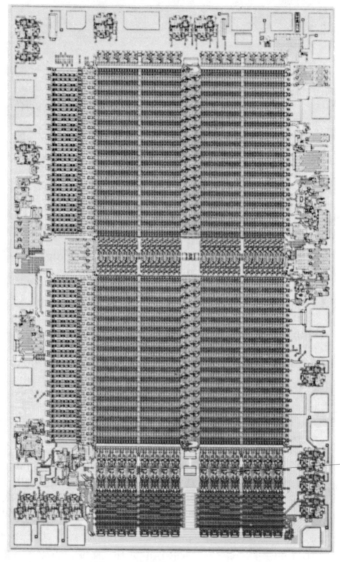

Figure 39: 4096 bit dynamic RAM Photo credit: Intel Corporation.

It's just that other documentation, other sorts of diagrams would be needed. You don't see that kind of thing very often because there's not much you can do with it. If a microprocessor chip doesn't work, you can't very well go in armed with a circuit diagram, a microscope, and a pair of tweezers hoping to fix the offending little mound of silicon. You throw the chip away and get another one.

Q 436 The disposable computer. If it breaks, you throw it away. How 20th century.

A The other blow up is of a RAM chip. Specifically, it's Intel's version of a 2107 4096 bit dynamic RAM.*

Q 437 It's a lot more regular . . .

A One memory location looks like the next when you don't know what's stored in them.

Let me show you some other diagrams of the same chip. The photograph gives structural information about the internal circuitry. Another sort of diagram you'll see is a **pin configuration diagram**, which shows what signals should be attached to each pin on the package the chip comes in.

RAM Q 51

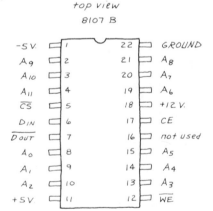

top view
8107 B

$-5V.$	1	22	GROUND
A_9	2	21	A_8
A_{10}	3	20	A_7
A_{11}	4	19	A_6
$\overline{CS}$	5	18	$+12V.$
D_{IN}	6	17	CE
$\overline{D_{OUT}}$	7	16	not used
A_0	8	15	A_5
A_1	9	14	A_4
A_2	10	13	A_3
$+5V$	11	12	$\overline{WE}$

$A_0 - A_{11}$ address (need 12 lines since $2^{12} = 4096$)

D_{IN} Data in (bit to be stored at location given by $A_0 - A_{11}$)

$\overline{D_{OUT}}$ Data out (complement of bit stored at location given by $A_0 - A_{11}$)

$\overline{WE}$ Write Enable (if this is high, **read**, if low, **write**)

CE Chip Enable

$\overline{CS}$ Not Chip Select (used to control refresh cycle)

Figure 40   Pin configuration diagram —
4096 bit dynamic RAM chip

Q 438 I'm still not too sure about your division into functional
and structural information. What would you say this diagram is in those terms?

A   I'd say it's a mixture, but why don't you tell me what
you think it is?

Q 439 I guess it's structural information because it shows what
the pins on the actual chip look like. But on the other
hand, it seems functional because the descriptions below
the drawing tell what it does, sort of.

A   Yeh. That's the way it seems to me too. A mixture. How
about this diagram? It's a **logic symbol,** that is, it's the
way you'd show the chip on a circuit diagram.

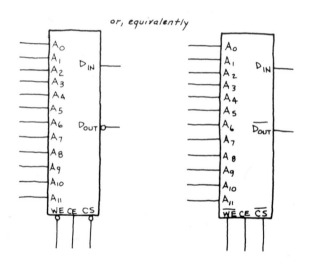

*Figure 41   Logic symbol - 4096 bit
dynamic RAM chip*

Q 440 I guess it's mostly functional . . . when would you use
these kinds of diagrams?

A   You use the **logic symbol** when you're making a diagram
showing how the circuit works, how the functional proper-
ties of each of the components are combined to make
the overall circuit. You use the **pin configuration diagram**
when you're showing structural details of how the actual
components are to be placed on the circuit board, and
what pins to solder to what.

Maybe it would help if we looked back at the corresponding
two diagrams of a **nand.**

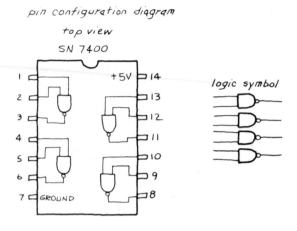

pin configuration diagram

top view

SN 7400

logic symbol

Figure 42   Pin configuration diagram and logic
symbol for quad 2-input nand.

Let's look at some more diagrams that use these kinds
of symbols and it'll come clear.

Q 441 The little circles on the logic symbol . . . I mean on the
RAM chip . . what does that mean there beside D_{out}. That
the D_{out} signal is negated?

A   Right. With this particular technology, it's easier to produce the negation (the **not**) of the stored bit for some
reason. If you store a 1, then when you read from that
location, you get back a 0.

Q 442 Doesn't that cause trouble?

A   Not as long as you know about it. You can design the
RAM board so it negates that signal before placing it on
the data bus.

Q 443 One last question. If this chip stores just one bit at each
address . . .

A   Then what do you do if you want your memory to store
a *byte* at each location?

Q 444 Right.

A   You use eight chips, one per bit. I think I saw a diagram
that shows something like that in the stack you brought
. . . let's see.

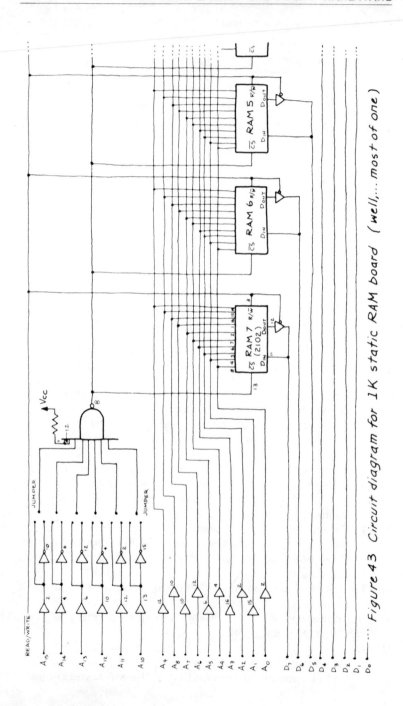

Figure 43 Circuit diagram for 1K static RAM board (well,...most of one)

Circuit diagrams

OK. This is a **circuit diagram,** or **schematic,** of a 1K RAM board. It uses a different kind of RAM chip than the one we just looked at. Probably we should look up the details of that chip, but assuming there's no mistakes in the schematic (not always a very good assumption), we can figure out most of the details from it.

Q 445 If you pulled this board out of a computer, is this what it would look like?

A Well, not exactly, but somewhat. The components are indicated by their logic symbols, i.e. by their functions, but if you look closely, you can see some little numbers beside some of the elements that indicate **pin numbers** on the actual chips. So it's sort of a hybrid diagram. Using it, you can find your way around on the actual board, even though the interconnections are shown in a stylized form. This is the sort of diagram you'd use if you were

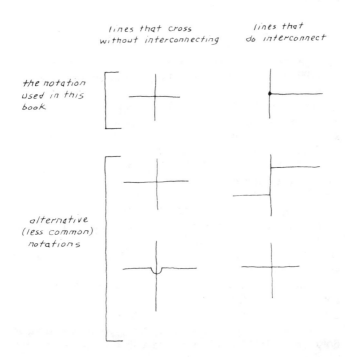

Figure 44 Ways of showing lines that cross versus lines which interconnect

trying to trouble shoot the board. It gives you enough
of the functional details so you can figure out what sorts
of signals you should be seeing, plus it gives enough
structural information so you can tell what pin to measure
from.

Let's see. Are all the symbols obvious? Is it clear what
the difference is between lines that cross and lines that
interconnect?

I assume you know the symbol for ground? And for
resistors?

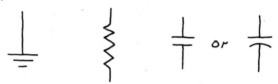

electrical ground   resistor   capacitor

Q   Yes. Sure.

A   Ok. Let's see what we can deduce from the schematic.
First of all, we can see the 16 address lines A_0 through
A_{15} coming to the board from the address bus — at the
left of the diagram. Lines A_{10} through A_{15} go storming into
a **nand** gate, and A_0 through A_9 get sent to each chip.
If 10 address lines get sent to each chip, that must be
because there are $2^{10} = 1024$ different memory locations
on the board.

Q 446 But there are 8 RAM chips on the board . . .

A   Yeh, but just like the last RAM chip we saw, each chip
stores only one bit. See, you can tell that by looking at
the data lines D_0 through D_7. One goes to each chip. So
each of the 1024 different addresses corresponds to one
byte, one bit per chip.

Q 447 So this must tie in to the way they describe memory chips
in the ads like 256x1 RAM, 32x8 ROM, so on?

A   Right. From the schematic, we can tell that the 2102 RAM
chips must be of the 1024x1 type.
OK. We've accounted for 10 of the address lines. What
are the other ones (A_{10} through A_{15}) doing?

Q 448 They go through a **nand** and then to the chips . . . at
a place marked CS. What's that mean?

A   Let's back up a bit.
It's unlikely that a home computer system would have
only 1K of RAM, so this board will be one of several.
Obviously, each memory location has to have a unique
address, so the other six address lines . . .

Q 449 The other address lines must somehow be telling which
board?

A   Something like that, right. By choosing what values of A_{10} through A_{15} the RAM chips on this board respond to, we can choose where this 1K of memory is in the address space of the controller.

Q 450   **Address space?**

A   Since there are 16 lines on the address bus, the processor is capable of specifying $2^{16} = 65\,536$ different memory addresses. Those 65 536 possible addresses make up the **address space** of the controller. When you add memory to the system, you can select which block of addresses will refer to that block of memory. That means that you're selecting which part of the address space the memory lies in. Unless you need (and can afford) 65 536 bytes of memory, you won't fill the entire range of possibilities, you'll leave part of the address space empty.

So now let's go over how the address lines A_{10} through A_{15} can be used to fix what region of the address space this board will be in.

Q 451   If I bought a board like this, I'd have to decide that, right?

A   Right. It's not hard, but since you need to know what addresses to use when you write programs, you want to make a reasonable choice.

Q 452   Wouldn't you just start at zero and keep working up as you got more memory?

A   That would be reasonable in a lot of cases, but sometimes you need some memory at the very top of the address space. For instance, the 6800 chip has some instructions that implicitly address memory locations $FFF8_{16}$ through $FFFF_{16}$. So, if you want to use those instructions at all, you'll need some memory at the top of the address space. Also, . . .

Q 453   What on earth do those instructions do?*
interrupts Q 488

A   They're used with interrupts. But let's go over that later. Let's get back to this specific board. You can tell from the circuit diagram that you choose the addresses by putting wires **(jumpers)** in the appropriate places. You have the choice of connecting the big **nand** up to each address line as it is, or a negated version of it, see? Look. There where it says "jumpers", at the upper left?

Q 454   Go on. I see where you mean, but how does it work? And what is that resistor doing that runs to V_{cc}?

A   Oh. The resistor. That's a little bit of structural reality creeping in. Most logic gates like **nands** come with either 2, 4, or 8 inputs. Since in this case, there are 6 inputs that we want to run into the **nand** (the 6 derived from address lines A_{10} through A_{15}), there are two unneeded inputs to the (8 input) **nand**. Remember that the output of a **nand** is low only if all its inputs are high? If we didn't make sure the unused inputs were kept at a high level, they'd get in the way, they'd affect the output of the **nand**. Tying the unused lines to the high voltage level is a way to make an 8 input **nand** act like a 6 input one. OK? Now. Let's suppose that we've decided to place the memory in locations 0400_{16} = 00000100 00000000$_2$ up to $07FF_{16}$ = 00000111 11111111$_2$ Then we'd put jumpers on $\overline{A}_{15}$, $\overline{A}_{14}$, $\overline{A}_{13}$, $\overline{A}_{12}$, $\overline{A}_{11}$, and A_{10}. That means that the output of the **nand** will be high unless A_{11} through A_{15} are low and A_{10} is high. OK so far?

Q 455 No.

A OK, let's work it out.

nand $\overline{(\overline{A}_{15}, \overline{A}_{14}, \overline{A}_{13}, \overline{A}_{12}, \overline{A}_{11}, A_{10})} = \overline{\overline{A}_{15} \cdot \overline{A}_{14} \cdot \overline{A}_{13} \cdot \overline{A}_{12} \cdot \overline{A}_{11} \cdot A_{10}}$
which, using DeMorgan's Theorem is
DeMorgan's Theorem Q 363

$$= A_{15} + A_{14} + A_{13} + A_{12} + A_{11} + \overline{A}_{10}$$

So it's like I said. The only time the output will be low is when the address lines A_{15} down to A_{10} have the values 000001.

Q 456 All right. Let's see. The output of the **nand** goes to each RAM to a pin marker $\overline{CS}$, which stands for . . .

A "Not Chip Select", which is a signal that tells the chip whether it should do anything. If that pin is high, it means that that chip isn't **selected,** that it should ignore its other inputs.

The only time the chips *are* selected is when the address lines A_{10} through A_{15} are in the states we said.

Q 457 I see. So if the chip *is* selected, then the lines A_0 through A_9 tell which location on the chip . . .

A Right.

Let's follow through what happens when a specific address is placed on the address lines, and a WRITE operation is taking place. I'll draw wiggly lines on the pathways that the relevant signals take. Pick an address, any address.

Q 458 How about zero?

A Well, that's not a real good choice, since the way we picked the jumpers, this board isn't supposed to respond to that address, but here.

See, since CS stays at 1, the chips aren't selected, and nothing happens.

Pick another address.

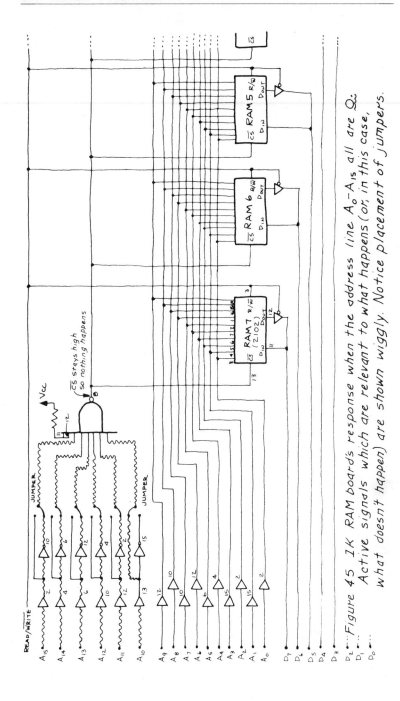

Figure 45 1K RAM board's response when the address line A_0-A_{15} all are 0. Active signals which are relevant to what happens (or, in this case, what doesn't happen) are shown wiggly. Notice placement of jumpers.

Q 459 All right. Let me see. A_{10} has to be 1, doesn't it.

A   Right. And A_{11} through A_{15} have to be 0.

Q 460 How about 0000010000000111?

A   OK. Something should happen for that. And what byte do you want stored at that location?

Q 461 What *byte*?

A   We're doing a write operation, so there needs to be some value on the data lines, something to store.

Q 462 Oh. How about, uh, 11111100.

A   OK. Here goes.

First, you can see that the upper six bits of the address make the output of the **nand** go to 0, so $\overline{CS}$, is low to all the RAM chips, enabling them.

Then, since we're doing a write operation, the **read / write** line will be low.

Q 463 That comes from the controller?

A   Right.

So that sets up the RAM chips to accept a value on their D_{in} pins, and that value comes zinging in from the data lines.

Q 464 There's something complicated going on in the circuit beside each RAM chip . . . where the D_{in} and D_{out} pins go.

A   Well, you can see that there's just one data line for each chip: data line D_0 goes to RAM 0 only, and D_1 goes to RAM 1 only, and so on. But on each chip, there are *two* pins for data. One marked D_{in} for data to enter the chip during a write operation, and a separate pin marked D_{out} for data to leave the chip during a read operation.

You could say that the data bus is **bi-directional** and the chip pins are **uni-directional**. The circuitry there beside each chip sorts the incoming signals from the outgoing ones. I think if you stare at it for a while you'll be able to figure it out.

System configuration diagram

Q 465 I came across this diagram — it's just like one you drew the first day. Do you have anything more to say about it?

A   I feel pretty talkative today, I'm sure I can come up with something more to say about it.

It's called something like a **system configuration diagram.** It's much less specific than the last diagram we looked at. It shows the flow of information between the microprocessor chip and the various things it interacts with

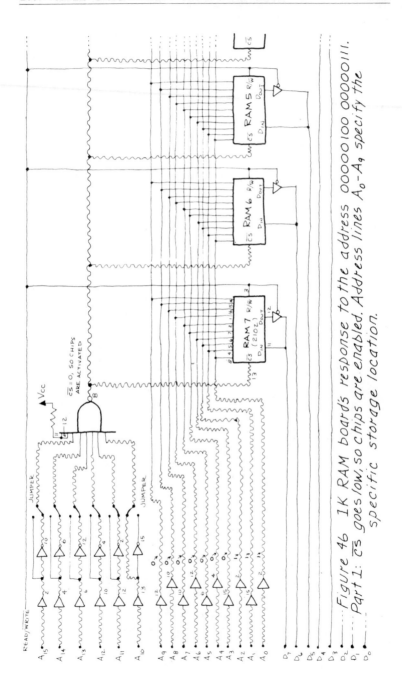

Figure 46 1K RAM board's response to the address 0000 0100 0000 0111. Part 1: $\overline{CS}$ goes low, so chips are enabled. Address lines $A_0 - A_9$ specify the specific storage location.

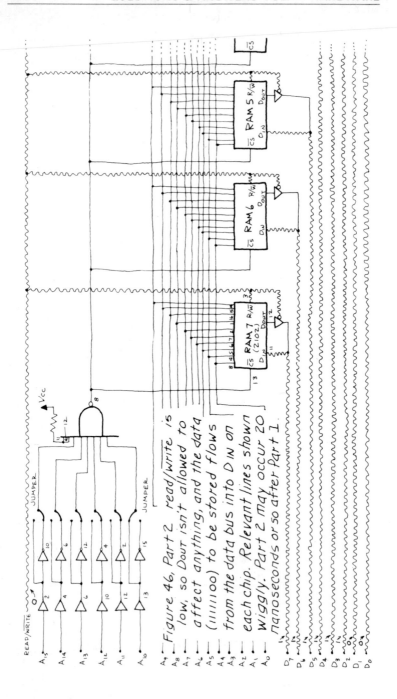

Figure 46, Part 2. read/write is low, so Dout isn't allowed to affect anything, and the data (1111100) to be stored flows from the data bus into Din on each chip. Relevant lines shown wiggly. Part 2 may occur 20 nanoseconds or so after Part 1.

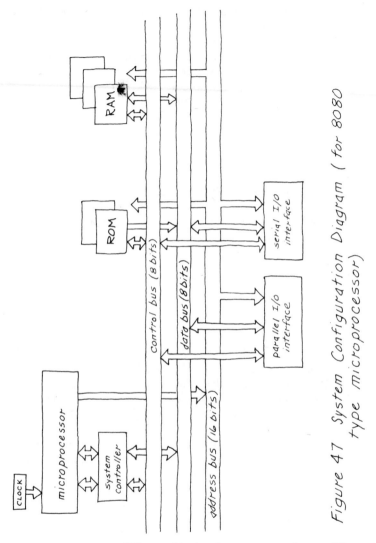

Figure 47 System Configuration Diagram (for 8080 type microprocessor)

— here, two different kinds of memory and two different kinds of peripheral device interfaces.

Q 466 You covered the address bus and the data bus pretty well before. [Q 87 — 100] What exactly is the **control bus**?

A It carries the control signals the controller sends and receives from the other devices. We've already seen a number of the control signals that are necessary. For instance, the **read / write** signal that determines whether the RAM chips are supposed to supply a stored value or accept a new value to be stored comes to the RAM board through the control bus.

I wonder if I've made it clear enough that the division of the wires interconnecting the parts of a computer system into **address, data,** and **control** busses is just a functional description. If you take the cover off a home computer and look at the busses, they're just a bunch of wires . . .

Let's see. Other signals that go over the wires in the control bus are ones that let peripheral devices make requests to the controller, for interrupts and direct memory access operations. . .

Q 467 All right. I want to go into those, but first tell me when and how you actually use a diagram like this.

A   OK. It's a high level (i.e. abstract, with few specific details) diagram. It just gives an overview of the way the various parts of the system are tied together. If you were being introduced to a new computer system, this would be one of the very first things you'd want to look at, so that as you got into more and more detail, you could keep everything in perspective.

Q 468 But aren't all computer systems organized like this?

A   No. A lot of the earlier computer systems didn't use a bus organization at all, and not all systems that do use it do it quite this way. Some of them save a few wires by using a single bus for different things at different times. That's called a **multiplexed** bus organization. If you do that, then of course, you need additional circuitry to put the right signals on the bus at the right time, to sort out what's what.

Also, not all computer systems have ROM memory . . .

Q 469 You said that the busses are really just a bunch of wires . . . how do you . . . I guess I'm asking if you can't get more specific information from the diagram. . .

A   I'm not real sure what you want to know . . . On some systems, the busses take the form of ribbon cable. I'm sure you've seen ads for that stuff. It's flat, plastic coated cable that has a number (maybe as many as 50 or 100) of individual wires in it, side by side. That makes it easy to add new devices that won't fit in the cabinet your microcomputer comes in . . . you run a length of ribbon cable from one device to the next, making the necessary connections.

On home computers that come with huge cabinets, like the Altair 8800 series or the Imsai 8080, there's a big printed circuit board (called a **mother board**) that has the bus wires printed on it. To hook a new chunk of memory onto the bus, for example, you buy a connector, solder it to the bus lines on the mother board, and then plug the new memory card into the connector.

Does that answer anything?

Q 476 Not completely.

But before I forget it, what's a **mother board**? You just mentioned it and I've come across the term several times.

A   A **mother board** is a large board that has other boards (**daughter boards**) mounted on it.

Q 471 That's all? It doesn't mean anything else?

A   No. What were you thinking of?

Q 472 Never mind . . .

I think you should go into more detail on how busses work. It seems like we keep coming across them. They seem to be what holds everything together.

How do busses work?

A   OK. Remember the idea behind them? Instead of running separate wires to and from each device you want the processor to communicate with, and having to add logic to sort out what goes where each time you add a new memory board or i/o interface, you hang everything on a common set of wires called a **bus.** Of course, when you do that, you have to make sure that only one device affects the bus at a time.

Q 473 Right. I remember that.

A   There are two different popular ways to build busses. One is the so-called **open-collector** technique, and the other is the **tri-state** bus I think we mentioned before.

Let me draw a box with a transistor sticking out the end to represent a device that has the open-collector type of output.

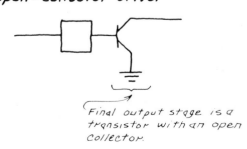

open-collector driver

Final output stage is a transistor with an open collector.

The output is either a high resistance or a short to ground, depending on whether the input to the final transistor is 1 or 0, respectively.

The tri-state driver has three different outputs, namely, short to ground (for a 0 output), a voltage source (for a 1 output), and an extremely high resistance (virtually an open-circuit). The last condition is the tri-state output.

tri-state driver

Q 474 Wait a minute. I thought I was following you . . . but I don't see how the open-collector thing works. I see that a short to ground makes the output voltage zero, so that corresponds to a 0, but how does it put out the voltage to make a 1 signal?

A Ah. The circuit designer has to do that for it. You do it by adding a **pull-up resistor.** Like this

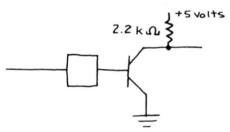

Q 475 And that does what, exactly?

A Let's look at the two possible cases. If the device is transmitting a 0, the output transistor conducts, effectively shorting the output to ground. So, the circuit component the output leads to sees zero volts — a 0 signal.

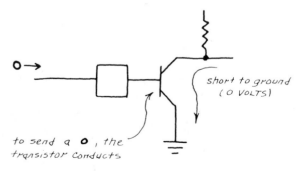

Q 476 All right, I'll buy that.

A   In the other case, when the device is putting out a 1 signal,
        the output transistor isn't conducting, and presents a high
        resistance. To make it easier to see what's going on, we
        can assume that in this situation, the transistor acts like
        an open circuit. (It isn't quite, and that can cause trouble
        if a large number of open-collectors devices are used
        together.)
        If the transistor presents an open circuit, the output line
        must be at 5 volts, because no current is flowing through
        the pull-up resistor. That gives us the 1 signal.

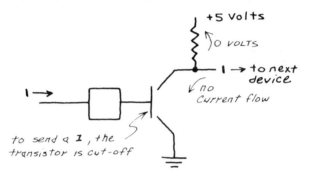

To form a bus using open-collector devices, you hang them
all on a common wire. Then, if any one of the devices
goes into the 0 state (becomes a short circuit), the whole
bus goes to 0. Otherwise a pull-up resistor keeps the whole
line at +5 volts, indicating a 1.

Q 477 My circuit theory is a little rusty, but that seems clear
        enough, I guess. In fact, it seems like it would be simpler
        to use than the tri-state method because you don't need
        a separate signal to put the driver into the tri-state.

A   There are two main reasons people use the tri-state
        scheme. First, when you use an open-collector type of bus,
        you have to arrange things so that any signal that the
        microprocessor needs to communicate or receive involves
        at least some of the lines going to 0. Do you see that?
        Because the pull-up resistor keeps the bus at a 1 signal
        unless . . .

Q 478 No, I see why. I guess that makes the bus a little less
        convenient to use.

A   The second reason is that when the open-collector device
        is in the 1 state, it isn't *quite* an open circuit — it puts
        a measurable load on the bus line. So if you have a lot
        of things on the bus, it can start to draw a lot of current.
        And hand in hand with that, the open-collector arrange-

ment is more prone to noise problems. Oh . . . Also, I think that tri-state drivers (at least the way they're made now) are faster. . .

All in all, it's just cleaner to use a tri-state bus.

Q 479 All right. And to make a tri-state bus you just hook all the driver outputs to the same line?

A   Until you said that, I thought you were following all this. If you mean exactly what you said, then the answer is no. Think of a data bus for a minute, and let's imagine hooking up several RAM boards to it. On each board, there's a bus driver for each bit, right? Because data gets transferred to and from memory a byte at a time.

All the drivers that correspond to bit position 0 on all the memory boards attach to the same wire in the data bus, all the ones that correspond to bit 1 attach to their own wire, all the ones that correspond to bit 2 attach to yet another wire, so on.

Q 480 That's what I meant. I meant, you don't have to do anything fancy.

A   OK. You also have to design the system so that no more than one device uses a bus at once. When *no* devices are using a bus, it's said to be **floating.**

Q 481 Floating? Why floating? Why not empty . . . or unchartered?

A   Unchartered? . . . oh. Hah.

Floating because it's not tied to ground or to a voltage source, it's just, well, floating. Maybe with a small signal on it from electrical noise.

Q 482 Do you know off hand which manufacturer's use which kind of bus?

A   Not really. I know that DEC machines like the PDP-11 series (including the LSI-11 microcomputer) use the open-collector scheme. The Altair 8800's, the Imsai 8080, the Sphere systems use tri-state busses. I think that most computers made especially for the home market use tri-state busses.

Obviously if you're going to go hanging more memory or i/o interfaces on a specific computer system, you'd better find out which kind of bus it uses. They're not compatible.

Q 483 I guess that covers busses.

A   Oh no. That's just some background info so you'll have an idea what people are talking about when they mention a specific kind of bus — you also need to know more about how they're used. I thought I'd go over the main ideas.

Q 484 Wait a minute . . . I'm getting a little bit lost here. When you say "use a bus", are you talking about how you design things to hook on it, or are you talking about what signals go over it, or . . .

A   Mmmm. Both. Plus if you're programming in machine or assembly language, you need to know something about communicating with i/o interfaces through the busses. I thought I'd just sketch in the overall picture. You'll have to dig the details out of the manual for whatever system you wind up with.

There are two different communications schemes, called **synchronous** (or **strobed**) and **asynchronous** (or **handshaking**). Let me concentrate on devices that send values *to* the controller, just to keep us from getting swamped with details.

In the **synchronous** situation, the controller sends a signal to the device, informing it that it wants a value, and it's up to the device to provide the data in time. Typically, the device puts the data value on the data bus and keeps it there for some length of time. At some point during that time (if all goes well), the controller will read whatever's on the data bus into the accumulator. That's called **strobing** the data into the controller.

Q 485 Why **strobing**?

A   Well, I suppose it's the same idea as a strobe light . . . like they used to use at dances? Some activity is going on, and a brief flash of light illuminates it so you see it at that one point. Here, a value is placed on the data bus, and the controller reads it during a short time interval.

Anyway, synchronous data communication is easier to write programs for, but of course, it can be used only when the process is guaranteed to be able to produce the data within a fixed length of time.

If that's not the case, you need some form of **asynchronous** communication.

Q 486 And that's called **handshaking**?

A   Often. Here's a typical arrangement. There are two flip-flops, and the signals stored by them are called Busy and Done.

Q 487 For each one?

A   What? Oh. No. One flip-flop is called **Busy,** and the other is called **Done**. In addition, there'll be a buffer to store the value returned by the external device (again, let's stick with input operations). Let's take, oh say, a paper tape reader. The controller tells the device to start reading the next character on the paper tape by setting Busy (i.e. by causing the Busy flip-flop to enter the 1 state). Some time later, after the reader finishes reading the next character on the tape, and the value is stored in the buffer, the reader sends a signal to the interface that sets the Done flip-flop (to indicate that now there's a new piece of data available) and resets Busy (to indicate that the device is no longer is use). Since the two flip-flops completely specify the state of the paper reader, the controller can always tell what the situation is by testing the Busy and Done flip-flops, no matter how slowly the reader responds.

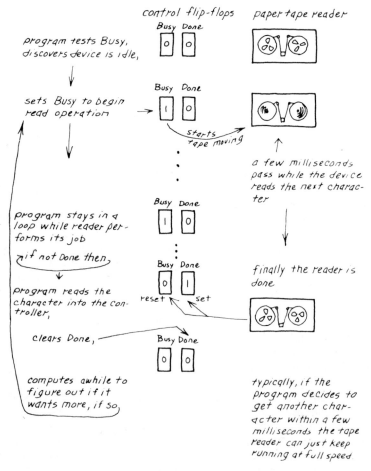

Figure 48 Typical sequence of events — handshaking between the processor and a peripheral device

[Editor's note: Most microcomputer systems use a synchronous bus organization, thus when dealing with asynchronous input or output, the necessary control signals (which A chooses to call "Busy" and "Done") are *themselves* communicated in a synchronous manner.]

Sometimes the Done flip-flop is hooked to the **interrupt** line so that the controller doesn't have to keep testing to see if the device is done, it can go on carrying out some other program . . .

What are interrupts?

Q 488 Why don't you tell me what an **interrupt** is, since you keep bringing it up? Or were you through with busses? I hope so . . .

A   I suppose I'm through, for all practical purposes. What's an **interrupt**? Mainly, it's just what it says. It's a process by which the controller can interrupt what it's doing (the program it's running), go do something else, and then return to the original program, with no loss of information. It's sort of like a selective attention mechanism, if you know what . . .

Q 489 But how does it work?

A   Well, it works a little differently on every different microprocessor, and there are several different kinds of interrupts . . .

Q 490 Why are you always so vague?

A   Come on. I'm not trying to be vague, there's just so many different possibilities. Why are you always so . . .

Q 491 Give me an example.

A   OK, OK, already. Here's the main idea. The controller is chugging along carrying out some program when all of a sudden, some external device needs attention.

Q 492 It got lonely?

A   Either it has a piece of data ready for the processor to read, or it's ready for the next piece of output from the processor. Here's an example. Suppose you're running some kind of game program that puts a complicated picture on your TV screen, some kind of display that's always changing, so that the controller has to keep running the program that updates the display. And suppose that, as part of the game, you get to type in commands, like . . . I know. Let's imagine that we have a sailboat race game. You get to play the skipper, and you type in commands like a real captain would issue. Instead of your crew members carrying them out, they affect parameters in the program. All the while, the TV screen is showing the sailboat riding the waves, trimming its sails, so on.

Q 493 Wow! Do you have a game like that around we can play?

A   I'll give you the classic answer. "Almost. It's almost de-bugged, it's not quite ready yet, but be sure to send your money in now so you can be sure of getting the first copy on your block." No, I don't. But it's certainly possible. [Editor's note: This seems questionable. The amount of computation required to generate a realistic image of a sail flapping in the wind is probably prohibitive. This section does, however, give a feeling for using interrupts, so it has been retained.] Anyway, here's the point. The controller has to keep running the program that determines what the TV screen should be showing, keep the boat rocking up and down, the sails flapping in the wind, . . . But what happens when you start to type in a command, like COME ABOUT? If the controller switches to a program which accepts letters from the keyboard, and keeps processing characters until you've typed in the complete command, the TV display will freeze. You don't want that, you want the ship to continue toward the rocks while you frantically type in your next command. Right?

Q 494 All right . . . So what do you do?

A   One way to solve the problem is to use **interrupts.** Each time you hit a key on the keyboard and the character is received by the i/o interface, it can request an interrupt. The controller momentarily stops updating the TV display, and runs a program which stores the character you typed. Then it tests the character to see if it was a **carriage return** (the character which corresponds to the RETURN key on the keyboard), and if it wasn't, it goes right back to the TV display update program. If it *was* a carriage return, that means that the user has finished entering a command, and the controller has to switch to the program that carries out that command, and then go back to the display program. Get the idea?

Q 495 I think I do, but I don't have the slightest idea how I'd go about writing the programs to do all that.

A   I wouldn't claim that it's a program for a beginner to tackle, but once you've done a fair amount of assembly language programming, it wouldn't be too hard. Anyway, for now, I'm just trying to give you a feeling for what interrupts are and what they can be used to do.

Q 496 All right. But I don't see what's been gained here. Won't the controller have to leave the picture on the TV screen alone while it carries out your command?

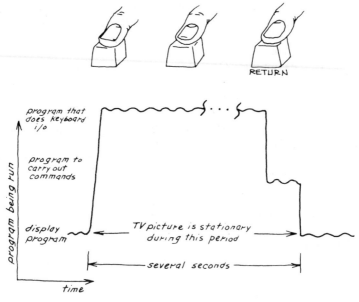

Once person starts typing in a new command, this scheme
stays in the i/o routine until the person finishes. Then it
interprets the command, and finally resumes the display program.

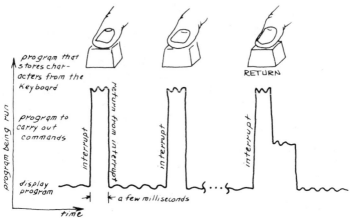

As each character is typed, the display program is interrupted
just long enough to store that one character. Once the complete
command has been entered, it's interpreted and the display program is
resumed.

Figure 49

A   Right. But don't forget how much faster microprocessors run compared to how fast you can type. It might take you several seconds to type in a complete command. You'd certainly notice it if the picture stood still for a couple of seconds. But with our second scheme, using interrupts, when the controller goes to carry out the command, the whole command is already stored in memory, so the whole process can run at full speed. There's no need to update the TV display more than, oh, 50 or 60 times a second, because your eye can't respond that fast anyway. That means that the microprocessor can carry out a few thousand operations between display updates. If a command was so complex that it required more than that amount of computation, it might cause a momentary glitch in the display, but most likely, everything would look continuous.

Q 497 I've come across that word somewhere.

A   What word?

Q 498 **Glitch.**

A   A **glitch** is a transitory, undesirable phenomenon. If you have a fast oscilloscope, sometimes you can see little voltage spikes in digital signals. They're called **glitches** and are caused by noise or timing problems. I guess you can tell how I was using it—to refer to a momentary hesitation in the display. We're getting even farther off the subject (I seem to remember that we were supposed to be going over a bunch of diagrams!), but while we're at it, I might as well define another common term— **kludge.** [Pronounced "kloooge", sometimes spelled **kluge.**] To **kludge something together** (it's used to refer to hardware and software both) means to assemble it in a slip-shod, spur-of-the-moment fashion. "I didn't have all the parts I needed, so I kludged it together with bailing wire and chewing gum." Or, "The program wasn't handling the carriage return right, so I kludged in a fix."
As a noun, obviously, it refers to something that has been kludged together. The more common noun-form is **kludge-job.** "Phew! This subroutine is a real kludge-job. Ech."
Kludges in hardware often cause glitches.

Q   You're not well, are you.

A   Hah.

Q 499 Let me try again. What's an **interrupt**?

A   OK . . . it's a process. Here's what you want to happen. When an external device informs the controller that it wants attention, namely when it activates the **interrupt request**

line in the control bus, you want the controller to stop running the current program, save enough information about where it was (so it can start the program up again later) and then inform the interrupting device that an interrupt has occurred and it has the controller's "attention". Then the controller has to start running the program that will deal with the interrupting device.

Q 500 But specifically how does that happen?

A What can I say? It's different on different processors. Typically, when the interrupt signal is received by the processor, the following things happen. First, the processor completes the current instruction. Then, further interrupts are disabled, that is, are ignored to prevent a mixup in case two devices request an interrupt at virtually the same time. Then, typically, the contents of the program counter, the accumulator, and the status flags are stored. Finally, the microprocessor does some specific thing to get to the program which will handle the device that requested the interrupt. On the 6800, what happens next is that the value stored in memory locations $FFF8_{16}$ and $FFF9_{16}$ is used as the address of the interrupt handling routine. That means when you write the routine, you also have to store its starting address in memory locations FFF8 and FFF9.

If there's more than one device that could have generated the interrupt, then the program has to figure out which one it was so it can respond properly.

Q 501 Good grief . . . how can it do that? This is getting complicated . . .

A Again, it depends. On some systems, there are actually a number of interrupt request lines, and the exact pattern of signals on those lines can specify the device. On others, the controller sends out an **interrupt acknowledge** signal on the control bus, and the device that was requesting the interrupt responds by putting a value identifying itself on the data bus.

At any rate, after the routine has determined which device needs attention, then it can either re-enable the interrupts and branch to the program which will deal with the device, or it can just branch to that program, leaving the interrupts disabled. If it re-enables interrupts (sometimes called **arming** the interrupts), that means that the interrupt handling routine can *itself* be interrupted. After the device that requested the interrupt has been serviced, the routine has to restore the controller's registers to their old values and re-start the program that was running when the whole mess started.

Q 502 Whoa. That seems pretty unwieldy, but . . .

A   Wait. You wanted specifics, and I'm nowhere near through. That's one way interrupts are implemented. On the 8080, it's different. There, when the interrupt is acknowledged, it's the responsibility of the interrupting device to place a (one-byte) instruction on the data bus. The processor finishes its current instruction, disables the interrupts, and then carries out that instruction.

Q 503 And what would that be?

A   It can be anything you want. Almost always, though, it's an RST (ReSTart) instruction, which is a special branch instruction to one of 8 specific memory locations, which you'd use as the starting addresses of different interrupt handling routines.

Q   And . . .

A   I'm not through yet. On the PACE chip, there are four different interrupt lines, and the controller takes the interrupt handling routine's starting address as one of four different locations depending on which line went high.

Q 504 All right. All right! I get the idea.
        I had a question a while back. You said that you didn't have to allow the program that was handling one interrupt to be interrupted itself. Wouldn't you always want to? You don't want to miss anything, do you?

A   Well, you might have devices that run at wildly different speeds. If your system was responding to an interrupt from a disc, and just then the Teletype starts screaming, you'd want to go ahead and finish, but if the order were reversed, you'd want the disc to interrupt the Teletype, because the Teletype runs so slowly that you can afford to let it wait.

Q 505 One last thing. I came across an ad that mentioned a **vectored interrupt.**

A   That refers to a scheme in which more than just one signal is delivered to the controller, where most of the work in deciding which device has requested the interrupt is done by hardware. The first method I mentioned isn't a vectored interrupt scheme. The others are.

Q 506 All right. What next?

A   What next? I don't remember what got us into all this. Oh well. What other diagrams do you have there?

A timing diagram

Q 507 I have this **timing diagram.**

A   OK. We've already gone over what a timing diagram is, that it's a representation of the signals you'd see if you put an oscilloscope on the leads carrying the signals whose names appear to the left of the diagram. This particular one is more complicated than the one we went over . . .

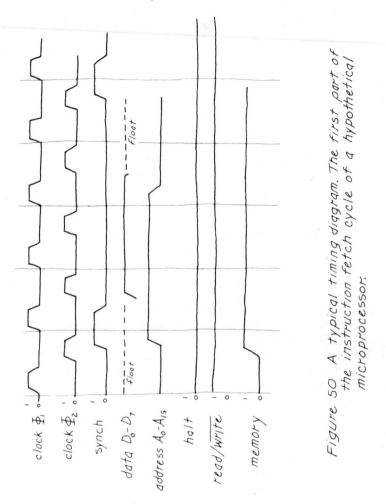

Figure 50 A typical timing diagram. The first part of the instruction fetch cycle of a hypothetical microprocessor.

Q 508 It says **instruction fetch cycle**. So it must be showing something about how the controller gets instructions from memory, right?

A   Sure must. Let's see . . . it seems to be showing signals that are inputs to and outputs from the microprocessor chip itself. That is, it's not showing how the memory responds, and it's not showing the details of what's going on *inside* the microprocessor.

Q 509 Why are there two different signals called **clock**?

A   Well, each basic machine cycle involves a number of different operations, and the clock signals are used to coordinate events on the chip. The two different clock signals are called **phases,** since they're used to identify different phases or stages of performing the functions of the processor. The vertical lines in the timing diagram mark off **basic machine cycles.** The clock pattern repeats once between each pair of vertical lines. When they say that a microprocessor uses a (say) 2 megahertz clock, that would mean that there are two million machine cycles per second, or, in this case, that the time between vertical lines was

$$\frac{1}{\frac{2\,000\,000\ \underline{\text{cycles}}}{\text{second}}} \qquad = 400\ \frac{\text{nanoseconds}}{\text{cycle}} \qquad = .5\ \frac{\text{microseconds}}{\text{cycle}}$$

Q 510 So that tells how fast the controller can carry out instructions, right?

A   Basically, that's right. Different instructions consume different numbers of machine cycles, depending on how complex they are. For instance, on the 8080, the fastest instruction takes 4 basic machine cycles, and the slowest 18. But let me get back to the timing diagram.

To fetch an instruction, obviously, the processor has to be running. So naturally, the **halt** signal is going to be 0 all the while.

Q 511 The **halt** signal does what, exactly?

A   It indicates that the processor isn't doing anything. Isn't running a program. Computers with front panels have a switch that stops the processor. Flipping it sends a signal that makes the processor enter the **halt state,** and the **halt** line goes to 1 to indicate that fact.

Now. Since to fetch an instruction, the controller has to read it from memory, of course the **read/write** line needs to be placed in the high state to . . .

Q 512 That's the signal we saw on the RAM board*, right?

A   Right. The controller sets it high to inform the memory that it wants to **read** a value (and **not write** one).

RAM board Q 445-464

Q 513 What's the signal marked **memory** for?

A   Ah. The microprocessor you took this diagram from must have explicit i/o instructions. That signal indicates that the value on the address bus is to be used as a **memory address,** not as an **i/o device number.**

OK. To fetch the next instruction, the address stored in

the program counter has to be placed on the address bus so the memory knows what location to read.

The plots labeled **address** and **data** are a little different in meaning from the others. Since there are sixteen address lines, and the address changes all the time, obviously they can't draw the exact signal that's going to appear on each line. So where it shows the address as rising up to the 1 level . . . it doesn't mean that the address is always 11111111 11111111.

Q 514 Come on. You must be getting tired. I can see what the diagram means. It must just mean that at that point the value will be on the address lines.

A   Just out of curiosity, why did that seem obvious to you?

Q 515 Partly from what you said, and partly because it doesn't just say **address,** it says **address A_0-A_{15}.**

A   Humph. I would have thought that it would be sort of confusing.

Oh well.

So now what have we got? We're not in a **halt state,** the **memory** is being accessed, the **address** is on the address bus, a memory **read** is taking place. Then after some time, the memory places the desired value on the data bus. The diagram shows that happening during the second machine cycle.

Q 516 What are those dotted lines doing there before that?

A   It looks like this particular microprocessor lets the data bus float before then.

Q 517 Float?

A   You remember. Be in the **tri-state?**

Q 518 Oh. Right. Why do that?

A   Well, once the processor has received a particular value from the data bus, it stores it internally (in some register), and until it's ready for another value, it doesn't want anything that happens on the data bus to affect it, I guess. Oh. I know what it is. Other devices can access the memory at times (that's called a **direct memory acess, DMA**), so the controller has to leave the data bus alone unless it absolutely needs it.

Q 519 Do you really know what you're talking about?

A   Usually, usually.

Aren't you going to ask when this diagram would be of use to you?

Q 520 All right.

A   Glad you asked. For one thing it helps you get a feeling for how the microprocessor really works. But its main use would be if you were designing some piece of circuitry that was going to interact with the controller over the busses. Then you'd need to take the timing details into account, to make sure that your circuit makes the right responses at the appropriate times.

State transition diagram

Q 521 What's a **state valence diagram?**

A   A what?

Q   A **state valence diagram.**

A   Good grid! I have no idea. Where did you come across it? It sound like some kind of chemical thing.

Q 522 Here. Right here . . . ooops. Sorry, it's called a **state transition diagram.**

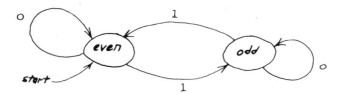

Figure 51   State transition diagram of a parity checker

A   Oh. It's a visual portrayal of a machine's function. Typically it shows each possible state as a **node** (drawn as a circle), and has an arrow out of that node for each possible input to the machine, showing what state comes next, given that input.

The one you have here shows the functional characteristics of a device that has two states, called **even** and **odd.** Well, you can see how it works. If the input is a 0, the thing stays in the same state. If it's a 1, it switches to the other state. Apparently it always starts out in the state called **even.** Then if an even number of 1's have come in, it'll be in the state called **even,** and if an odd number of 1's have come in, it'll be in the **odd** state. You could use it as a **parity checker.**

Q 523 Did you mention that before?

A   **Parity?** I don't think so. It's a method of detecting errors. Somewhere along the line I'm sure I said that the standard (ASCII) scheme for transmitting characters uses a string of 7 bits?

Q 524 Right.

A   Typically, 8 bits are used to convey the data, with the 8th bit chosen so the total number of 1's is even (called **even parity**) or odd (called **odd parity**).

Character	ASCII code	for even parity send	for odd parity send
A	1000001	01000001	11000001
B	1000010	01000010	11000010
C	1000011	11000011	01000011
•	•	•	•
•	•	•	•
•	•	•	•
Z	1011010	01011010	11011010

As the 8 bits come into the i/o interface, they could be run into a device that implements the state transition diagram we just saw. If you were using even parity, then after all 8 bits had gone through the device, if it ends up in the state called **odd,** you'd know there had been a transmission error.

Q 525 You mean the circuitry could detect that there had been a transmission error. You don't look at it yourself.

A   No, of course not.

Q 526 When do you use them?

A   What? Parity checkers?

Q 527 No. State transition diagrams.

A   Well, they're convenient for showing the operation of fairly small circuits that have memory. They can get sort of unwieldy if you try to use them to describe really elaborate machines. You see them fairly often in the chip manufacturer's literature, to show relationships among the main microprocessor states (**halt, wait, interrupt,** etc.).

Q 528 Wait. How were you using the word **memory** there. I got the feeling you didn't mean RAM or ROM, somehow . . .

A   RAM and ROM are certainly examples of circuits that have memory, but they're not the only ones that do.
It's kind of a technical definition. A circuit with **memory** is one in which what's happened in the past affects how it responds now.
For example, a **nor** gate *doesn't* have that property. It's said to be **memory-less.** Its output is completely determined by its current inputs.
On the other hand, a flip-flop's behavior *does* depend on what's happened in the past. Why don't we draw out a state transition diagram for a J-K flip-flop?*

* J-K flip-flop Q 402

Q 529 Be my guest.

A   Well, why don't you do it. I already know how.

Q 530 I don't remember exactly how it works.

A   OK. You remember that there are two different states, right? Corresponding to Q=0 and Q=1. So draw two circles for the two states.

Q 531

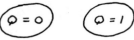

A   Let's ignore the C input, and draw what happens for the various combinations of J and K values. If J=0 and K=0, Q doesn't change.

Q 532 Like this?

A   Great. Here. I'll write down the transition table and you finish the state transition diagram.

J^n	K^n	Q^{n+1}
0	0	Q^n
0	1	0
1	0	1
1	1	$\overline{Q^n}$

Q 533 How's this?

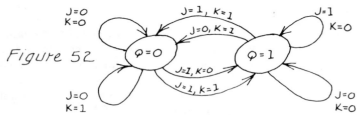

Figure 52

A   That's got it, or you could make it easier to read, maybe.

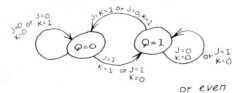

or even

Figure 53

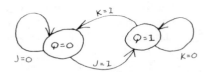

Q 534 It seems like there's a tremendous number of different kinds of diagrams . . . different ways to do everything . . . where does it all end?

A Mmph. It's not so bad once you get over the initial shock. Once you get familiar with the basic ideas, you can usually figure out how to read a new kind of diagram you come across. If you can't, then maybe it's the fault of the person who drew the diagram. After all, they're supposed to communicate something to the person reading them, so if you need a tremendous amount of specialized knowledge to read a particular diagram, it probably wasn't done very well to begin with.
What next?

Q 535 I've got another diagram here.

Actually hooking things up

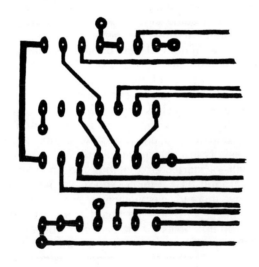

Figure 54

*A small portion of a typical **etch and drill guide** for making a handmade printed circuit board. All copper plating except for the pattern shown in black is etched off the bottom of the board; circuit components are mounted on the top of the board, soldered on the bottom. Oval shapes are for pins on ic chips, circles are for jumpers. On commercial boards, the problem of crossing paths is solved by printing the circuit on both sides of the board instead of using jumpers.*

A Ah. This is an **etching and drilling guide** for a printed circuit board. It's the other extreme from the state transition diagrams. They were concerned completely with functional information. This one is completely structural. It gives you the actual wiring pattern. You can use it to make a printed circuit board. To complete it, you solder the components in.

Q 536 Explain all that.

A   What's to explain? Obviously you can't make a decent piece of equipment by just hooking a bunch of components together with wires. You need to fasten everything down on a board so they don't move around and short each other out.

Q 537 But aren't there different ways to do that? I've run across the term **wire-wrap,** and things like **sockets** . . . what is all that?

A   Ah. I see what you want.
       There are three main ways. All involve mounting the components (logic gates and other integrated circuit chips, resistors, capacitors, connectors, diodes) on boards that are made of some kind of insulating material (fiberglas, epoxy, different kinds of plastic).
       Here's one thing you can do that requires virtually no special equipment. You buy a board that is drilled with a regular pattern of holes, spaced to fit the pins on integrated circuit packages. You stick the pins (or leads, in the case of resistors and capacitors) through the holes, and solder wires to the tips sticking through the board.
       The second method, and probably the most popular among hobbyists is to use **printed circuits.** You can make them yourself—a starter kit that has the chemicals you need costs around $10, I think. You use a pattern like the one you have there to selectively etch away some of the copper that's been plated on the board you start with.
       Then you drill holes for the pins on chips and for the leads on other components, insert them and solder them down. There are a number of advantages to using printed circuits. Probably the most important one is that you're less likely to hook things up wrong.

Q 538 But that just applies if you're copying somebody else's plan, right? I mean, what do you do if you make a mistake when you draw out your own wiring plan?
       And what if you can't draw a circuit without having wires cross each other? What do you do then?

A   The printed leads can't cross each other, but you can put jumpers on the board to make connections across a lead. Also, you can use both sides of the board—you can etch a pattern on both sides, and make connections through holes drilled in the board to get from one side to the other.

Doing very much of that gets pretty tricky to do at home, though.

Let's see. Your other . . . What if you've made the printed circuit board and you suddenly discover that there's a mistake in the wiring pattern? (Incidentally, the "suddenly" there might well have been preceeded by three days of wracking your brains trying to figure out why it doesn't work.)

If it's a big mistake, you'll have to throw the board away and start over. If it's a small mistake, you're still OK. If you left out a connection, you can just run a wire to make it. If there's an incorrect connection of the board, you can scrape a break in the offending pathway.

It's pretty easy to make mistakes. The old "yellow wire" phenomenon.

Q 539 What's that?

A Just an old saying. You pick up a printed circuit board someone has made, and it looks absolutely beautiful. The leads all run straight and true, everything looks immaculately well organized, the components are all neatly placed, . . . but there's this one little yellow wire running from here, way over to there.

Q 540 Because of a mistake?

A Right.

In hardware work, just like in programming, it's so easy to make little mistakes, little mental lapses, that you have to be on your toes all the time, and use every trick you can to prevent errors. It's not a bad idea to type identifying numbers or notes on little pieces of paper and glue them right on the board, so a year from now, when something is going wrong, you have some hope of recapturing what it was you thought you were doing when you designed the thing. Keep good notes, re-copy your circuit diagram if it gets messy because of changes, . . .

Q 541 And obey the Scout Laws.

A Hah.

The third method is called **wire-wrap.** It's especially popular in bigger labs that can afford the equipment. It's fast to do, and it lets you put more components in the same space.

You start with a board that's drilled with a regular pattern of holes. You buy a wire-wrap socket for each device. The sockets have little spring loaded metal connections, one for each pin on the component you're mounting. On the other side of the socket, there are metal posts, one for each of the pins on the component. You push the posts

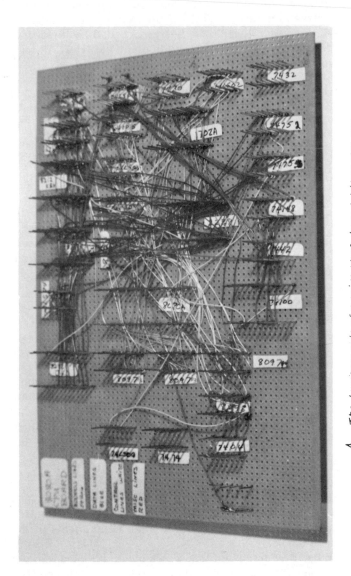

A   The business side of a **wire wrap** board. Wires are run point to point instead of being neatly bunched into cables in order to lessen noise problems.

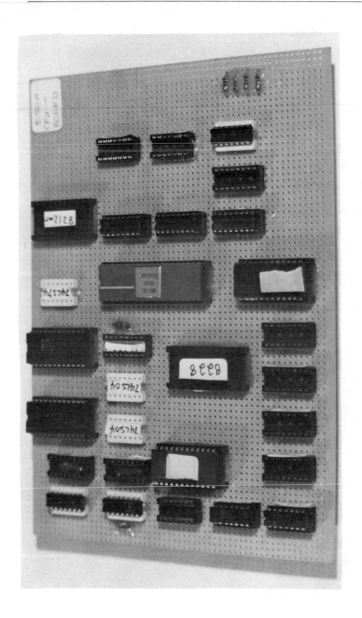

B The top side of the board shown in A. Notice how closely components can be placed—compare with the (much larger) printed circuit board chip placements (in C).

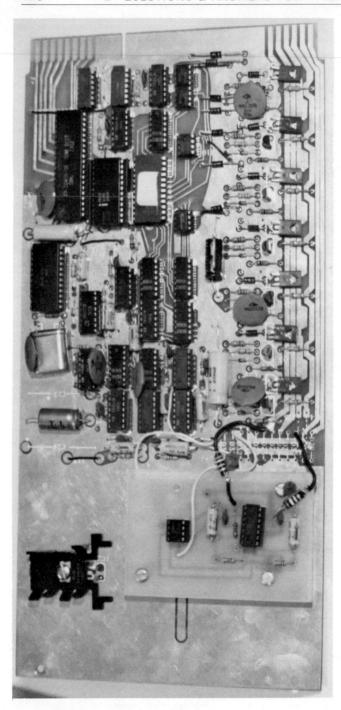

Figure 55   Circuit boards   c   A printed circuit board. Traces may be seen running the length of the board. Soldering is done on the other side. This particular board is made to plug into an edge connector.

through the holes in the board so they stick out on the back of the board. That's where you do the wiring.

Q 542 But why's that called wire-wrap?

A Oh. The posts have a square cross section, so they have fairly sharp edges. You attach a wire to a post using a special tool (a wire-wrap gun) that winds it around the post so tightly that the edges of the post cut into the wire a little, forming a good electrical connection.

Q 543 Can you just wind the wire around the post by hand, or do you really have to have a special tool?

A There are some inexpensive tools called something like **wiring pencils** that you can use, but after you've finished wiring a post with those, usually you go ahead and solder the whole thing to make sure you have a good, sound electrical connection. You can't afford to screw around trying to save a few minutes when it comes to wiring. Suppose the method you use gives you 99% good connections. It's not uncommon to have a thousand connections on a complex board, and that means that on the average you'll have 10 bad connections to track down. There's nothing quite so frustrating as a marginal solder joint. As you put your measuring probe near a connection, you may move it just enough to make it conduct. For a while.

Q 544 What technique would you recommend I use, since I'm just getting started.

A Let me go over one more thing. So far I've talked about sockets just with respect to wire-wrapping. You can buy sockets to use with the other methods too. There's a big advantage to using sockets. It makes it easy to remove chips from the circuit to check that they're getting the proper signals. And if you suspect that a particular component is bad, you can just pop a new one into the socket instead of trying to unsolder it. So sockets make troubleshooting easier.

Q 545 So you should use them, then.

A Overall they're probably worth it, but there are two drawbacks. One is the additional cost. The other is that sometimes the pins on the chips don't make good connections with the socket, and sometimes the chips seem to move around a little if you pull the board out of the computer very often.

There's another advantage — you do all your soldering to the socket, not the IC chips, so you don't run the risk of damaging your chips with excess heat.

Q 546 So they're good for beginners.

A   Yeh, but if you're not very good at soldering, you're going to have a lot of trouble anyway. A computer kit is no place to learn to solder.

Q 547 All right . . . but this doesn't seem to be telling me what I really want to know. Tell me specifically what it's like to put a microcomputer kit together.

A   It's too late to do that today . . . let's do that next time, OK?

DAY 4: WHAT'S IT LIKE TO ASSEMBLE A MICROCOMPUTER KIT?

Kits

Q 548   What's involved in assembling a microcomputer kit? In detail.

A   I've got a plan for going over that, but first, let me impress something on your mind.

Q 549   What's that?

A   *Caveat emptor.* When you're thinking about buying a home computer, kit *or* assembled, keep chanting it to yourself. *Caveat emptor, caveat emptor.* "Let the buyer beware." OK. Now here's my plan. There's . . .

Q 550   Wait a minute. What are you getting at?

A   Well, since we're getting into the details of specific products, I didn't want you to get the idea that I'm recommending one brand over another. And more important: Don't Believe Everything You Read in the Ads.

Q 551   So what else is new?

A   Look. I'm not talking about some theoretical situation. It's really something to worry about.

Q 552   Get to the *point.* This is a pretty weird way to start talking about kits.

A   I know this is sort of negative . . . but it's really important. There have been a lot of problems with companies promising things, accepting people's money, and then taking two or three or four times as long as they promised to deliver anything. And there has been at least one case in which the company found out they *couldn't produce* the product they'd been advertising and accepting orders for. When you're deciding what to get, make sure you talk to someone who's dealt with that company. Go to your local computer store and get your hands on the machine you're interested in. If they don't stock it, ask them why not. Go to meetings of your local computer club and ask around. *But don't send your hard earned cash off in the mail to some company just because their ad sounds good.*

[Editor's note: This problem seems to be lessening as the manufacturers become more experienced. Although unforgivable, no doubt, to those cusomers who have sat waiting for their computers for months on end, the problem is understandable — no one had ever produced microcomputers before, so how were realistic estimates to be made?]

Anyway, here's my plan. At this point, there are two main classes of home computers — those based on the 8080 microprocessor, and those based on the 6800.

Q 553 What about the Z-80? I've seen a lot of ads for that in the magazines I have.

A I'm lumping that in with the 8080 type systems. But you're right, there are home computers available based on a number of other chips. The ones we'll go over are typical, though.

Anyway, since I haven't put together an 8080 based system myself, I called the local computer store, and they said we can come down and talk to someone who has. After we do that, I'll tell you about my experiences with a 6800 based home computer. Sound OK?

Q 554 Sure.

A OK. Let's go. Grab the tape recorder, would you?

later

Q 555 It's running . . .

A OK. Ah. There's the woman I talked to on the phone. Hi! How are things going?

W Oh, fine, fine. We're selling a lot of video terminals all of a sudden.

Did you just stop in to browse, or can I help you with something?

A Uhmmm. I called you yesterday. We wanted to talk about what was involved in putting a kit together. Remember?

W You have to put *every*thing together. It just comes in a bunch of little pieces.

A No two pieces come together, huh?

Q (Come on.)

A Is there anybody here who's put one together?

W   Skip. He's put some together.

Q   Thank you.

A   Can we ask you a few questions?

S   Suppose.

Q 556 We wanted to know exactly what's involved in building one of the kits.

S   Here. I put this one together. It's the first one I ever did.

A 557 It's an Imsai 8080. But you'd done other electronics things before?

S   (nods)

A 558 Well, first, what tools did you use?

S   Let's see. I used a soldering iron, a pair of wire cutters . . ., a set of hex drivers . . . You know what they are?

A   Yeh.

Q 559 What are they?

A   It's a gadget for screwing nuts on. It's got a handle like a screwdriver, but instead of having a blade, it's got a thing that holds hexagonal shaped, uh, wrenches.

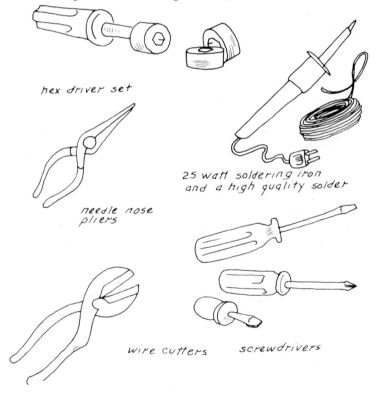

hex driver set

needle nose pliers

25 watt soldering iron and a high quality solder

wire cutters   screwdrivers

Figure 56

S   Let's see. And a pair of needle nose pliers. Oh. Did I mention screwdrivers?

Q   No.

S   I used a regular screwdriver, a philip's head screwdriver, and a real small regular one . . . for bending things.

Q 560 For bending things?

S   Un huh. Sometimes I had to push a capacitor or something over a little to fit something else in.

A 561 OK. So what did you start on?

S   First I put the chassis together. It goes right together with screws and nuts. It's all bent to shape, and all the screw holes are drilled, so you just stick it together. No problem. Took about a half hour.
     Then I put the power supply together. That's here. You mount all the parts, solder everything in. I tested it right away. Wanted to check everything as I went. Took about 3 hours.

Q 562 That big silver cylinder is . . .

A   A filter capacitor. And look there. Four big diodes hooked together in a bridge — it converts the transformer output to DC.

S   Next I put together the mother board. Well, there's nothing to put together, you just solder in the connectors, one for every board you're going to put in. There's a hundred solder connections per plug. We put in eight connectors, so we can have up to eight boards.

A 563 There's just one card in there now. Is that what comes with the basic kit?

S   Yep. That's the CPU card. It has the 8080 on it . . .
     But let's see . . . After you solder all the connectors onto the mother board, you mount it in the chassis, using spacers and nuts and machine screws. Then you have to test it to make sure none of the pins on the connectors are shorted out against the chassis. With some of the earlier kits, there was a problem with that. All in all, counting the 800 solder connections, I think it took about 3 hours.

A 564 And did you do the card with the microprocessor next?

S   I could have, but I didn't. I did the front panel next. That was far and away the hardest part.
     Here. Look down from the top here. It's made up of two boards, and it's covered with stuff. Then this plexiglas panel goes in front of that.

A 565 It looks nice! Was it easy to do?

S   Not particularly. See, all these LEDs [**light emitting diodes**] that show through the plexiglas are mounted on the circuit board and you have to play around with them so they line up and look even from the front. Oh. And you have to cut this mask where the LEDs show through. All in all, it took a little over 8 hours to do the front panel.

A 566 And how did the processor board go?

S   Easy. It's all down hill after the front panel. The CPU board went right together. About 2 hours.

A 567 I see you have sockets on all the ICs.

S   Yep, but they didn't come with the kit.

Q 568 So you must feel they're worth it.

S   Oh, jeez, yeh. It would have been a real pain to de-bug if it weren't for the sockets.

A 569 I take it it didn't work right away?

S   No, no. It took another, oh, day and a half to get it running. About 12 hours.

A 570 What was the problem? Bad solder joint?

S   No, there were some bad components.
       The voltage regulator on the front panel was bad, and when we turned on the power, apparently that blew out some of the MOS chips. And then, after we figured all that out, it still didn't work right. We finally tracked it down to this capacitor, here on the front panel.
       Imsai was real good about replacing the bad components.

A 571 I guess you've got to expect some bad ones out of that many.

S   Surprisingly few . . . I think they must be pretty careful. Is there anything else? I'm going to have to go. It's my lunch hour.

A   Thanks a million.

Q   Yes, really appreciate it, Skip.
       I guess we should go too.

A   Wait a minute. I want to buy a copy of Finite State Fantasies before we go.

Q   You've already got a copy. I saw it on your coffee table.

A   On my coffee table?

Q   You know. That old vegetable crate in your front room.

A   Oh well. Got to help keep the store in business.

(later)

Q 572 I'm glad we're finally getting down to the real thing.
        Now why don't we go over the one you put together. This
        is it here, right? What is it?

A   It's a Sphere 330. Based on the 6800 microprocessor.
        As you can see, it comes with a keyboard instead of a
        front panel like the Imsai.

Q 573 Why don't you start from when it showed up, and go
        over what you did, what it took to put it together . . .

A   OK. Here's the general idea.

        step 1: Look for a packing list, for special instructions
                about unpacking the thing (none found in this
                case).

        step 2: Study the manual and any instructions that come
                with it, watching especially for warnings about
                parts that require special handling. Get a feeling
                for what's involved in putting it together. (Take
                a few days here. Don't rush.)

        step 3: Go over each board, trying to understand what
                it does, and checking against the parts list to see
                if anything's missing. After you've gone over ab-
                solutely everything, go back to the store and get
                any missing parts. Or, if you got your system
                through the mail, write the company requesting
                the missing parts. (Then pray a lot.)

Q 574 I take it there were a few missing parts in your kit?

A   A few. The keyboard, all the ROMs, all the ribbon cable
        for the busses.

Q 575 And did they send it all to you, as soon as you let them
        know it was missing?

A   Let's not go into that with the tape running.[!]

        step 4: Set up a place to work, a place with good lighting,
                where you have access to a good electrical ground,
                where you have room to spread out.

step 5: Carefully solder the parts to each board, starting with the simplest, so you can get used to the particular notation used by the manufacturer. (I started with the circuit board for the keyboard.)

Here's some tips on soldering: If it's been a while since you've done much soldering on circuit components, be sure to start with things you can't hurt by overheating.

Q 576 Like resistors.

A Yeh, or the sockets. And if you've never soldered electronic components before, *don't start with a computer kit.* Buy a cheap calculator kit to learn on.
One more thing. If you're soldering integrated circuit chips directly (i.e. not using sockets), you should be able to make a good solder connection and still not leave the iron on any one pin long enough to make the chip get warm. Turn the board over and touch the chip with your finger. If it's very warm after you've soldered it in, you're doing something wrong. Maybe your soldering iron tip isn't clean enough (use a good soldering paste and a rag or sponge to clean it after every few joints). Maybe your tip is too powerful (a 25 watt iron does fine). Maybe you're using crummy solder. If you're not making good solder joints, you're in for real trouble.

Q 577 These marks on the chips show which way is up, right?

A Right. That's another important point — be sure the components are mounted in the proper orientation. It doesn't matter which way you mount the resistors and ceramic capacitors, but every other component goes in only one way.
The only other problem that comes to mind right now is that sometimes, on a crowded board, it may not be completely obvious which hole to stick a particular resistor or capacitor in. You resolve those problems by carefully following the traces on the board to see what each of the holes in question is connected to, and then using the circuit diagram to see what the components in question are supposed to be hooked to.

Q 578 Some of the ICs here have sockets and some are soldered right to the board.

* post-soldering tips Q 587

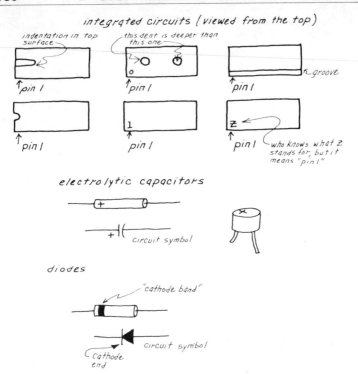

Figure 57 Component orientations

A   Right. Sphere provides sockets for all the delicate ICs (ones made using MOS or CMOS technology). Those particular chips are fairly fragile. They're sensitive to stray electrical charges. When you handle them, you have to make sure that you're not carrying any built up static charge (like you get when you scuff your feet on a wool rug), so you ground yourself before you handle them. To be really safe, you can attach a wire to your wrist and run it to ground through a large resistor (say, 10 Meg ohms).

But back to putting the kit together.

Step 6: After you've mounted all the components (except the ones that plug into sockets), plug the thing in, and go over each board, checking to make *sure* the proper supply voltages are being delivered to the right pins. Check everything you can.

step 7: Using all due precaution, plug in the remaining parts, plug it in, and stand back.

step 8: Start trying to figure out why it doesn't work.

Q 579 Surely there's a chance that everything'll work right the first time, isn't there?

A   I suppose, I suppose. But more than likely, you'll have to do some trouble shooting. The key idea is to develop and test hypotheses about what's causing the trouble, not to just start replacing components at random. You can use a vacuum tube voltmeter to measure steady signals, and you can use a pulse-catcher [see articles such as ''The Logic Grabber'', *73 magazine,* August, 1976, p. 60 or ''Build a TTL Pulse Catcher'', *Byte,* February, 1976, p. 58; also available commercially] to trace transient signals. Better yet, make friends with someone who works in an electronics lab so you have access to a decent oscilloscope. Keep the circuit diagram by your side at all times. Take the time to understand how the circuit is supposed to work.

Q. 580 And think clean thoughts.

       Give me some feeling for how hard it is to do all this.

A   I can tell you how long it took me to assemble what you see here:

Module	assembly time
controller (6800 and related circuitry, ROM, etc.)	4 hours
Keyboard circuitry.	1 hour
video display unit	3 hours
i/o interface board (for keyboard, cassette tape units)	3 hours
16K RAM board.	4 hours
putting the boards in the chassis, hooking up the power supply, attaching the bus cables, trim	1 hour

The last entry doesn't include the time I spent tracking down someone who knew how to do it — no instructions came with the kit! And it took about 5 hours to de-bug it.

Q. 581 So you can do it in a couple of days.

A   Well, *I* couldn't have.

Q. 582 If all the parts had come right away.

A   No, that's not what I meant. I find that if I solder for more than an hour straight, I start to flip out. I start to lose my concentration, start trying to go too fast, get error-prone. I have to go in spurts. An hour here, an hour there. Overall it took about 20 hours, spread over a couple of weeks.

Q. 583 What happened when you first turned it on?

A   Well, I didn't ''first turn it on''.

       Fortunately, I have a friend who has an oscilloscope, and was able to do a lot of checking around before inserting any of the expensive chips.

Q 584 And you found some things wrong?

A   Right. First of all we went over the power connections, checking to see that the right voltages were being supplied to the right pins. We found that one of the voltages that was supposed to be supplied to the bank of RAMs (there's 4K of RAM on the same board as the microprocessor on this system) wasn't getting there. After a little searching, we found that I'd left out a jumper.

      Oh. I forgot to tell you something I did before I started checking it out.

Q 585 Which is?

A   One of the problems you can run into is **solder splashes.** Some of these printed circuit boards are pretty crowded, and the traces run close together. Sometimes when you're soldering, a little hot solder will spit out of the joint . . . and if you're unlucky, short two circuit traces together. It's never happened to me (far as I know), but it's something you've got to check for.

Q 586 What do you mean, far as you know? It would cause something to fail, wouldn't it?

A   Right, right. But I was thinking that even if I had had one, what Nick told me to do might have gotten rid of it before I found it. See, he blew up his microprocessor chip once, so he's pretty sensitized to the problem.

Q 587 A solder splash did that? Made it blow up?

A   Yeh. Well, not *blow up,* I mean it didn't work anymore. It melted one of the little wires that run to the little pads on the chip — remember, the pads we saw in the picture? Anyway, he told me to take a toothbrush and some methyl alcohol, and scrub the solder joints I'd made, to scrub the back of the printed circuit boards.

Q 588 And that gets rid of solder splashes?

A   It might get rid of real minor ones. The idea is that the methyl alcohol dissolves the rosin that's left from soldering. With all the rosin cleaned off you've got a much better chance of spotting solder splashes. And while you're looking, you should also check all your solder joints. Resolder any that don't look good. They should look kind of shiny, and there should be enough solder so there aren't any holes showing.

Q 589 All right. So you finally had the power connections straightened out.

A   Oh. Right. Then we started checking other signals. We discovered that one of the clock signals that was

  * photograph of an 8080 chip Figure 38

supposed to be supplied to the microprocessor wasn't there. After a while, we traced the problem to one specific chip.

Q 590 It wasn't any good?

A   No, it was OK. I (blush) had mounted it upside down.

Q 591 Hah! You mounted it upside down! Why'd you do that? Hah! Was it hard to read the marking?

A   No excuse, sir. Just one of those things that happens sometimes. Anyway, since it wasn't in a socket, we had to take it off . . .

Q 592 That's what I was going to ask. How do you take a chip out?

A   OK. There's a gadget called a **solder sucker** (or something like that) that you cock by pushing its plunger. You hold the solder sucker over a solder joint, heat up the joint with your iron, and when the solder starts to flow, you press the trigger on the sucker and *slurp*! it sucks most of the solder out of the joint. You do that to all of the pins, then you try to break the pins away from the remaining solder. Then you turn the board over and pry the chip up. If you're lucky, it'll come off.

Q 593 And were you lucky?

A   Yeh. We cleaned out the holes in the board, inserted the chip the right way, soldered it down, and now the clock signals were OK.

Q 594 What did you do next?

A   Are you sure you want me to go through all this?

Q 595 Yes, it's giving me an idea of what all's involved.

A   Let me see . . . what did we do next?
Oh. I held my breath and inserted the 6800 chip, the ROM chips, and the RAM chips in their sockets. Then we hooked the bus cables up from the processor board to the TV display generator board, ran a piece of coaxial cable to the TV monitor, and plugged it in again.

Q 596 What did you see on the TV screen?

A   I don't know how to describe what I saw. It was sort of like a salt and pepper storm with a wavy white line squirming along the right edge.

Q 597 I gather that wasn't what you expected?

A   Well, we didn't know exactly what the problem was. We wound up taking the TV interface board out of Nick's machine (fortunately, it's the same as mine) to see what that would do. Now the screen was filled with a constantly changing array of characters, some half formed, with weird little flecks of white flashing through it.
We found that by holding down the RESET key on the

keyboard (which stops the processor), we could stop the display from changing. It was still just a random bunch of characters, though.

Q 598 That would mean that the processor was making the picture change, wouldn't it? If the picture stopped changing when you . . .

A Right. But why? After about two hours of puzzling over the problem, checking signals, pouring over circuit diagrams, swapping parts from his machine to mine, Nick hit on the problem. Subroutine returns weren't working right. We replaced the RAM chips, and *voila!*, there was the cursor (a little white square) blinking on and off once a second — the machine was waiting patiently for us to enter a command on the keyboard.

Q 599 Your problems were over.

A Well, not really. It took a while to get my TV interface board to work, but there's no need to go into that, I think you get the idea.

Q 600 Could you have gotten it working if you didn't have an oscilloscope to use?

A I *think* so, but I'm not sure. Even if so, it would have taken much, much longer. Even with the use of a scope, and the help of someone who had gone through it before, it wasn't a trivial job.

Q 601 Do you think this system is going to satisfy your needs, or are you already planning to add to it?

A I'd say this system is potentially adequate. I can't honestly guess how long it'll take me to round up the software packages I need. Some, I'm sure, I'll have to write myself.

Q 602 But in terms of the hardware?

A This is fine, as of right now. I don't anticipate maintaining any huge data bases, so I wouldn't consider getting a disc, even if I could afford one. The one thing I'll be on the lookout for is a decent quality hard copy output device so I can print out finished copies of manuscripts I've entered and edited using the keyboard and TV . . . but that's got to wait a while.

Q 603 All right. Now you're sort of a special case, right? You've had a lot of experience using computers before and . . .

A I don't see that that matters, and besides, a large percentage of computer hobbyists have had some kind of exposure to computers at school or in their jobs . . .

Q 604 Wait. What I want to know is if you really think you're going to be satisfied with a microcomputer when you've been used to huge computers.

A Yes. Absolutely. These things are really powerful general purpose computers. For years, I've been aching to have my own computer, one I can use any time I want, for any kind of crazy scheme I think up. And now I do! I think it's fantastic!

Are you a coward if you buy pre-assembled equipment?

Q 605 It doesn't seem too hard to put a kit together . . . except for the trouble shooting part. I'm not sure I know enough to do that, if there was something seriously wrong. And I think it would take me a lot longer to put together some of those boards . . . you must solder pretty fast.

A   It doesn't really cost that much more to buy an assembled microcomputer. Not if your time is worth anything to you. There's a strange sort of **macho aura** associated with building your home computer from a kit. It's true that it does require a certain amount of bravery . . . you're dealing with a lot of unknowns. But it's also true that you're not going to learn very much about computers just by assembling a kit. All the design work has been done already; basically you just become a worker on a one-time assembly line. And you're not in a good position for dealing with the company if your computer doesn't work — they can always take the position that the reason it doesn't is that you didn't assemble it properly (and justifiably so). My personal opinion is if you have any question about your ability to put together a complex electronics kit, the only rational thing to do is get a pre-assembled system, and get on with the really fun, creative part of home computing — using it.

What sort of things are available?

Why don't we look at a couple of things that are available right now and compare the kit and assembled prices?

Q 606 As long as we're going over specific products, why don't you list some i/o devices?

A   I'm all ready for you today. I drew out a table showing a bunch of peripherals.

Before you look at it . . . there's a unit of measure I'd better explain. I used it in the table, and you see it in a lot of ads. The **baud. Baud** is a unit of speed of signal transmission. It's equivalent to one signal change per second. If you're sending a string of binary pulses, then one baud is one bit per second. If you're sending a signal that consists of pulses that have four possible states, say

Figure 58: A random sampling of currently available products.

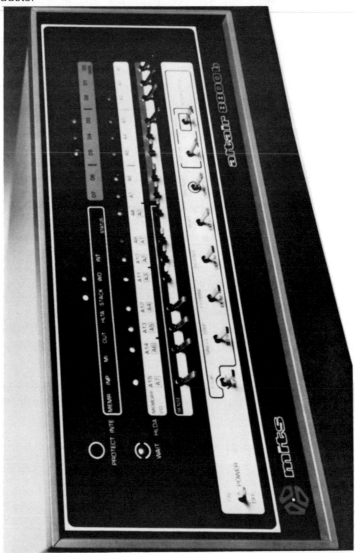

Figure (58A): The latest offering from the company that "started it all". Based on the 8080 microprocessor. Kit versions start at $840, assembled at $1100. A full line of options (memory, i/o interfaces, software) is available. 16K static memory boards cost $765 in kit form, $945 assembled. MITS, Albuquerque, New Mexico.

Figure (58B): A system based on the 6800 microprocessor. Basic unit (shown) consists of cover, chassis, power supply, 2 K static RAM, serial i/o interface, microprocessor, and a monitor [Q209] in ROM. Kit price is $395. Southwest Technical Products Corporation, San Antonio, Texas.

Figure 58B cont'd: the insides of the SWTPC 6800.

Figure (58C): A system based on the Z-80 microprocessor. Basic system (the box behind the keyboard) price is $895 kit, $1295 assembled. Includes Z-80 microprocessor, 10K memory, i/o interface, TV interface, power supply, motherboard, chassis, cover. System shown includes keyboard, TV monitor, two cassette tape drives, 26K memory, sells for approx. $2100 kit, $2700 assembled.

The Digital Group, Denver, Colorado.

Figure 58D: The ADM-3 video display terminal kit.
Basic unit displays 12 lines of up to 80 (upper case)
characters each. Has a number of switch selectable
options. List price $995. Plugs into RS232C stand-
ard interface on your computer. Extra cost options
include lower case characters, ability to move the cursor anywhere on the screen under program control
(useful for graphic effects). Lear Siegler, Inc., Ana-
heim, California.

Figure 58E: The assembled ADM-3.

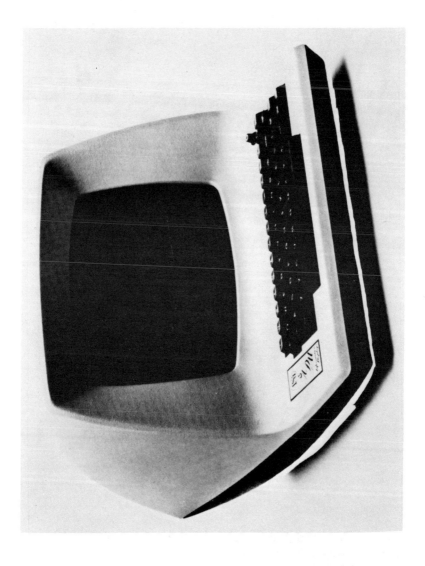

Figure 58F: "Old faithful." The ASR-33 Teletype. (ASR = Automatic Send Receive. Models without paper tape reader obviously can't send automatically, and are called KSR = Keyboard Send Receive.) Runs at 110 band (= 10 characters/second), costs $1070 as shown, $1034 without stand. Teletype Corporation, Skokie, Illinois.

+10 volts, +5, −5, and −10; and one pulse is transmitted each second, that's also a rate of one baud (even though in information theoretic terms you're now sending 2 bits

Table 5 Typical peripheral devices (page 1 of 3)

device	basic use	approx. speed	cost range (new)	comments
keyboard	input	faster than you can type	$20–$80	A keyboard itself is just a bunch of switches—you also need circuitry which figures out what key was pressed and generates the appropriate bit pattern for your machine's i/o interface.
TV display	output	depends on hardware, faster than you can read	$100–$300 +TV set	Typically the circuitry includes RAM (one byte for each character position on the display). Least expensive versions are organized as 16 lines of up to 32 characters each, which can make it hard to develop large programs (unless you also have a hard copy listing, you forget what you can't see). High density displays may not work on cheap (or misaligned) TV sets.
video terminal	i/o	often selectable 110 baud – 9600 baud	$900–$4000	Keyboard and TV-like display all in one package. A wide variety of models is available. Less expensive video terminals display upper case letters only, are less flexible to use. More expensive terminals include microprocessors which implement editing facilities, etc., (in a half serious, half tongue-in-cheek way) such devices are called intelligent terminals). Figures 58 B and E show a dumb terminal.
hard copy terminals	i/o	110 baud 660 baud	$900 – $3,000	The advantages and disadvantages of hard copy over video terminals are obvious: you can quickly look at all parts of a large program listing, mark changes, you can keep copies of important programs—but—you have to pay for the paper and put up with the noise and slower operation. Teletypes (see Fig. 58F) have been around for a long time (and are by no means an endangered species). The less expensive models print upper case letters only, are slow and noisy—but keep working. Some hard copy terminals use quiet, fast electronic printing which requires special (read costly) paper.

per second). Since virtually all the communications involved with computers is binary in form, you're pretty safe if you read **bits per second** where it says **baud**.

* bit Q 41

Table 5 - continued - (page 2 of 3)

device	basic use	approx speed	cost range (new)	comments
hard copy terminals -continued-				For around $2500 - $3,000 you can get terminals (e.g Diablo Hi-Term II) which can produce immaculate copy, including figures (made by utilizing the variable spacing features), with an extensive (changeable) character set. Great for producing camera-ready copy for publications. Small publishers, magazines, writers, take note!
printers	output	40 char/line 75 lines/min	$200 - $500	The relevant variables on printers are character set (cheaper ones print the 64 ASCII characters, more expensive ones the full ASCII character set), column width, speed (usually gives in **lines/minute**), and reliability. **Dot matrix** printers construct characters from ▒▒▒, are usually faster & cheaper. **Chain** printers have the characters on a moving chain or band, a little hammer slams the character onto the page at the right moment. Not all printers can handle **special forms** (i.e. mailing labels, carbon copies etc.)
		80 char/line 70 lines/min	$1500 - $2500	
		132 char/line 100-300-500 lines/min	$2000, $4000, $10,000	
paper tape reader, punch	permanent storage of programs, data in machine readable form	100 baud - 1000 baud	$100 - $2000	Some models of Teletype (such as the one in Figure 58 F) include a paper tape reader and punch. Thus, quite a few programs are available on paper tape. Inexpensive paper tape readers may require you to pull the tape through by hand. For home use, cassette tape recorders are probably better — more economical, more convenient, let you do the same things.

Q 607 Explain what **ASCII** means again? You listed **64 ASCII characters** there beside the printer heading.

see Appendix ASCII characters

Table 5 - continued - (page 3 of 3)

device	basic use	approx speed	price range (new)	comments
Cassette tape	off-line storage	300 - 2400 baud	$50 - $200	Inexpensive, used by most hobbyists. The Kansas City standards for using cassette tapes allow the use of inexpensive ($30 or up) cassette tape recorders, reads and writes data at 300 baud. Faster systems are available, but there are no standards for them (yet), so you probably won't be able to trade programs with people using different systems than your own
floppy disc	random access mass storage	~100K baud once right location is found, 200-600 milliseconds search time	$600-$2000	The **floppy disc** (in which the storage medium is a flexible, thin, magnetically impregnated disc) is a much cheaper, more convenient, slower, smaller version of rigid disc systems. Typical system can store 100 K bytes/disc. Newer technologies (**charge coupled devices, magnetic bubble devices**) may soon prove competitive, providing the same capabilities as a disc, but a higher speed since they have no moving parts. Floppy disc drives themselves run $350 - $800. You also need a disc controller (interface) which runs $600-$1000.

Table 6   Exotic peripherial devices   (page 1 of 2)

name	use	comments
joystick	input of position information — 2 or more axes of angular displacement	A joystick is a device which has a movable shaft — you move the shaft (stick) by hand (and with some, you can twist it too, plus there may be a button on it you can push with your thumb). The motion of the shaft alters the settings of variable resistors. By sensing the resistance, your computer can detect the position of the stick. Requires a voltage source & some form of A/D conversion (can be cheap since you can't move the stick very fast). Used in a number of electronic games, for moving a cursor around on a screen, etc.
slide switch, potentiometer	input of position along one axis	one axis version of joystick
mouse	input of two-dimensional position information	Similar idea to joystick, except you move the mouse over a flat surface. Two wheels set at right angles detect movement along the two axes. Good way to control position of a cursor for text editing, etc.
lightpen	interaction with a visual display	A lightpen is a simple device which detects sudden changes in light intensity. A program rapidly (and repeatedly) brightens each position on the display (in order). When the position the lightpen is being held over flashes, the lightpen sends a signal, thus identifying its position.
humidity, pressure, temperature, etc. sensor	input of sensor reading	Any device that changes its electrical characteristics in accordance with the quantity being sensed can serve as an input device. May need to amplify the signal before running into an A/D converter. May need to provide electrical isolation to protect digital logic.

input devices

Table 6 Exotic peripheral devices (page 2 of 2)

name	use	comments
speech synthesizer	produces signals mimicking human speech sounds	A number of kits and assembled systems are available. Typically, the hardware synthesizes an audio signal for each phoneme, which you specify by having your program send a character to the device. You have to figure out how to pronounce each part of each word you want to output. The units produce understandable, but unnatural sounding "speech".
music synthesizer	play music generated under program control; control a moog synthesizer	Several kits are available. Limited music can be produced by hooking the output of a D/A converter into your stereo system—most micro-processors aren't fast enough to generate really complex waveforms. The music synthesizers let the computer control oscillators instead of having to compute instantaneous voltage levels.
graphics	display arbitrary visual patterns	The most common form displays the contents of a block of memory. Changing the contents of memory location changes the scene. There are also vector generators" which draw lines between points instead of working on a point-by-point basis.
lights, motors, coffee pots, burglar alarms, etc.	control appliances, etc. with appropriate programs	Silicon control rectifiers, triacs, or relays can be used to turn electrical appliances on & off under program control.

output devices

A   Let's see. **ASCII** stands for the American Standard Code for Information Interchange. It's a standard way of assigning characters (A,B,C, . . . ,Z,a,b,c, . . . ,z,0,1,2, . . . ,9,'',#,$,%,&,',(,),*,+, etc.) to seven bit binary values. Since $2^7 = 128$, there are 128 ASCII characters in the full set (about 90 of which are displayed — the rest are control characters.)

Obviously, the fewer different characters a printer has, the cheaper it will be to build, so a lot of equipment is made to print a subset of the full ASCII characters. (There's a standard for the subset too.) The subset has 64 characters in it. The most noticeable omission in the 64 character set is the lower case letters.

Q 608 **Character set** just means . . . collection of possible characters?

A   Exactly.

As long as we're on standards, I might as well mention a couple more. You'll probably run into references to **RS-232 compatible devices.** RS-232 is a standard that specifies electrical characteristics for inputs and outputs on peripheral devices. So if you buy an RS-232 interface with your home computer, you can hook up to any RS-232 compatible device with no hassle. You literally should be able to just plug it in.

Just as with the ASCII standard, not *all* equipment is designed to meet the standard, but quite a bit of the newer equipment does. And then there's the (to date) one and only standard agreed to by computer hobbyists, the so-called **Kansas City Standard,** which specifies a uniform method for using inexpensive cassette tape recorders to store binary data. It's relatively slow as mag tape schemes go (300 baud, or about 27 characters per second*), but it serves a really useful purpose, namely, letting hobbyists share tapes with each other. Hopefully, there will be quite a few more standards agreed upon in the next few years. Any more questions about the peripherals in the table?

Q 609 Are the prices going to come down?

A   They're probably going to drift lower . . . but certainly no where near as fast or as much as the price of pure electronics . . .

Q 610 All right. I have a few more questions, but I guess I can find out what I want to know by reading the ads. Why don't we give up for today?

---

* if you're wondering why that's 27 characters per second instead of 300/7 ≃ 42, don't forget parity, start, and stop bits, which mean you send 11 bits for each character.

A   OK. How about starting into some detail about microprocessors next time?

Q 611 That's a good idea . . . we've been talking about them for days now, and you still haven't told me what's really inside them.

DAY 5:
SOME SPECIFIC
MICROPROCESSORS

The organization of specific microprocessors

A   Here's my plan for today. I know you want to know, in detail, what a microprocessor is really like to program, how it's organized, and so on. Instead of taking one specific microprocessor chip and going over it inside and out, I thought it would be better to cover two chips, each in a little less detail. That way . . .

Q 612 Why?

A   The most important thing is for you to be able to read the manufacturer's literature for whatever chip you wind up with. Although the basic ideas are similar, it seems that each manufacturer uses slightly different terminology. There's no reason for you to completely memorize all the details of one specific microprocessor . . . then you'd be lost when the next one comes along.

Q 613 Go on. I'll see how it goes . . . my hunch is that I'll want more specifics. You have a tendency to go off into outer space with your generalizations.

A   Let's start from the outside in.
      Microprocessors like the 8080 (designed by Intel) and the 6800 (designed by Motorola) come in 40 pin dual in-line packages that are (typically) 2 inches long and a half inch wide. **Dual in-line package (DIP)** just means that there are two rows of pins, with standard spacings.
      A microprocessor, by itself, can't do much.

Q   I think you've already covered that . . .

A   First, you need a power supply. Different microprocessors have different power requirements. For instance, the 8080 needs three different voltages, namely, + 5, -5, and + 12 volts. The 6800 needs just one (5 volts), as does the Z-80. The RCA COSMAC chip (CDP 1802) can run on a single power supply of anywhere from 3 to 12 volts. OK. A microprocessor and a power supply can't do much by themselves either.

Q 614 You need memory and i/o, of course.

A   Besides that, most microprocessors need an external source of their **clock signals.** For example, Intel offers a chip (the 8224) which generates the necessary clocking signals, and Motorola makes the 6871. The 8080 also need some external circuitry to interact with its busses. There's the Intel 8228 System Controller chip for that. And then, as you mentioned, you need memory and i/o interfaces. So the moral is, just because you see a micro-processor chip for sale for $20, don't be misled into thinking you can whip a microcomputer together for just $100 or so.

        The newer microprocessor chips are coming with more and more circuitry packed in them, so you need less external circuitry to have a working system. Zilog's Z-80 goes the farthest along that route so far. It has built-in parallel and serial i/o interfaces, built-in dynamic memory refresh circuitry, and a number of other features that you have to provide externally with the older chips. Of course, it also costs more . . . but not that much when you consider everything.

Q 615 If I buy an assembled computer, or a kit, I don't have to worry about all that, right?

A   Right . . . although you do need to know something about what you've got — so you'll be able to read the circuit diagrams if you have to trouble shoot some problem.
        I'm going to concentrate on the 8080 and the 6800. I think once you understand those two chips, you'll be able to figure out the manufacturer's descriptions of any other chip you might come across. Here's the basic organization of the 8080. [Fig. 59]
        You can see that there's one **accumulator,** and six **general purpose registers** called B,C,D,E,L, and H . . .

Q 616 Why on earth did they pick those letters?

A   I don't . . . well, H stands for High-order byte and L stands for Low-order byte — there are a number of instructions that use the contents of the H and L registers as a memory address. As for the others, they're just in alphabetical order. A stands for the Accumulator, and after that, it's just B,C,D,E.

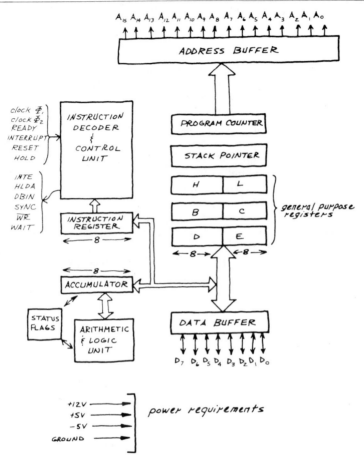

Figure 59 8080 Architecture

There are two other registers both 16 bits long since they hold memory addresses, the **stack pointer register** and the **program counter**. I guess we haven't talked about stacks yet.

Q 617 True.

A   <u>**Stacks**</u> are data structures — a technique for organizing memory. Having a **stack pointer** in hardware makes certain kinds of very commonly occurring programming problems easier.

    You remember what the **program counter** is, right?

Q 618 It tells where the next instruction in the program is stored in memory, right?

A   Right.

Let's see . . . what else? The **status flags.** The **accumulator** is the register you use to manipulate data, do additions, subtractions, logic operations, complements, so on. After some operation has been performed on the value in the accumulator, the status flags are set to indicate something about the result. The 8080 has 5 status flags. We'll be concerned with 4 of them.

Q 619 Hold it. What is a **flag?**

A A **flag** is something that has a true / false value. It's a one-bit memory that's used to keep track of something. I'm being vague because the term is used in hardware (where it's usually implemented as a flip-flop) *and* in software (where it's a value stored in memory).

I don't know where the term came from.

Let me tell you what the **status flags** are (sometimes they're also called **status bits,** sometimes **condition codes**) and I think you'll see what it means.

There's one called **Z** (for Zero) that is **true** (has the value **1**) if the last operation left a zero result (i.e. if the accumulator now contains 00000000).

There's one called **C** (for Carry) which is 1 if an add instruction resulted in a carry out of the most significant bit, or if a subtract resulted in a borrow into that bit.

Q 620 Again?

A OK. Suppose the accumulator has 00000101 in it, and we add the value 11111011 to it. What do you get?

Q 621
$$
\begin{array}{r}
00000101 \\
+\,11111011 \\
\hline
1\ \ 00000000
\end{array}
$$

A So, after that, the Carry flag would have the value **1**, and so would the Zero flag.

There are two other flags, the Sign flag (S), and the Parity flag. The sign flag has the same value as the most significant bit in the accumulator, and the parity flag is 1 if there is an even number of 1's in the accumulator. So the 8080 makes it really easy to test a value for even or odd parity.*

parity Q 522-Q 525

Q 622 How do you use the flags, though?

A There are instructions that have different results depending on the values of the status flags. But we'll get to that in a minute. First, I wanted to show you the 6800 innards.

Q 623 Oh. I forgot to ask you something from the last picture. What does **buffer** mean exactly?

A In this context, it means the same as **latch.** In general, it means a subsystem that serves as a go-between for two

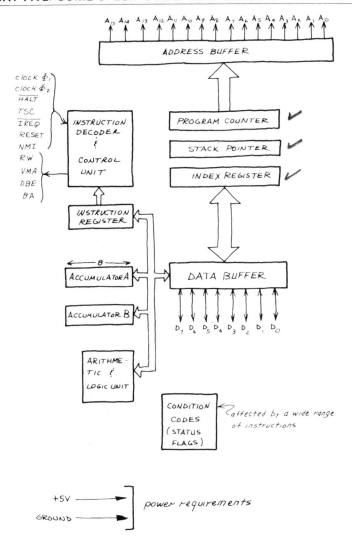

A_{15} A_{14} A_{13} A_{12} A_{11} A_{10} A_9 A_8 A_7 A_6 A_5 A_4 A_3 A_2 A_1 A_0

ADDRESS BUFFER

clock ϕ_1
clock ϕ_2
$\overline{HALT}$
TSC
$\overline{IREQ}$
RESET
NMI
RW
VMA
DBE
BA

INSTRUCTION DECODER & CONTROL UNIT

PROGRAM COUNTER

STACK POINTER

INDEX REGISTER

INSTRUCTION REGISTER

← 8 →
ACCUMULATOR A

DATA BUFFER

ACCUMULATOR B

D_7 D_6 D_5 D_4 D_3 D_2 D_1 D_0

ARITHMETIC & LOGIC UNIT

CONDITION CODES (STATUS FLAGS) — affected by a wide range of instructions

+5V ——→
GROUND ——→] power requirements

Figure 60 6800 Architecture

other sys . . .

Q 624 No, that's what I don't get. What's the difference between a **buffer** and an **interface**?

A   It's a strange language at times, isn't it? A **buffer** is a particular kind of interface. Usually, a buffer is an interface between two systems that have different speed or timing requirements. And (at least in all the cases I can think

Interfaced memory

of) a buffer includes some form of memory. The idea here is that the control unit lets a 16 bit value flow from (say) the program counter into the address buffer, and the address buffer holds it while it's broadcast over the address bus.

Q 625 I've got a question about the 6800. You show two accumulators . . .

A   Right. The 6800 has three 16 bit registers, the **program counter, stack pointer,** and **index register,** and two 8 bit **accumulators.**

Q 626 I can see that. What I wanted to know was this: if the status flags tell things about the status of the accumulator, why aren't there two sets of status flags? Or are there?

A   Interesting you'd notice that.

OK. There's just one set of status flags. On the 6800, the flags are affected by a great many instructions, so here it makes more sense to think of them as being set by the most recent instruction, no matter which accumulator (if any) was involved.

Q 627 Oh.

The 8080 didn't have an **index register***, did it? What's that for?

A   For referring to memory.

Q 628 That's not much of an answer — obviously the 8080 has to refer to memory too.

A   Yeh, it's just done differently on the two processors.

Since the **architecture** (machine organization) of the two is different, the **instructions sets** are different.

Q 629 **Instruction set** just means the basic machine instructions?

A   Right. **Set** used to mean collection. Anyway, obviously, one of the ways the instruction sets must be different is in how the two processors can access memory, since they have different registers to use.

Q 630 Does every computer have a different instruction set?

A   Almost . . . it's fun to design instruction sets, and each designer thinks he or she can do a better job than the last, so it's fairly rare for two different models to have identical instruction sets. Of course that just adds to the (already bad) software compatibility problem.

There are a couple of microprocessors that have the instruction sets of older minicomputers (the Micro Nova comes to mind), and the advantage there is that you can use all the programs that were developed for the mini.

Also, there are a few examples of microprocessors whose

---

* index register Q 654 Table 7

instructions sets include all the instructions of some other machine (and more besides). The Z-80 includes all the instructions of the 8080 (with one small exception), and quite a few more.

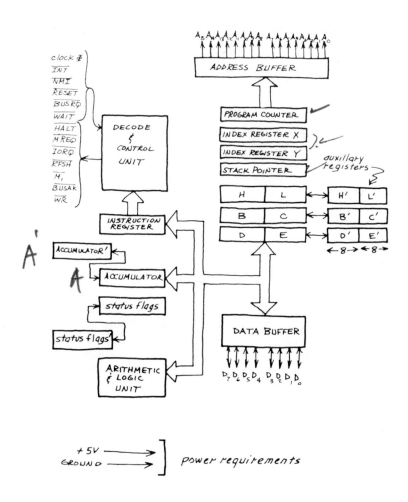

Note: there are no instructions which operate directly on the auxillary registers, accumulator, and status flags. There are instructions for swapping the contents of the main and auxillary registers

Figure 61   Z-80 Architecture

Q 631 Well, what are they? The instructions, on the 8080, say.

A   Let's think about it a bit.

Both the 6800 and the 8080 are byte oriented machines, and their instruction registers, therefore, are eight bits wide. So how many different types of instructions can there be?

Q 632 You're asking how many different 8 bit patterns there are, I guess . . .

2^8, which is $2^6 \times 2^2 = 64 \times 4 = 256$.

But wait a minute. Why did you say different *types* of instructions? There must just be 256 different instructions, right?

A   Don't forget that the instructions don't have to be just one byte long . . . Well, actually, I guess I'm being a little sloppy in my terminology here. Let me distinguish between a **command** and an **instruction**.

Q 633 They don't mean the same thing?

A   Not exactly.

Both the 8080 and the 6800 have a transfer of control command called JMP (for JuMP). To use it, you put the command in one byte in memory, and then in the next two bytes, you store the memory address you want the controller to JuMP to for its next instruction. Let's call the JMP by itself a **command,** and the JMP with the address (three bytes in all) an **instruction**. That way JMP to address 00000000 00000001 and JMP to address 00000000 00000010 are two *different* **instructions**, but both involve the *same* **command**. OK? So what I meant to say before was that both the 6800 and the 8080 allow for 256 different commands, and using those commands, you can write a huge number of different instructions. Now. Neither the 6800 nor the 8080 actually uses all the possible patterns for commands. Let's figure out what sorts of things they must have.

Remember the conceptual computer I drew a while back, I think it was the first day?

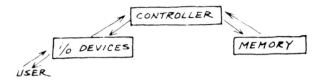

Q 634 Yes.

A   If we think in terms of that, we'll be able to figure out what sorts of commands any computer needs.

        You need a number of commands that allow you to interact with memory. Commands that bring values from memory into the controller, to store values into memory, and you need to be able to move values around in the registers in the controller. I'll call them **memory access commands.** Then you need some method of interacting with i/o devices. The 8080 includes **explicit i/o instructions,** the 6800 doesn't.

Q 635 You already mentioned something about that. You can treat i/o devices the same as memory locations, or something like that.
        [Q 91-96]

A   Right. On the 6800, it's left to hardware outside the controller to determine if a value on the address bus refers to memory or to an i/o device.

        OK. Then you need a range of **operate commands,** like add, subtract, shift, complement, and, or, exclusive-or, and so on. You need a range of **branching instructions,** kinds of jump commands that are conditional on the values of the status flags. And finally, you need some additional commands that don't fit in the other categories, like a **halt command** (which stops the controller), maybe some specialized commands for dealing with interrupts, commands for setting the status flags, and usually there's a NOP (for No OPeration) command which doesn't do anything.

Q 636 Really? It doesn't do *anything*?

A   Well, it does do something — it takes up a byte in memory, and it takes time for the processor to do it . . .

Q 637 It takes time to do nothing?

A   Just as with any other instruction, the processor has to **fetch** it from memory, **decode** it, update the **program counter** to get ready for the next instruction, so it takes time to do all that. It's just that that's *all* that happens for a NOP instruction. You can use it for a couple of things. One is to take up space (on some computers, you have to make sure certain instructions start at the right place in memory, so you can use NOPs to pad unwanted space. . .).

        You can use them in a timing loop.

Q 638 A **timing loop**?

A   Yeh. Suppose that you're using some kind of relatively slow i/o device and you want to do most of the timing in your program instead of buying a more costly i/o interface. Then you can repeat the NOP instruction some specific number of times to make the processor wait a given length of time before accessing the i/o device.

Q   Hmmm.

Instructions that access memory

A   I don't know how we managed to start with the NOP instruction — it's an oddball one. Let's really start with the **memory access instructions,** OK?

Q 639 Sure. It seems like a simple thing, you just need to bring a byte from memory into the controller and vice versa, right?

A   It's a simple idea, all right, but it's one of the most confusing parts of microcomputers when you get down to the details. See, there are a number of different situations you can get into when you're writing a program, and different ways of accessing memory can be more or less convenient depending on the situation. So, the person who designed the instruction set gives you a number of options. To make things even more complicated, there's very little agreement on what to *call* the various schemes, so what one manufacturer calls, say, **direct addressing,** the next calls **extended addressing,** and a third may call something else again.

Fortunately, though, there is a fair amount of agreement on a notation we can use to figure out what's going on. Here it is.

(name)

means ''the contents of the storage location identified by *name*''. So, for example, if there's a memory location that we choose to call LOC1, then (LOC1) is the value stored there, that is, the **contents** of LOC1.

Q 640 That's *it*? That's the notation that's going to bring order out of chaos?

A   That's most of it. There's one other symbol we need, and then I can start explaining the memory access instructions. If I write

(LOC1)←00000000

it means "store the value to the right of the arrow in the place on the left." It says "make the contents of LOC1 be 00000000".

OK so far?

Q 641 Sure, sure.

A Then let me start with some of the instructions that move values around among the registers and the accumulators.

8080 command mnemonic*	6800 command mnemonic	action performed
MOV B,A	TAB	$(B) \leftarrow (A)$
MOV A,B	TBA	$(A) \leftarrow (B)$

See how the notation works?

other 8080, 6800 instructions: Appendix — 8080 Instruction Set
Appendix — 6800 Instruction Set

Q 642 I don't see why you're making such a big deal out of this. It's obvious. The first instruction takes the contents of A and sticks it in B.

A Right.

Q 643 I hope you're not going to go rushing on to something else, though, because the notation is about the only thing that makes sense there. For one thing, I think you've got the 8080 instructions backwards.

A Just another example of how each manufacturer makes up its own notation . . . at least the notation I'm using is unambiguous. MOV B,A means, in Intel lingo, "MOVe the Accumulator to register B".
They list the **destination** first.
The 6800 mnemonic TAB reads "Transfer the contents of accumulator A to accumulator B". They list the **source** first.
OK. The 6800 has just the two accumulators, and no other 8-bit registers you can use, but the 8080 has seven 8-bit registers A,B,C,D,E,H, and L. There's a MOVe command for each possible combination, like MOV D,C and MOV H,A and so on. So right there we've used up 49 of the 256 possible commands.
Now let's start in on some of the instructions that access ROM or RAM.
The terminology starts to get really wild here. Let's look

* mnemonic Q 178

at commands which load a value from a specific place in memory into an accumulator. Virtually every computer ever built has a command that does that, and they're almost all called **LDA** (for LoaD Accumulator).

8080 command mnemonic	6800 command mnemonic	action performed
LDA *addr*	LDA A *addr*	(A) ←(addr)
	LDA B *addr*	(B) ←(addr)

addr stands for some specific memory address, and it's given in the second and third bytes of the instruction.

Q 644 So these are three byte long instructions.

A   Right. I forgot to mention that the MOV and TAB instructions we saw before are one byte long. The LDA instruction has to be three bytes long because it includes a memory address. Let me call the second and third bytes of a three byte instruction *byte$_2$* and *byte$_3$*. Both the 8080 and the 6800 LDA instructions require that the memory address of the value you want brought into the accumulator be stored in *byte$_2$* and *byte$_3$*, but they require it to be stored in a different order. I can explain it easier if I use our notation.
On the 8080, the LDA instruction has this effect

(A) ←((*byte$_3$*) (*byte$_2$*))

Q 645 Wait. What have you got there? The contents of the contents of *byte$_3$* . . .

A   Maybe an example will help. Let's suppose the memory location we want to access is 00000000 00111111. Then the instruction will look like this in memory (because the op code for LDA is 00111010 on the 8080).

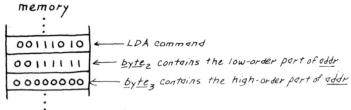

memory

00111010	←——— LDA command
00111111	←—— *byte$_2$* contains the low-order part of *addr*
00000000	←—— *byte$_3$* contains the high-order part of *addr*

So, by following through our notation, we can figure out what happens when this instruction is carried out.

(A) ←((*byte$_3$*) (*byte$_2$*))

in this case is

(A)←(00000000 00111111)

so A is loaded with the contents of memory location
00000000 00111111, just as we wanted. OK?

Q 646 All right. I guess that makes sense.

A   Now let me run through the same thing, but for the 6800.
I'll show an instruction that'll load accumulator A from
memory location 00000000 00111111. The op code
for LDA A is 10110110 and on the 6800, it does this

(A) ←((*byte*₂) (*byte*₃))

So, the whole instruction is

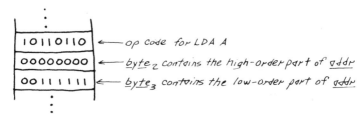

and interpreting our notation, we see that we get

(A)←(00000000 00111111)

I hope you can see that if you think in terms of what's
going on, and use the notation I'm suggesting, you won't
get hopelessly lost in all the quirky little details. A number
of the specific details *are* different from machine to machine, but the general ideas are remarkably similar.

Q 647 But why do you put the two parts of the address in
differently on the 8080 and the 6800?

A   Don't ask me, I just work here.

Different designers make different decisions.

Incidentally, we're not quite done with the details yet. On
the 8080 the LDA instruction doesn't affect any of the
status flags, but on the 6800 it does. Specifically, carrying
out an LDA sets the V (oVerflow) flag to 0, and alters
the N (sign) flag and Z (Zero) flag appropriately.
Everything OK?

Q 648 I guess so. I'm just amazed at all the little details . . .

A   There really aren't that many basic ideas . . . few enough
that you won't have any trouble remembering them. But
there are *scads* of little details . . . so many that you'll

have to keep the manual by your side.

Now let's go over another way to access memory.

Q 649 Before you go on, why don't you tell me what **effective address** means? I came across it in an article I was reading, and it seemed kind of complicated.

A The **effective address** in a memory reference instruction is just the address you finally wind up with . . . the place in memory the instruction ultimately refers to. That isn't a complicated idea in and of itself. What *can* get complicated is the process the controller goes through to obtain the effective address from the information provided in the instruction.

In the case we've seen so far, it's pretty simple. The effective address in an 8080 LDA instruction is

$(byte_3)$ $(byte_2)$

But we'll get to some that are more involved. Here's one that's slightly more complex.

In a number of situations, the address of the memory location your program needs to refer to next will have been stored in one of the registers in the controller by previous steps in your program. So it would be convenient to have instructions that use one of the registers (or a *pair* of registers if each register is only 8 bits long) to specify the memory address. I'm going to call that **register indirect addressing,** although it's sometimes called **implied addressing.**

8080
command   action
mnemonic   performed

| LDAX B | (A) ← ((B) (C)) |
| LDAX D | (A)   ((D) (E)) |

Let me set up an example we can follow through. [Fig. 63]

There's the situation. I'll tell you that the op code for LDAX B is 00001010, and that's all. What happens?

Q 650 I don't know quite where to start.

A The **program counter** tells where to get the next instruction. Start there. With the **instruction fetch.**

Q 657 Right. Fetch the instruction. So 00001010 gets brought into the controller and put in the instruction register. And you said that was a LDAX B instruction. But there's no address after it.

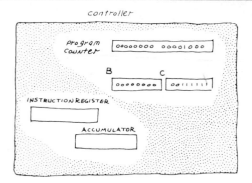

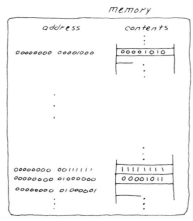

Figure 63   Situation at the beginning
of the instruction fetch. The
value stored at memory address
00000000 00001000 is 00001010 which
is an LDAX B instruction

A   Right. It's just one byte long, since it uses the B and C
         registers to form the effective address. That's another
         reason for using it. The program is shorter than if we had
         to use the LDA we saw before.

Q 652 I see what's going on, . . . the instruction does this

         (A) ← ((B) (C))

         so I have to take the contents of B and C. Register B
         has all zeros in it . . . so I've got

         (A) ← (00000000 00111111)

There.

A What do you mean "there"? Now you've got the effective address, so go ahead and carry out the instruction.

Q 653 Oh. All right. Memory location 00000000 00111111 has all 1's in it, and I'm supposed to load that in the accumulator. There.

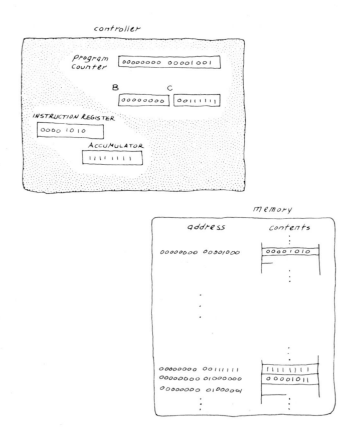

Figure 64 After the LDAX B has been carried out. No change has been made to memory.

Table 7   Common addressing schemes (page 1 of 2)

common name	other names for something	effective address	comments (apply to byte oriented systems – 8080, 6800, Z-80, etc.)
direct	absolute, extended	$(byte_2)(byte_3) \leftarrow 6800$ or $(byte_3)(byte_2) \leftarrow 8080$	A **load direct** instruction requires 3 bytes. The last two bytes contain the address of the value which is to be brought into the controller.
register	inherent	register named in instruction	A **register move** instruction is 1 byte long. Typically, two registers (called the **source** and **destination**) are specified within that one byte. The contents of the **source** are copied into the destination.
immediate		(program counter) $+1$	A **load immediate** instruction occupies 2 bytes. The value to be loaded is stored as the second byte of the instruction. (Called **immediate** because no memory reference is required beyond that needed to fetch the instruction itself.)
register indirect	implied	(16-bit register) or (pair of 8-bit registers)	A **register indirect** load instruction is 1 byte long. It specifies a register (or pair of 8-bit registers) whose contents are used as the address of the value to be brought into the controller. (Other instructions must have previously placed that address into the register [or registers].)
indexed		(16-bit register) $+ (byte_2)$	An **indexed** memory reference instruction is 2 bytes long. The effective address is obtained by adding the contents of the second byte of the instruction to the value stored in a register (usually surprise — an index register). Some microprocessors treat the value stored in the second byte as a positive number (between 0 and 255_{10}), others treat it as a signed (two's-complement) number (-128 to $+127$).
indirect		$((byte_2)(byte_3))$	An **indirect** memory reference instruction occupies 3 bytes. The address of the value being referenced is taken from the two memory locations which begin at the address given in $byte_2$ and $byte_3$ of instruction. Sort of like a treasure hunt.

Table 7 Common addressing schemes (page 2 of 2)

common name	other names for same thing	effective address	comments (apply to byte oriented systems - 8080, 6800, Z-80, etc.)
paged	base paged, page/offset	$(8\text{-bit register})(byte_2)$	2 byte instruction. The value stored in the second byte of the instruction is appended to the value stored in a register (often a special register called the **base register** or **page register**. Thus, the register provides the high-order byte of the effective address and $byte_2$ provides the low-order byte (or **offset**).
base page	direct, page zero	$00000000(byte_2)$	The contents of the second byte of the instruction are appended to 00000000 to form the effective address. Allows direct reference to the first 256_{10} memory locations in a 2 byte instruction.
page relative	paged direct	$(\text{high order byte of program counter})(byte_2)$	The contents of the second byte of the instruction are appended to the high-order byte of the program counter (i.e. to the current page) to form the effective address.
relative	program relative	$(\text{program counter}) + (byte_2)$	The contents of $byte_2$ are added to the current value of the program counter to form the effective address. The contents of $byte_2$ are treated as a signed number (-128 to $+127$) on most microprocessors.

A   One last thing. The program counter will have been incremented. Other than that, you've got everything.

Q 654   And I suppose the 6800 has something similar?

A   Similar, but a little more general. It's usually called **indexed addressing**. Here's how it works.

6800
command   action
mnemonic   performed
LDA A *offset*, X $(A) \leftarrow ((\text{index register}) + (byte_2))$
LDA B *offset*, X $(B) \leftarrow ((\text{index register}) + (byte_2))$

It's like the last scheme we saw in that a register which stores an address is involved, but now it's a two byte long instruction, and the second byte specifies an *offset* value which is added to the contents of the index register to get the effective address.

Q 655   I think I see what's going on . . . if the offset is 0, then it works pretty much like the last one, right?

A   Right.

There are quite a few more addressing schemes, but if you understand how to read the notation, you'll be able to figure them out. Also, of course, for each of the instructions we've seen there's a complementary one which goes the other way — **stores** a value in memory instead of bringing one from memory. Like, corresponding to the LDA instructions there are STA (STore Accumulator) instructions, and so on.

[Editor's note: This is the end of the first five days. From this point on, Q and A's conversations are concerned with matters dealing with software, and are contained in the last five days.]

Powers

Here are some powers of 2, 8, and 16, along with the program that was used to generate them.

RUN POWERS OF? 2

```
 0   1
 1   2
 2   4
 3   8
 4   16
 5   32
 6   64
 7   128
 8   256
 9   512
10   1 024
11   2 048
12   4 096
13   8 192
14   16 384
15   32 768
16   65 536
17   131 072
18   262 144
19   524 288
20   1 048 576
21   2 097 152
22   4 194 304
23   8 388 608
24   16 777 216
25   33 554 432
26   67 108 864
27   134 217 728
28   268 435 456
29   536 870 912
30   1 073 741 824
31   2 147 483 684
32   4 294 967 296
33   8 589 934 592
34   17 179 869 184
35   34 359 738 368
36   68 719 476 736
37   137 438 953 472
38   274 877 906 944
39   549 755 813 888
40   1 099 511 627 776
41   2 199 023 255 552
42   4 398 046 511 104
43   8 796 093 022 208
44   17 592 186 044 416
45   35 184 372 088 832
46   70 368 744 177 664
47   140 737 488 355 328
48   281 474 976 710 656
49   562 949 953 421 312
50   1 125 899 906 842 624
```

```
 0   1
 1   8
 2   64
 3   512
 4   4 096
 5   32 768
 6   262 144
 7   2 097 152
 8   16 777 216
 9   134 217 728
10   1 073 741 824
11   8 589 934 592
12   68 719 476 736
13   549 755 813 888
14   4 398 046 511 104
15   35 184 372 088 832
16   281 474 976 710 656
17   2 251 799 813 685 248
18   18 014 398 509 481 984
19   144 115 188 075 855 872
20   1 152 921 504 606 846 976
21   9 223 372 036 854 775 808
22   73 786 976 294 838 206 464
23   590 295 810 358 705 651 712
24   4 722 366 482 869 645 213 696
25   37 778 931 862 957 161 709 568
26   302 231 454 903 657 293 676 544
27   2 417 851 639 229 258 349 412 352
28   19 342 813 113 834 066 795 298 816
29   154 742 504 910 672 534 362 390 528
30   1 237 940 039 285 380 274 899 124 224
31   9 903 520 314 283 042 199 192 993 792
32   79 228 162 514 264 337 593 543 950 336
33   633 825 300 114 114 700 748 351 602 688
34   5 070 602 400 912 917 605 986 812 821 504
35   40 564 819 207 303 340 847 894 502 572 032
36   324 518 553 658 426 726 783 156 020 576 256
37   2 596 148 429 267 413 814 265 248 164 610 048
38   20 769 187 434 139 310 514 121 985 316 880 384
39   166 153 499 473 114 484 112 975 882 535 043 072
40   1 329 227 995 784 915 872 903 807 060 280 344 576
41   10 633 823 966 279 326 983 230 456 482 242 756 608
42   85 070 591 730 234 615 865 843 651 857 942 052 864
43   680 564 733 841 876 926 926 749 214 863 536 422 912
44   5 444 517 870 735 015 415 413 993 718 908 291 383 296
45   43 556 142 965 880 123 323 311 949 751 266 331 066 368
46   348 449 143 727 040 986 586 495 598 010 130 648 530 944
47   2 787 593 149 816 327 892 691 964 784 081 045 188 247 552
48   22 300 745 198 530 623 141 535 718 272 648 361 505 980 416
```

```
 0   1
 1   16
 2   256
 3   4 096
 4   65 536
 5   1 048 576
 6   16 777 216
 7   268 435 456
 8   4 294 967 296
 9   68 719 476 736
10   1 099 511 627 776
11   17 592 186 044 416
12   281 474 976 710 656
13   4 503 599 627 370 496
14   72 057 594 037 927 936
15   1 152 921 504 606 846 976
16   18 446 744 073 709 551 616
17   295 147 905 179 352 825 856
18   4 722 366 482 869 645 213 696
19   75 557 863 725 914 323 419 136
20   1 208 925 819 614 629 174 706 176
21   19 342 813 113 834 066 795 298 816
22   309 485 009 821 345 068 724 781 056
23   4 951 760 157 141 521 099 596 496 896
24   79 228 162 514 264 337 593 543 950 336
25   1 267 650 600 228 229 401 496 703 205 376
26   20 282 409 603 651 670 423 947 251 286 016
27   324 518 553 658 426 726 783 156 020 576 256
28   5 192 296 858 534 827 628 530 496 329 220 096
29   83 076 749 736 557 242 056 487 941 267 521 536
30   1 329 227 995 784 915 872 903 807 060 280 344 576
31   21 267 647 932 558 653 966 460 912 964 485 513 216
32   340 282 366 920 938 463 463 374 607 431 768 211 456
33   5 444 517 870 735 015 415 413 993 718 908 291 383 296
34   87 112 285 931 760 246 646 623 899 502 532 662 132 736
35   1 393 796 574 908 163 946 345 982 392 040 522 594 123 776
36   22 300 745 198 530 623 141 535 718 272 648 361 505 980 416
```

LIST

```
10    REM :GENERATE LOTS OF POWERS OF X.
20    REM :"X" IS GIVEN BY THE USER.
30    REM :THE ARRAY "N" STORES LARGE NUMBERS, ONE
40    REM :DECIMAL DIGIT PER MEMORY CELL.
50    REM :THE ARRAY "T$" IS USED TO GET PROPER SPACING
60    REM :WHEN PRINTING THE RESULTS.
70    REM :"P" IS THE CURRENT POWER OF "X"
80    REM :"C" IS THE CARRY OUT OF EACH LOCATION.
90    DIM N (50), T$(9)
100   REM :INITIALIZE.
110   GO SUB 2000
120   PRINT "POWERS OF";
130   INPUT X
140   PRINT
150   PRINT
200   REM :MAIN LOOP. FIRST PRINT LATEST POWER OF "X".
210   GO SUB 3000
220   LET P=P+1
230   REM :NOW MULTIPLY LATEST VALUE BY "X"
240   GOSUB 4000
250   REM :IF CARRY OUT OF LEFT-MOST DIGIT, QUIT. ELSE GO ON.
260   IF C=0 THEN 200
270   STOP

2000  REM :SUBROUTINE TO INITIALIZE RELEVANT VARIABLES.
2010  LET P=0
2020  REM :HANDLE "N0" DIGITS IN ALL.
2030  LET N0=50
2040  REM :START "N" AT 000 . . . 0001
2050  LET N(1)=1
2060  FOR D=2 TO N0
2070    LET N(D)=0
2080    NEXT D
2090  LET C=0
2100  REM :INITIALIZE "T" TO STORE STRING VERSION OF
2110  REM :DIGITS (USED TO GET SPACING RIGHT).
2120  FOR D=0 TO 9
2130    READ T$(D)
2140    NEXT D
2150  DATA "0", "1", "2", "3", "4", "5", "6", "7", "8", "9"
2160  RETURN

3000  REM :SUBROUTINE TO PRINT LARGE NUMBERS
3010  PRINT P,
3020  REM :SKIP LEADING ZEROS.
3030  FOR D=N0 TO 1 STEP -1
3040    IF N(D)<>0 THEN 3060
3050    NEXT D
3060  REM :PRINT VALUE, LEAVING A BLANK EVERY 3 DIGITS.
3070  LET V$=T$(N(D))
3080    LET D=D-1
3090    IF D=INT(D/3)*3 THEN 3200
3100    LET V$=V$ + T$(N(D))
```

```
3110     LET D=D-1
3120     GO TO 3090
3200     REM :GOT A BLOCK OF 3—PRINT 'EM.
3210     PRINT V$ + " ";
3220     REM :DONE WITH THE WHOLE NUMBER?
3230     IF D>0 THEN 3060
3240   PRINT
3250   RETURN

4000   REM :SUBROUTINE TO MULTIPLY LARGE NUMBERS BY "X"
4010   FOR D=1 TO NO
4020     LET N(D)=N(D)*X + C
4030     REM :HAVE A CARRY?
4040     IF N(D) > 9 THEN 4080
4050     REM :NO CARRY—CONTINUE.
4060     LET C=0
4070     GO TO 4110
4080     REM :DO HAVE A CARRY.
4090     LET C=INT(N(D)/10)
4100     LET N(D)=N(D)-C*10
4110     NEXT D
4120   RETURN
10000  END
```

APPENDIX B

HOME COMPUTERS
2^{10} Questions and Answers
Volume 2

Contents

APPENDIX C

ASCII Character Set
(American Standard Code for Information Interchange)

7-bit value

(8-th bit chosen to
give even or odd parity)

binary	octal	hex	symbol printed	
0000000	0	0	NULL	
.	.	.	.	
.	.	.	.	non-printing control
.	.	.	.	characters
.	.	.		
0011111	37	1F	US	
0100000	40	20	space	
0100001	41	21	!	
0100010	42	22	,,	
0100011	43	23	#	
0100100	44	24	$	
0100101	45	25	%	
0100110	46	26	&	
0100111	47	27	'	
0101000	50	28	(	
0101001	51	29	)	
0101010	52	2A	*	
0101011	53	2B	+	
0101100	54	2C	,	
0101101	55	2D	-	
0101110	56	2E	.	
0101111	57	2F	/	
0110000	60	30	0	
0110001	61	31	1	
0110010	62	32	2	
0110011	63	33	3	
0110100	64	34	4	
0110101	65	35	5	
0110110	66	36	6	if a product says it
0110111	67	37	7	supplies "64 ASCII
0111000	70	38	8	characters", you get these
0111001	71	39	9	
0111010	72	3A	:	
0111011	73	3B	;	
0111100	74	3C	<	
0111101	75	3D	=	
0111110	76	3E	>	
0111111	77	3F	?	
1000000	100	40	@	
1000001	101	41	A	
1000010	102	42	B	
1000011	103	43	C	
1000100	104	44	D	
1000101	105	45	E	
1000110	106	46	F	
1000111	107	47	G	
1001000	110	48	H	

1001001	111	49	I
1001010	112	4A	J
1001011	113	4B	K
1001100	114	4C	L
1001101	115	4D	M
1001110	116	4E	N
1001111	117	4F	O
1010000	120	50	P
1010001	121	51	Q
1010010	122	52	R
1010011	123	53	S
1010100	124	54	T
1010101	125	55	U
1010110	126	56	V
1010111	127	57	W
1011000	130	58	X
1011001	131	59	Y
1011010	132	5A	Z
1011011	133	5B	[
1011100	134	5C	\
1011101	135	5D	]
1011110	136	5E	^
1011111	137	5F	_
1100000	140	60	`
1100001	141	61	a
1100010	142	62	b
1100011	143	63	c
1100100	144	64	d
1100101	145	65	e
1100110	146	66	f
1100111	147	67	g
1101000	150	68	h
1101001	151	69	i
1101010	152	6A	j
1101011	153	6B	k
1101100	154	6C	l
1101101	155	6D	m
1101110	156	6E	n
1101111	157	6F	o
1110000	160	70	p
1110001	161	71	q
1110010	162	72	r
1110011	163	73	s
1110100	164	74	t
1110101	165	75	u
1110110	166	76	v
1110111	167	77	w
1111000	170	78	x
1111001	171	79	y
1111010	172	7A	z
1111011	173	7B	{
1111100	174	7C		
1111101	175	7D	}
1111110	176	7E	~
1111111	177	7F	DEL

APPENDIX D

6800 Instruction Set*

The notation used to describe the meaning of each instruction is explained in Q639-646. [Editor's note: Recall that (x) is read "the contents of x".] The architecture of the 6800 is discussed in Q621-625 and Figure 60. Op codes are given in hexadecimal.

The 6800 provides six different memory addressing modes. One of the modes, **relative,** is used only with **branch** instructions. The other addressing modes have the following interpretations:

MOTOROLA name for addressing mode	name used in Table 7 (near Q655)	meaning	length
inherent	register	refers to registers on the 6800 itself. E.g. ASLA which affects accumulator A only, and does not refer to memory.	one byte
immediate	immediate	*effective address = byte$_2$*	two bytes except for CPX, LDS, and LDX which are three bytes long in their **immediate** forms.
direct	bottom page	*effective address =* 00000000$_2$ (*byte$_2$*) i.e. instructions using the **direct** mode can refer to memory locations with addresses in the range 0 to 255$_{10}$ only.	two bytes
indexed	indexed	*effective address = (index register) + (byte$_2$)* (*byte$_2$*) are treated as an unsigned positive value	two bytes
extended	direct	*effective address = (byte$_2$) (byte$_3$)*	three bytes

*Thanks to MOTOROLA Semiconductor Products, Inc. for permission to include this material.

The 6800 has six **status flags.**

status flag	abbreviation	meaning for instructions which affect the flag
carry	C	if an arithmetic operation resulted in a carry or a borrow out of the leftmost bit, *carry* = 1.
overflow	V	if an operation resulted in a two's complement overflow, *overflow* = 1, i.e. if the leftmost bit (which indicates whether the value is positive or negative) has been changed improperly.
zero	Z	if the result of an operation is zero (all bits = 0), *zero* = 1.
sign	N	if the leftmost bit of the result is 1, *sign* = 1.
interrupt mask	I	if I = 1, the processor will ignore interrupt requests.
half carry	H	carry out of bit 3, used in dealing with BCD values

Other abbreviations

The second and third bytes of multibyte instructions are identified as $byte_2$ and $byte_3$

A — accumulator A (an 8-bit register)
B — accumulator B (an 8-bit register)
pc — the **program counter** (a 16-bit register)
sp — the **stack pointer** (a 16-bit register)

Branch instructions

Branch instructions on the 6800 are all two bytes long, and use **relative** addressing.

As with any instruction, the first step that is taken is to increment the **program counter** so that it contains the address of the next instruction. Since branch instructions are two bytes long, that means $(pc) \leftarrow (pc) + 2$. Next, the test associated with the branch instruction is carried out. If it fails, no further action is taken. If it succeeds, $(byte_2)$ are added to the **program counter** as a signed (two's complement) value. Thus, overall, if the test succeeds, the effect is $(pc) \leftarrow (pc) + 2 + (byte_2)$.

If you need to branch to a location which is more than 127 bytes [Editor's note: Actually the range is -126_{10} to $+129_{10}$ from the address of the branch instruction.] away, use the **(extended)** JMP instruction.

When you're dealing with signed (two's complement) values, BLT, BLE, BGE, BGT, BEQ, and BNE are appropriate. When you're dealing with plain 8-bit values, BCS, BLS, BCC, BHI, BEQ, and BNE are appropriate.

mnemonic	description	inherent	immediate	direct	indexed	extended	flags affected C	V	Z	N	I	H	meaning
ABA	Add accumulator B to accumulator A	1B					•	•	•	•		•	(A) ← (A) + (B)
ADCA	Add to A with carry		89	99	A9	B9	•	•	•	•		•	(A) ← (A) + (*effective address*) + (*carry*)
ADCB	Add to B with carry		C9	D9	E9	F9	•	•	•	•		•	(B) ← (B) + (*effective address*) + (*carry*)
ADDA	Add to A without carry		8B	9B	AB	BB	•	•	•	•		•	(A) ← (A) + (*effective address*)
ADDB	Add to B without carry		CB	DB	EB	FB	•	•	•	•		•	(B) ← (B) + (*effective address*)
ANDA	Logical **and** with A		84	94	A4	B4		0	•	•			(A) ← (A) ∧ (*effective address*)
ANDB	Logical **and** with B		C4	D4	E4	F4		0	•	•			(B) ← (B) ∧ (*effective address*)
ASL	Arithmetic shift left				68	78	•	•	•	•			same as ASLA, except (*effective address*) are shifted instead of (A)
ASLA	Shift A left arithmetic	48					•	•	•	•			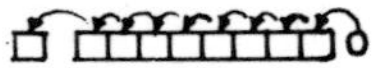 *carry* A [note that the rightmost bit of A is loaded with a 0]
ASLB	Shift B left arithmetic	58					•	•	•	•			same as ASLA, except (B) are shifted instead of (A)
ASR	Arithmetic shift right				67	77	•	•	•	•			same as ASRA, except (*effective address*) are shifted instead of (A)
ASRA	Shift A right arithmetic	47					•	•	•	•			 *carry* A [note that the leftmost bit stays the same — ''sign propagate'']
ASRB	Shift B right arithmetic	57					•	•	•	•			same as ASRA, except (B) are shifted instead of (A)
BITA	Bit test A		85	95	A5	B5		0	•	•			sets the status flags according to the value of (A) ∧ (*effective address*), doesn't affect the values in A or *effective address*
BITB	Bit test B		C5	D5	E5	F5		0	•	•			same as BITA except compares (B) to (*effective address*)

BRANCH [Branch instructions are listed immediately after this table (i.e. after the WAI instruction).]

mnemonic	description	inherent	immediate	direct	indexed	extended	C	V	Z	N	I	H	meaning
CBA	Compare accumulators	11					·	·	·	·			sets the status flags according to the value of (A) - (B) neither (A) nor (B) are altered
CLC	Clear carry	0C					0						(carry) ← 0
CLI	Clear interrupt mask	0E										0	(interrupt mask) ← 0 [enables interrupts]
CLR	Clear				6F	7F	0	0	1	0			(effective address) ← 00000000
CLRA	Clear A	4F					0	0	1	0			(A) ← 00000000
CLRB	Clear B	5F					0	0	1	0			(B) ← 00000000
CLV	Clear two's complement overflow bit	0A						0					(overflow) ← 0
CMPA	Compare A		81	91	A1	B1	·	·	·	·			sets the status flags according to the value of (A) - (effective address). neither (A) nor (effective address) are altered
CMPB	Compare B		C1	D1	E1	F1	·	·	·	·			sets the status flags according to the value of (B) - (effective address). neither (B) nor (effective address) are altered
COM	Complement				63	73	1	0	·	·			(effective address) ← (effective address) [all 0's change to 1's and vice versa]
COMA	Complement A	43					1	0	·	·			(A) ← (Ā) [all 0's change to 1's and vice versa]
COMB	Complement B	53					1	0	·	·			(B) ← (B̄) [all 0's changed to 1's and vice versa]
CPX	Compare index register		8C	9C	AC	BC		·	·	·			sets the status flags according to the value of (index register) - (effective address) (effective address + 1) neither (index register) nor (effective address) nor (effective address + 1) are altered

mnemonic	description	inherent	immediate	direct	indexed	extended	C	V	Z	N	I	H	meaning
DAA	Decimal adjust A	19					•	•	•	•			converts the value in A to binary-coded decimal (BCD) representation after additions
DEC	Decrement				6A	7A		•	•	•			(effective address) ← (effective address) - 1
DECA	Decrement A	4A						•	•	•			(A) ← (A) - 1
DECB	Decrement B	5A						•	•	•			(B) ← (B) - 1
DES	Decrement stack pointer	34											(sp) ← (sp) - 1
DEX	Decrement index register	09							•				(index register) ← (index register) - 1
EORA	**Exclusive-or** with A		88	98	A8	B8		0	•	•			(A) ← (A) $\oplus$ (effective address)
EORB	**Exclusive-or** with B		C8	D8	E8	F8		0	•	•			(B) ← (B) $\oplus$ (effective address)
INC	Increment				6C	7C		•	•	•			(effective address) ← (effective address) + 1
INCA	Increment A	4C						•	•	•			(A) ← (A) + 1
INCB	Increment B	5C						•	•	•			(B) ← (B) + 1
INS	Increment stack pointer	31											(sp) ← (sp) + 1
INX	Increment index register	08							•				(index register) ← (index register) + 1
JMP	Jump				6E	7E							(pc) ← (index register) + (byte$_2$) indexed, or (pc) ← (byte$_2$)(byte$_3$) extended
JSR	Jump to subroutine				AD	BD							first the (pc) are updated to point to the next instruction (the **return address**) then the low order byte of the pc is pushed on the stack, followed by the high order byte. Finally the pc is set as in the JMP instruction.
LDAA	Load accumulator A		86	96	A6	B6		0	•	•			(A) ← (effective address)
LDAB	Load accumulator B		C6	D6	E6	F6		0	•	•			(B) ← (effective address)

mnemonic	description	inherent	immediate	direct	indexed	extended	C	V	Z	N	I	H	meaning
LDS	Load stack pointer		8E	9E	AE	BE	·	0	·	·			$(sp) \leftarrow$ (effective address) (effective address + 1)
LDX	Load index register		CE	DE	EE	FE	·	0	·	·			(index register) $\leftarrow$ (effective address) (effective address + 1)
LSR	Logical shift right				64	74	·	·	·	0			same as LSRA except (effective address) are shifted instead of (A)
LSRA	Shift A right logical	44					·	·	·	0			(diagram) $0 \rightarrow \boxed{\quad} \rightarrow$ carry, A
LSRB	Shift B right logical	54					·	·	·	0			same as LSRA except (B) are shifted instead of (A)
NEG	Negate				60	70	·	·	·	·			(effective address) $\leftarrow$ - (effective address) [two's complement]
NEGA	Negate A	40					·	·	·	·			$(A) \leftarrow -(A)$
NEGB	Negate B	50					·	·	·	·			$(B) \leftarrow -(B)$
NOP	No operation	01											do nothing (except, of course, increment pc to prepare for next instruction)
ORAA	Inclusive or with A		8A	9A	AA	BA		·	·				$(A) \leftarrow (A) \vee$ (effective address)
ORAB	Inclusive or with B		CA	DA	EA	FA		·	·				$(B) \leftarrow (B) \vee$ (effective address)
PSHA	Push A onto stack	36											$((sp)) \leftarrow (A)$; $(sp) \leftarrow (sp) - 1$
PSHB	Push B onto stack	37											$((sp)) \leftarrow (B)$; $(sp) \leftarrow (sp) - 1$
PULA	Pull top of stack into A	32											$(sp) \leftarrow (sp) + 1$; $(A) \leftarrow ((sp))$ [pop the stack]
PULB	Pull top of stack into B	33											$(sp) \leftarrow (sp) + 1$; $(B) \leftarrow ((sp))$
ROL	Rotate left				69	79			·				same as ROLA except (effective address) are affected instead of (A)

flags affected: C V Z N I H

mnemonic	description	inherent	immediate	direct	indexed	extended	C	V	Z	N	I	H	meaning
ROLA	Rotate A left	49					•	•	•	•			carry ← [◯◯◯◯◯◯◯◯] A
ROLB	Rotate B left	59					•	•	•	•			same as ROLA except (B) are affected instead of (A)
ROR	Rotate right				66	76	•	•	•	•			same as RORA except (effective address) are affected instead of (A)
RORA	Rotate A right	46					•	•	•	•			carry ← [◯◯◯◯◯◯◯◯] A
RORB	Rotate B right	56					•	•	•	•			same as RORA except (B) are affected instead of (A)
RTI	Return from interrupt	3B					•	•	•	•	•	•	the status flags (stored in one byte), (B), (A), (index register) [2 bytes], and (pc) [2 bytes] are popped [PULled] off the stack [in the order given].
RTS	Return from subroutine	39											the 2 top bytes on the stack are popped [PULled] off and stored in pc, i.e., (pc) ← ((sp) + 1) ((sp) + 2), (sp) ← (sp) + 2
SBA	Subtract accumulators	10					•	•	•	•			(A) ← (A) - (B)
SBCA	Subtract from A with borrow		82	92	A2	B2	•	•	•	•			(A) ← (A) - (effective address) - (carry)
SBCB	Subtract from B with borrow		C2	D2	E2	F2	•	•	•	•			(B) ← (B) - (effective address) - (carry)
SEC	Set carry	0D					1						(carry) ← 1
SEI	Set interrupt mask	0F									1		(interrupt mask) ← 1 [disable interrupts]
SEV	Set two's complement overflow bit	0B						1					(overflow) ← 1
STAA	Store A			97	A7	B7		0	•	•			(effective address) ← (A)
STAB	Store B			D7	E7	F7		0	•	•			(effective address) ← (B)

mnemonic	description	inherent	immediate	direct	indexed	extended	C	V	Z	N	I	H	meaning
STS	Store stack pointer			9F	AF	BF		0	•	•			(effective address) ← high order byte of (sp); (effective address + 1) ← low order byte of (sp)
STX	Store index register			DF	EF	FF		0	•	•			(effective address) ← high order byte of (index register); (effective address + 1) ← low order byte of (index register)
SUBA	Subtract from A		80	90	A0	B0	•	•	•	•			(A) ← (A) - (effective address)
SUBB	Subtract from B		C0	D0	E0	F0	•	•	•	•			(B) ← (B) - (effective address)
SWI	Software interrupt	3F									1		(pc) ← (pc) + 1, then (pc), (index register), (A), (B), (status flags) are pushed onto the stack, then (pc) ← ($FFFA_{16}$) ($FFFB_{16}$)
TAB	Transfer from A to B	16						0	•	•			(B) ← (A)
TAP	Store A in status flags	06					•	•	•	•	•	•	$(status\ flags) \leftarrow (A) \begin{bmatrix} bit_0\ of\ A \rightarrow C & bit_3 \rightarrow N \\ bit_1\ of\ A \rightarrow V & bit_4 \rightarrow I \\ bit_2\ of\ A \rightarrow Z & bit_5 \rightarrow H \end{bmatrix}$
TBA	Transfer from B to A	17						0	•	•			(A) ← (B)
TPA	Store status flags in A	07											(A) ← (status flags)
TST	Test				6D	7D	0	0	•	•			status flags set according to the value of (effective address)
TSTA	Test A	4D					0	0	•	•			status flags set according to the value of (A)
TSTB	Test B	5D					0	0	•	•			status flags set according to the value of (B)
TSX	Transfer from stack pointer to index register	30											(index register) ← (sp) + 1
TXS	Transfer from index register to stack pointer	35											(sp) ← (index register) - 1
WAI	Wait for interrupt	3E											(pc) ← (pc) + 1, then (pc), (index register), (A), (B), (status flags) are PUSHed onto the stack. Then execution is suspended until an interrupt occurs.

Branch instructions

	description	op code	meaning
BCC	Branch if carry clear	24	if $(carry) = 0$ then $(pc) \leftarrow (pc) + 2 + (byte_2)$ otherwise $(pc) \leftarrow (pc) + 2$ (i.e. if $(carry) = 0$ branch otherwise go on in sequence)
BCS	Branch if carry set	25	if $(carry) = 1$ then branch [as specified in $byte_2$] otherwise go on in sequence
BEQ	Branch if equal	27	if $(zero) = 1$ then branch, otherwise go on
BGE	Branch if greater than or equal to zero	2C	if $(sign) \oplus (overflow) = 0$ then branch, otherwise go on
BGT	Branch if greater than zero	2E	if $(zero) \wedge [(sign) \oplus (overflow)] = 0$ then branch, otherwise go on
BHI	Branch if higher	22	if $(zero) \wedge (carry) = 0$ then branch, otherwise go on
BLE	Branch if less than or equal to zero	2F	if $(zero) \vee [(sign) \oplus (overflow)] = 1$ then branch, otherwise go on
BLS	Branch if lower or same	23	if $(zero) \vee (carry) = 1$ then branch, otherwise go on
BLT	Branch if less than zero	2D	if $(sign) \oplus (overflow) = 1$ then branch, otherwise go on
BMI	Branch if minus	2B	if $(sign) = 1$ then branch, otherwise go on
BNE	Branch if not equal	26	if $(zero) = 0$, then branch, otherwise go on
BPL	Branch if plus	2A	if $(sign) = 0$, then branch, otherwise go on
BRA	Branch always (unconditional)	20	branch [i.e., $(pc) \leftarrow (pc) + 2 + (byte_2)$]
BSR	Branch to subroutine	8D	increment (pc), PUSH (pc) onto the stack, then branch
BVC	Branch if overflow clear	28	if $(overflow) = 0$ then branch, otherwise go on
BVS	Branch if overflow set	29	if $(overflow) = 1$, then branch, otherwise go on

APPENDIX E

8080 Instruction Set*

The notation used to describe the meaning of each instruction is explained in Questions 639-646. The architecture of the 8080 is discussed in Q614-620 and Figure 59. Op codes are given in binary.

Some of the instructions include references to specific registers. For instance, the MOV r_1, r_2 instruction takes the value stored in register r_2 (called the **source** register) and stores it in register r_1 (called the **destination** register). The three bit value used to identify the source is shown as SSS in the op code; the three bit value used to identify the destination is shown as DDD. The correspondences between registers and three bit values are

	register	SSS or DDD
(accumulator)	A	111
	B	000
	C	001
	D	010
	E	011
	H	100
	L	101

Thus, the op code for MOV A, B is

$$\overset{\displaystyle DDD}{01\overbrace{111}000}$$
$$\underset{\displaystyle SSS}{\underbrace{000}}$$

The 8080 (and the 8085) has five **status flags** (also called **condition flags** or **condition codes**).

status flag	abbreviation	meaning for instructions which affect the flag
zero	Z	if the result of an instruction is zero (all bits 0), *zero* = 1, otherwise *zero* = 0.
sign	S	if the leftmost bit of the result is 1, *sign* = 1, else 0.
carry	CY	if an arithmetic operation resulted in a carry or a borrow out of the leftmost bit, *carry* = 1.
parity	P	if there is an even number of 1's in the result, *parity* = 1.
auxiliary carry	AC	carry out of bit 3. Used when dealing with binary coded decimal values (see DAA instruction).

Other abbreviations

The second and third bytes of multibyte instructions are identified as $byte_2$ and $byte_3$.

pc	—	the **program counter** (a 16-bit register)
r	—	a register, one of A, B, C, D, E, H, L
sp	—	the **stack pointer** (a 16-bit register)

*Thanks to Intel Corp. for permission to include this material.

mnemonic	description	op code	Z	S	P	CY	AC	clock cycles	length	meaning
ACI	Add immediate to A with carry	11001110	•	•	•	•	•	7	2	$(A) \leftarrow (A) + (byte_2) + (carry)$
ADC M	Add memory to A with carry	10001110	•	•	•	•	•	7	1	$(A) \leftarrow (A) + ((H)(L)) + (carry)$
ADC r	Add register to A with carry	10001SSS	•	•	•	•	•	4	1	$(A) \leftarrow (A) + (r) + (carry)$
ADD M	Add memory to A	10000110	•	•	•	•	•	7	1	$(A) \leftarrow (A) + ((H) (L))$
ADD r	Add to register to A	10000SSS	•	•	•	•	•	4	1	$(A) \leftarrow (A) + (r)$
ADI	Add immediate to A	11000110	•	•	•	•	•	7	2	$(A) \leftarrow (A) + (byte_2)$
ANA M	And memory with A	10100110	•	•	•	•	•	7	1	$(A) \leftarrow (A) \wedge ((H)(L))$
ANA r	And register with A	10100SSS	•	•	•	•	•	4	1	$(A) \leftarrow (A) \wedge (r)$
ANI	And immediate with A	11100110	•	•	•	•	•	7	2	$(A) \leftarrow (A) \wedge (byte_2)$
CALL	Call unconditional	11001101						17	3	$((sp) - 1) \leftarrow$ (high order byte of pc) $((sp) - 2) \leftarrow$ (low order byte of pc) $(sp) \leftarrow (sp) - 2$ $(pc) \leftarrow (byte_3) (byte_2)$ i.e. (pc) is pushed on the stack, control is transferred to $(byte_3) (byte_2)$
CC	Call on carry	11011100						11/17	3	same as CALL if $(carry) = 1$ otherwise continue in sequence (i.e. $(pc) \leftarrow (pc) + 3$)
CM	Call on minus	11111100						11/17	3	same as CALL if $(sign) = 1$ otherwise go on
CMA	Complement A	00101111						4	1	$(A) \leftarrow$ one's complement of (A) i.e. all 0's become 1's and vice versa
CMC	Complement carry	00111111				•		4	1	$(carry) \leftarrow (\overline{carry})$
CMP M	Compare memory with A	10111110	•	•	•	•	•	7	1	set status flags based on the value of $(A) - ((H) (L))$. (H), (L), and (A) remain unchanged
CMP r	Compare register with A	10111SSS	•	•	•	•	•	4	1	set status flags based on value of $(A) - (r)$. (A) and (r) remain unchanged

mnemonic	description	op code	Z	S	P	CY	AC	clock cycles	length	meaning
CNC	Call on no carry	11010100						11/17	3	same as CALL if (carry) = 0, otherwise go on
CNZ	Call on not zero	11000100						11/17	3	same as CALL if (zero) = 0, otherwise go on
CP	Call on positive	11110100						11/17	3	same as CALL if (sign) = 0, otherwise go on
CPE	Call on parity even	11101100						11/17	3	same as CALL if (parity) = 1, otherwise go on
CPI	Compare immediate with A	11111110	•	•	•	•	•	7	2	set status flags based on value of (A) - (byte$_2$). (A) remains unchanged
CPO	Call on parity odd	11100100						11/17	3	same as CALL if (parity) = 0, otherwise go on
CZ	Call on zero	11001100						11/17	3	same as CALL if (zero) = 1, otherwise go on
DAA	Decimal adjust A	00100111	•	•	•	•	•	4	1	convert the 8-bit value in A into 2 BCD digits (in A). used after additions on BCD values
DAD B	Add B & C to H & L	00001001				•		10	1	(H)(L)←(H)(L) + (B)(C)
DAD D	Add D & E to H & L	00011001				•		10	1	(H)(L)←(H)(L) + (D)(E)
DAD H	Add H & L to H & L	00101001				•		10	1	(H)(L)←(H)(L) + (H)(L)
DAD SP	Add stack pointer to H & L	00111001				•		10	1	(H)(L)←(H)(L) + (sp)
DCR M	Decrement memory	00110101	•	•	•		•	10	1	((H)(L))←((H)(L)) - 1
DCR r	Decrement register	00DDD101	•	•	•		•	5	1	(r) ← (r) - 1
DCX B	Decrement B & C	00001011						5	1	(B)(C)←(B)(C) - 1
DCX D	Decrement D & E	00011011						5	1	(D)(E)←(D)(E) - 1
DCX H	Decrement H & L	00101011						5	1	(H)(L)←(H)(L) - 1
DCX SP	Decrement stack pointer	00111011						5	1	(sp)←(sp) - 1
DI	Disable interrupts	11110011						4	1	ignore interrupt requests from now on
EI	Enable interrupts	11111011						4	1	respond to interrupt requests from now on
HLT	Halt	01110110						7	1	stop. i.e. don't carry out any further instructions.

mnemonic	description	op code	flags affected Z	S	P	CY	AC	clock cycles	length	meaning
IN	Input	11011011						10	2	place a value from the input port specified by (byte$_2$) in A
INR M	Increment memory	00110100	•	•	•		•	10	1	((H)(L))←((H)(L)) + 1
INR r	Increment register	00DDD100	•	•	•		•	5	1	(r) ← (r) + 1
INX B	Increment B & C registers	00000011						5	1	(B)(C)←(B)(C) + 1
INX D	Increment D & E registers	00010011						5	1	(D)(E)←(D)(E) + 1
INX H	Increment H & L registers	00100011						5	1	(H)(L)←(H)(L) + 1
INX SP	Increment stack pointer	00110011						5	1	(sp) ← (sp) + 1
JC	Jump on carry	11011010						10	3	same as JMP if (carry) = 1, otherwise go on in sequence
JM	Jump on minus	11111010						10	3	same as JMP if (sign) = 1, otherwise go on
JMP	Jump unconditional	11000011						10	3	(pc) ← (byte$_3$) (byte$_2$)
JNC	Jump on no carry	11010010						10	3	same as JMP if (carry) = 0, otherwise go on
JNZ	Jump on not zero	11000010						10	3	same as JMP if (zero) = 0, otherwise go on
JP	Jump on positive	11110010						10	3	same as JMP if (sign) = 0, otherwise go on
JPE	Jump on parity even	11101010						10	3	same as JMP if (parity) = 1, otherwise go on
JPO	Jump on parity odd	11100010						10	3	same as JMP if (parity) = 0, otherwise go on
JZ	Jump on zero	11001010						10	3	same as JMP if (zero) = 1, otherwise go on
LDA	Load A direct	00111010						13	3	(A)←((byte$_3$) (byte$_2$))
LDAX B	Load A indirect	00001010						7	1	(A)←((B)(C))
LDAX D	Load A indirect	00011010						7	1	(A)←((D)(E))
LHLD	Load H & L direct	00101010						16	3	(L)←((byte$_3$) (byte$_2$)); (H)←((byte$_3$) (byte$_2$) + 1

mnemonic	description	op code	Z	S	P	CY	AC	clock cycles	length	meaning
LXI B	Load immediate register Pair B & C	00000001						10	3	$(B) \leftarrow (byte_3)$, $(C) \leftarrow (byte_2)$
LXI D	Load immediate register Pair D & E	00010001						10	3	$(D) \leftarrow (byte_3)$, $(E) \leftarrow (byte_2)$
LXI H	Load immediate register Pair H & L	00100001						10	3	$(H) \leftarrow (byte_3)$, $(L) \leftarrow (byte_2)$
LXI SP	Load immediate stack pointer	00110001						10	3	$(sp) \leftarrow (byte_3)(byte_2)$
MVI M	Move immediate memory	00110110						10	2	$((H)(L)) \leftarrow (byte_2)$
MVI r	Move immediate register	00DDD110						7	2	$(r) \leftarrow (byte_2)$
MOV M,r	Move register to memory	01110SSS						7	1	$((H)(L)) \leftarrow (r)$
MOV r,M	Move memory to register	01DDD110						7	1	$(r) \leftarrow ((H)(L))$
MOV r₁r₂	Move register to register	01DDDSSS						5	1	$(r_1) \leftarrow (r_2)$, r_1 is the **destination** r_2 is the **source**
NOP	No-operation	00000000						4	1	don't do anything except increment (pc) to get the next instruction
Or memory with A — ORA M		10110110	•	•	•	0	0	7	1	$(A) \leftarrow (A) \vee ((H)(L))$
Or register with A — ORA r		10110SSS	•	•	•	0	0	4	1	$(A) \leftarrow (A) \vee (r)$
Or immediate with A — ORI		11110110	•	•	•	0	0	7	2	$(A) \leftarrow (A) \vee (byte_2)$
OUT	Output	11010011						10	2	send (A) to the port specified by $(byte_2)$
PCHL	H & L to program counter	11101001						5	1	$(pc) \leftarrow (H) (L)$, i.e. jump to $(H) (L)$
POP B	Pop register pair B & C off stack	11000001						10	1	$(C) \leftarrow ((sp))$, $(B) \leftarrow ((sp) + 1)$, $(sp) \leftarrow (sp) + 2$
POP D	Pop register pair D & E off stack	11010001						10	1	$(E) \leftarrow ((sp))$, $(D) \leftarrow ((sp) + 1)$, $(sp) \leftarrow (sp) + 2$
POP H	Pop register pair H & L off stack	11100001						10	1	$(L) \leftarrow ((sp))$, $(H) \leftarrow ((sp) + 1)$, $(sp) \leftarrow (sp) + 2$

flags affected

mnemonic	description	op code	flags affected Z	S	P	CY	AC	clock cycles	length	meaning
POP PSW	Pop A and Flags off stack	11110001	•	•	•	•	•	10	1	(status flags) ← ((sp)), (A) ← ((sp) + 1), (sp) ← (sp) + 2
PUSH B	Push register Pair B & C on stack	11000101						11	1	((sp) - 1) ← (B), ((sp) - 2) ← (C), (sp) ← (sp) - 2
PUSH D	Push register Pair D & E on stack	11010101						11	1	((sp) - 1) ← (D), ((sp) - 2) ← (E), (sp) ← (sp) - 2
PUSH H	Push register Pair H & L on stack	11100101						11	1	((sp) - 1) ← (H), ((sp) - 2) ← (L), (sp) ← (sp) - 2
PUSH PSW	Push A and Flags on stack	11110101						11	1	((sp) - 1) ← (A), ((sp) - 2) ← (status flags)
RAL	Rotate A left through carry	00010111				•		4	1	carry ↔ A [diagram]
RAR	Rotate A right through carry	00011111				•		4	1	carry ↔ A [diagram]
RC	Return on carry	11011000						5/11	1	same as RET if (carry) = 1, otherwise go on in sequence
RET	Return	11001001						10	1	(pc) ← ((sp) + 1) ((sp)), (sp) ← (sp) + 2, i.e. jump to address stored on the top of the stack
RLC	Rotate A left	00000111				•		4	1	carry ↔ A [diagram]
RM	Return on minus	11111000						5/11	1	same as RET if (sign) = 1, otherwise go on
RNC	Return on no carry	11010000						5/11	1	same as RET if (carry) = 0, otherwise go on
RNZ	Return on not zero	11000000						5/11	1	same as RET if (zero) = 0, otherwise go on
RP	Return on positive	11110000						5/11	1	same as RET if (sign) = 0, otherwise go on
RPE	Return on parity even	11101000						5/11	1	same as RET if (parity) = 1, otherwise go on
RPO	Return on parity odd	11100000						5/11	1	same as RET if (parity) = 0, otherwise go on

mnemonic	description	Z	S	P	CY	AC	op code	clock cycles	length	
RRC	Rotate A right						00001111	4	1	carry A
RST	Restart						11AAA111	11	1	push (pc) on the stack, then (pc) ← 0000000000AAA000 (for responding to interrupts)
RZ	Return on zero						11001000	5/11	1	same as RET if (zero) = 1, otherwise go on
SBB M	Subtract memory from A with borrow	•	•	•	•	•	10011110	7	1	$(A) \leftarrow (A) - ((H)(L)) - (carry)$
SBB r	Subtract register from A with borrow	•	•	•	•	•	10011SSS	4	1	$(A) \leftarrow (A) - (r) - (carry)$
SBI	Subtract immediate from A with borrow	•	•	•	•	•	11011110	7	2	$(A) \leftarrow (A) - (byte_2) - (carry)$
SHLD	Store H & L direct						00100010	16	3	$((byte_3)(byte_2)) \leftarrow (L)$ $((byte_3)(byte_2) + 1) \leftarrow (H)$
SPHL	H & L to stack pointer						11111001	5	1	$(sp) \leftarrow (H)(L)$
STA	Store A direct						00110010	13	3	$((byte_3)(byte_2)) \leftarrow (A)$
STAX B	Store A indirect						00000010	7	1	$((B)(C)) \leftarrow (A)$
STAX D	Store A indirect						00010010	7	1	$((D)(E)) \leftarrow (A)$
STC	Set carry				•		00110111	4	1	$(carry) \leftarrow 1$
SUB M	Subtract memory from A	•	•	•	•	•	10010110	7	1	$(A) \leftarrow (A) - ((H)(L))$
SUB r	Subtract register from A	•	•	•	•	•	10010SSS	4	1	$(A) \leftarrow (A) - (r)$
SUI	Subtract immediate from A	•	•	•	•	•	11010110	7	2	$(A) \leftarrow (A) - (byte_2)$
XCHG	Exchange D & E, H & L Registers						11101011	4	1	H — D, L — E

flags affected

mnemonic	description	op code	Z	D	P	CY	AC	clock cycles	length	meaning
XRA M	**Exclusive or** memory with A	10101110	•	·	•	0	0	7	1	$(A) \leftarrow (A) \oplus ((H)(L))$
XRA r	**Exclusive or** register with A	10101SSS	•	·	•	0	0	4	1	$(A) \leftarrow (A) \oplus (r)$
XRI	**Exclusive or** immediate with A	11101110	•	·	•	0	0	7	2	$(A) \leftarrow (A) \oplus (byte_2)$
XTHL	Exchange top of stack, H & L	11100011						18	1	$(L) \leftarrow ((sp))$, $(H) \leftarrow ((sp) + 1)$

Note: the newer 8085 microprocessor has all the above instructions plus two more:

RIM	read interrupt mask	00100000						4	1	$(A) \leftarrow (interrupt\ mask)$
SIM	set interrupt mask	00110000						4	1	$(interrupt\ mask) \leftarrow (A)$

APPENDIX F

Bibliography

There are literally hundreds of new titles published each year in the general computer, computer technology, programming, information processing area. At this moment, for example, there are over 80 books in print covering programming in Fortran, and somewhere between 30 and 40 on programming in Basic. In compiling this Bibliography, I've tried to include a good sample of books and magazines that are directly relevant to home computing. By browsing through technical bookstores and college libraries, watching the ads in the magazines, and talking to friends, you can uncover scads more.

Organization of the Bibliography

Hardware
    Books dealing mainly with hardware
    Manufacturers' literature
Software
    Books dealing mainly with software
    Textbooks covering specific languages
General Interest
Periodicals
    Popular magazines
    Trade magazines

Hardware

Books dealing mainly with hardware

C. Gordon Bell and Allen Newell, *Computer Structures: Readings and Examples,* McGraw-Hill, 1971, xix + 668 pages.
    This massive book provides a taxonomy of computer architecture, that is, an orderly classification of computers in terms of their hardware organization and instruction sets. It shows the historical and logical relationships between the designs of a huge number of different machines. It stops short of microprocessors, but all the design ideas used in microprocessor organization are covered many times over.

Thomas R. Blakslee, *Digital Design With Standard MSI and LSI*, John Wiley, 1975, $19.95, 357 pages.
    Updates a number of digital design techniques for use with the new generations of components.

Paul M. Chirlian, *Analysis and Design of Digital Circuits and Computer Systems,* Matrix Publishers, $16.95, 606 pages.
    Starts from scratch, gives general ideas about digital devices, tells how number systems work, develops Boolean algebra as a means of analyzing digital logic, takes you to the point where you can design major components of computers. Includes a separate 82 page booklet giving answers to exercises and problems.

Wayne Green (ed.), *Hobby Computers are Here*, 73 Inc., 1976, $4.95, 11″x8″, 95 pages. Reprints (from 73 Magazine) of articles and feisty editorials about getting started in hobby computing.

Don Lancaster, *TTL Cookbook,* Howard W. Sams & Co., 1974, $8.95, 335 pages.
    First 120 pages give descriptions of specific TTL components (official number, what logic is on the chip, what pins connect to what, switching speed, power requirements, special considerations). The rest of the book tells how to use TTL by covering a number of specific projects. Other Sams books by Don Lancaster include the *User's Guide to TTL* and the *TV Typewriter Cookbook.*

E. J. McCluskey, *Introduction to the Theory of Switching Circuits,* McGraw-Hill, 1965, $12.50, xv+318 pages.

The strong point of this book is its development of techniques for minimizing the number of gates required to implement at given logic expression. An old standard text.

Daniel R. McGlynn, *Microprocessors: Technology, Architecture, and Applications,* John Wiley, 1976, about $9, xi+207 pages.

Where Osborne's book (see entry immediately below) may have too fine a focus for the hobbyist, this book's focus may be too broad. Probably aimed at engineering management, it gives an overview of exactly what the title says. Good, understandable treatment of applications, interesting data on trends in microelectronics.

Adam Osborne, *An Introduction to Microcomputers,* Adam Osborne and Associates, 1975, $7.50, xix+397 pages.

If you have some familiarity with computers, and want to learn about microprocessors, this is an excellent book. If you're starting into computing for the first time, the particular slant of the book (it's aimed at people who want to use microprocessors in design, not as microcomputers), its fast pace, and its occasional typos will make it tough. On the other hand, there's not much else available. Now out in revised form as Vol. I and Vol. II — the second volume contains specifics about particular microprocessors.

Charles J. Sippl, *Microcomputer Dictionary and Guide,* Matrix Publishers, 1976, $17.95, approx. 700 pages.

More than just a dictionary for all the quirky acronyms you come across, this book contains a wide variety of useful information (despite its occasional tendency to lapse into descriptions of specific products instead of covering the broad meaning of the word being defined). For instance, entries beginning with **TTL** take up almost two full pages and include such topics as **TTL; TTL applications; TTL compatibility; TTL input/output; TTL logic· TTL logic features; TTL low power Schottky (LSTTL); TTL, Schottky; TTL vs. CMOS.**

Branko Soucek, *Microprocessors and Microcomputers,* John Wiley, 1976, $23.

Manufacturers' Literature
Each manufacturer provides some kind of descriptive material telling how to use its product. Here are some that were used in writing this book.

Microcomputer Handbook, Digital Equipment Corporation (DEC), 1976.

8080 Microcomputer Systems User's Manual, Intel Corporation, 1975.

M6800 Microprocessor Applications Manual, Motorola Semiconductor Products Inc., 1975.

TTL Data Book for Design Engineers, Texas Instruments Inc., $3.95, 640 pages.

Software
Books dealing mainly with software

C. William Gear, *Computer Organization and Programming,* McGraw-Hill, 1969, $14, xiv+397 pages.

Lots of good material at an understandable level. Unfortunately, most of the specific examples are written in IBM 360/370 assembly language. But that may not be as big a problem as it seems at first glance — the people who designed the 8080 were no strangers to the 360's architecture, and with just a little extra effort, you can figure out what's going on. Covers a very wide range of basic programming techniques.

Brian W. Kernighan and P. J. Plauger, *The Elements of Programming Style*, McGraw-Hill, 1974, $3.95, x+147 pages.
> This is a nice book to look at once you've assimilated the basics of programming in a higher-level language. It's filled with good tips for making your programs cleaner, easier to understand, and easier to debug.

Donald E. Knuth, *The Art of Programming*, Addison-Wesley, $29.95 per volume,
> Vol. 1 *Fundamental Algorithms*
> Vol. 2 *Seminumerical Algorithms*
> Vol. 3 *Sorting and Searching*

De rigueur among academics, widely used by all manner of professional programmers, this multi-volume (eventually there are to be seven), master work covers the ins and outs of programming technique. An excellent source for a long term study of specific algorithms, ways of devising algorithms, and the analysis of algorithms.

Jurg Nievergelt, J. Craig Farrar, Edward M. Reingold, *Computer Approaches to Mathematical Problems*, Prentice-Hall, 1974, xiii+257 pages.
> Provides a solid introduction to a number of advanced programming techniques. Especially suited to those who have a background in mathematics. Useful annotated lists of references. Anyone who plans to write a championship chess playing program should be familiar with the techniques covered here.

101 BASIC Computer Games, Digital Equipment Corporation, $7.50 and the companion

Understanding Mathematics and Logic Using Basic Computer Games, $4.50.
> The first popular book of computer games.

People's Computer Company (with Hewlett-Packard), *What To Do After You Hit Return or P.C.C.'s First Book of Computer Games*, 1975, approx. $7, 11''x15'', 158 pages.
> Fanciful descriptions and fun introductions to 48 computer games. Full listings (in Hewlett-Packard's version of extended Basic) for all of the games. A good place to start if you're looking for tips on designing your own games.

Jean E. Sammet, *Programming Languages: History and Fundamentals*, Prentice-Hall, 1969, xxx+785 pages.
> Gives history, syntax, example programs, discussion of merits for over a hundred programming languages. Virtually every language that saw the light of day before 1969 is covered. Contains an extensive section on all the languages I've seen covered in hobbyist publications except for Wirth's language PASCAL which is a more recent creation. Extensive bibliography.

Scelbi software books:
Scelbi's First Book of Computer Games for the 8008/8080, $14.95.

Scelbi's Galaxy Game for the 8008/8080, $14.95.

Scelbi 8080 Software Gourmet Guide and Cook Book, $9.95.

An 8080 Assembler Program, $17.95.

An 8080 Editor Program, $14.95.

etc.
> All include program listings you can copy for use on 8008 or 8080 based systems. More on the way!

Harold S. Stone, *Introduction to Computer Organization and Data Structures*, McGraw-Hill, 1972, $13.50, 320+pages. If you're getting tired of feeling slightly lost as you attempt a major program, but you have a good grasp of programming basics, going through the last half of this book (Chapters 6-11 on Data Structures) will yield a quantum jump in your programming abilities. Tells how and why to use **arrays, stacks, queues, lists, plexes, trees, heaps**—all manner of data structures.

Dennie Van Tassel, *Program Style, Design, Efficiency, Debugging, and Testing,* Prentice-Hall, approx. 250 pages. This book is crammed with helpful hints, tips, and ideas, all of real pracitcal value. Putting them in practice will make your program cleaner, easier to read, de-bug, and use. Also includes 101 programming problems—a good source of ideas for useful programs.

Gerald M. Weinberg, *The Psychology of Computer Programming,* $9.95, 288 pages. This is a fascinating book—it looks at the behavior of and patterns of interaction among computer programmers. Although it may be intended more for people who have to manage teams of programmers, it contains a number of ideas which are of direct practical value to the individual programmer. See especially the sections on **ego-less programming.**

Textbooks covering specific languages
Basic
Robert L. Albrecht, LeRoy Finkel, and Jerald R. Brown, *BASIC,* John Wiley, 1973, $4.95, 325 pages.
In a programmed instruction format. Patient and gentle.

Michel Boillet and Lister Horn, *BASIC,* West Publ. Co., 1976, xii+273 pages.
Good coverage, lots of good problems at the end of each chapter, many business oriented.

John G. Kemeny and Thomas E. Kurtz, *Basic Programming,* John Wiley, 1971 (2nd. ed.), $7.75, 8'' x 11'', 150 pages.
The ''old standard''. Moves quickly, has lots of really clever examples.

Robert E. Lynch and John R. Rice, *Computers: Their Impact and Use: Basic Languages,* Holt, Rinehart, and Winston, 1975, xi+398 pages.
The first half gives a broad overview of computing, the second half covers programming in Basic. Moves fairly rapidly, includes a number of nice, real world examples.

Paul W. Murrill and Cecil W. Smith, *Basic Programming,* Intext Educational Publishers, 1971, $6, 8'' x 11'', 155 pages.

Anthony P. Peluso, Charles R. Bauer, and Dalward J. Debruzzi *Basic BASIC Programming,* Addison-Wesley, 1972, $7.50, 8''x11'', 274 pages.
In a programmed instruction format, broad coverage.

My Computer Likes Me (When I Speak in BASIC), dilithium Press, 1972, $3.95, 64 pages.
Nice, mellow, friendly, very brief introduction in Basic. Good place to begin if you're starting completely from scratch.

etc.,etc.,etc.,etc.

Fortran
Rich Didday and Rex Page, *Fortran for Humans,* West Publ., 1977 (2nd. ed.), 1974 (1st ed.), approx. $9,xv+430 pages.
etc.,etc., etc., etc., etc.

LISP
John McCarthy, et. al., *LISP 1.5 Programmer's Manual,* MIT Press, 1962, $3,106 pages.

PASCAL
K. Jensen and N. Wirth, *PASCAL — User Manual and Report,* Springer-Verlag, 1976, $5.90, viii+167 pages.

PL/I

Frank Bates and Mary L. Douglas, *Programming Language/One,* 2nd. Ed., 1970, 432 pages.

SNOBOL4

R. E. Griswold, J. F. Poage, and I. P. Polonsky, *The SNOBOL4 Programming Language,* 2nd Ed., 1971, 8''x11'', 256 pages.

Note: before you rush out and buy any book on programming, stop in at a college library and look through the ones they have.

General Interest

David H. Ahl (ed), *The Best of Creative Computing, Vol. 1,* Creative Computing Press, 1976, $8.95, 8½''x11'', ix+317 pages.
If you want to get caught up with what *Creative Computing* (see entry under Popular magazines) did in their first six issues, this is the only way — they're sold out of back issues. Includes programs in Basic for a number of games, including the ever popular Hunt the Wumpus and Star Trek. (Note: Star Trek is a large program, and will have to be altered before it'll run on most home systems. A small version of Star Trek called "Star Trek Trainer" is given in the September 1976 issue of *Byte.*)

Robert Baer, *The Digital Villain: Notes on the Numerology, Parapsychology, and Metaphysics of the Computer,* Addison-Wesley, 1972, approx. 190 pages.

Stewart Brand, *II Cybernetic Frontiers,* Random House, 1974, $2, 96 pages.
Reports from two frontiers. The first, in the form of a conversation with anthropologist/cybernetician Gregory Bateson, asks what happens when you take the basic principles of the information sciences and use them to analyze the human condition. The second, in the form of a tour of late night activities at the Stanford Artificial Intelligence Lab, asks what happens when you take the techniques of the information sciences and let people play.

Rich Didday, *Finite State Fantasies,* Matrix Publishers, 1976, $1.25, 8½''x11'', 48 pages.

Charles and Ray Eames, *A Computer Perspective,* Harvard University Press, 1973, $15, 9''x9'', 175 pages.
An astonishing slice of computer history, shown in photographs, private notes, letters, circuit diagrams and early flowcharts of the founding fathers and mothers, pictures of early equipment, etc.,etc. It's historically accurate, incredibly well thought out, and absolutely fascinating. The book consists of materials gathered for a major display at the IBM Exhibit Center in New York City, and covers the rise of computing from Babbage up to the early 1950's. The snapshot (p. 133) of Goldstine and Eckert standing like proud papas holding a memory unit is worth the price of admission by itself. The unit is wider than the both of them, about a foot high, and stored *one* decimal digit!

John G. Kemeny, *Man and the Computer,* Charles Scribner's Sons, 1972, $1.45, 152 pages.
A non-technical piece done by one of the co-inventors of Basic. Develops the notion that humans and computers are symbiotic; presents and predicts their co-evolution.

Theodor H. Nelson, *Computer Lib/Dream Machines,* Hugo's Book Service, $7, 10''x14'', 128 pages (of course).
Welcome to the wonderful, wacky, zany, rib tickling, sloganeering, crusading world of Ted Nelson's mind. Full of useful information, funny anecdotes, gossip, diatribes against the powerful, nifty slogans ("Stamp Out Cybercrud! Computer Power to the People!")

Dennie L. Van Tassel, *The Compleat Computer*, SRA, 9''x12'', 216 pages.
A very tasty collection of news articles, cartoons, fiction, poetry, full color reprints of early computerish scific cover art, thought provoking articles, and references to other literature. All with the goal of giving the Big Picture of how computers fit into our society and our daily lives. Goes down easy — fun to read.

Joseph Weizenbaum, *Computer Power and Human Reason*, W.H. Freeman and Company, 1976, $9.95, 300 pages.
This widely read book explores the edge between computer technology and human values. For my money, it's said better in R. Pirsig's *Zen and the Art of Motorcycle Maintenance*.

Periodicals

Popular magazines

ACM Computing Surveys, published quarterly by the ACM (the computing world's professional society). The "Survey and Tutorial Journal of the ACM". Expensive if you don't belong to the ACM, contents frequently not relevant to home computing, but every so often, there's an invaluable piece. Browse at your local college library.

BrainTheory Newsletter, published 4 times a year by the Center for Systems Neuroscience, University of Massachusetts, Amherst, Massachusetts 01002, $5/year. Contains brief reports of current research; reviews of books and papers, controversies. If you have an interest in applying your knowledge of computers and information processing to the study of biological information processing systems, have a look here to see what's going on in this challenging field of study.

Byte (the small systems journal), published monthly by BYTE Publications, 70 Main St., Peterborough, New Hampshire 03458, $12/year. The first glossy, professionally conceived and carried out magazine exclusively aimed at the computer hobbyist. Articles to date have run ¾ hardware, ¼ software.

Communications of the ACM, published monthly by the ACM.
Reports on theoretical advances in computing. Currently undergoing a re-evaluation, may shift toward the practical end. Check it out at your local college library.

Computer, published monthly by the IEEE Computer Society. Articles tend to be practical (as opposed to theoretical), informative, and non-threatening. Each issue is usually organized around a central theme. Issues covering microcomputerish topics are available at most computer stores.

Computerworld, published weekly in Boston, is a tabloid/newspaper which covers the commercial computer world. Useful if you want to follow what the big manufacturers are up to, want to follow court decisions related to computing. Buried in the middle is an occasional article on computer hobbyists.

Creative Computing, subtitled "the magazine of recreational and educational computing", published bi-monthly, P.O. Box 789-M, Morristown, NJ 07960, $15/year.
Fun and informative reading on general topics. Good source of references to other literature. Each issue contains listings of games programs.

Dr. Dobb's Journal of Computer Calisthenics and Orthodontia, published 10 times a year, Box 310, Menlo Park, California 94025, $10/year. Each issue contains program listings (almost all in assembly language, very machine specific), teasers about upcoming hardware products. Main idea is to provide a source of free software products to computer hobbyists—has presented a number of different programs which implement subsets and variants of Basic (lumped under the name Tiny Basic). New projects are afoot. Good source of software ideas.

Interface Age, subtitled "microcomputing for home and small business", published monthly by McPheters, Wolfe & Jones, 6615 Sunset Blvd., Suite 202, Hollywood, CA 90028, $10/year. Introductory articles, product reviews, and a substantial Software Section.

Kilobaud, published monthly, Peterborough, NH 03458, $15/year. Main thrust is applications, i.e. What Can You Do With It? Wide range of solid articles relevant to the hobbyist as well as small businesses.

Microtrek, subtitled "the microcomputer magazine for the hobbyist & professional", published monthly, $10/year. — Now merged with Personal Computing

People's Computer Company is a bimonthly newsletter published by the People's Computer Company, Box 310, Menlo Park, CA 94025, $6/year, tabloid style. The PCC newsletter started out (I think in 1972 or so) bringing the word about computing to school aged people, is now shifting more into the computer hobbyist sphere. It must feel good to the people who started PCC to see what's happening—they're no longer a voice crying in the wilderness.

Personal Computing, published bimonthly by Benwill Publishing Corp., 167 Corey Road, Brookline, MA 02146. Premier issue was Oct/Nov 1976, $8/year.

Popular Electronics, published monthly at One Park Avenue, New York, NY 10016, $9.98/year. For the last couple of years, about one fifth of their material has been relevant to home computing. Some manufacturers use Popular Electronics articles to introduce new products. MITS's Altair 8800 and 680 microcomputers, Cromemco's TV Dazzler, and others have appeared first as Popular Electronics construction articles. Lots of good hardware info, no software to speak of so far.

Radio-Electronics, published monthly, subscriptions are $8.75/year from Radio-Electronics Subscription Service, Boulder, CO 80302. *Radio-Electronics* was the first major magazine to run articles on building a home computer (the Mark-8 microcomputer, 1974).

73 Magazine, published monthly by 73, Inc., Peterborough, NH 03458, $10/year. An amateur radio magazine at heart, with a dynamic section on microcomputers called I/O. The I/O section is edited by John Craig (who also edits *Kilobaud*), and has articles providing introductions to hardware (and some software) techniques. Good source of ads if you're shopping for circuit components.

SIGART Newsletter, published bimonthly by the ACM Special Interest Group on Artificial Intelligence, $12/year. Contains brief reports of current AI work, ongoing arguments, occasional bibliographies, reports of computer chess tournaments. Lively, fun to read.

Trade magazines
There's a tremendous number of magazines which make their living by getting computer and electronic manufacturers' ads on the right people's desks. Usually they include timely, well-written articles. If you are in the right category (your "professional profile" matches the image they want to portray), you can get some of them for free. Good way to get tips on what's about to happen, keep track of trends. Here are a few. If you think you might qualify, write for a subscription form.

Computer Decisions, "distributed computing for management", Hayden Publishing Co., P.O. Box 13802, Philadelphia, PA 19101.

Computer Design, "the magazine of digital electronics", PO Box 302, Winchester, MA 01890.

Datamation, 35 Mason St., Greenwich, CT 06830.

Data Processing, 134 N. 13th St., Philadelphia, PA 19107.

Digital design, "the magazine of digital systems", Benwill Publ. Co., P.O. Box 335, Winchester, MA 01890.

Electronic Design, Hayden Publishing Co., P.O. Box 13803, Philadelphia, PA 19101

Electronic Design News,

Mini-Micro Systems, 5 Kane Industrial Drive, Hudson, MA 01749. (Formerly called *Modern Data.*)

APPENDIX G

$$\overline{(A+B)} = \overline{A} * \overline{B}$$ De Morgan's Theorem

A	B	A+B	$\overline{A+B}$	$\overline{A}$	$\overline{B}$	$\overline{A} * \overline{B}$
0	0	0	1	1	1	1
0	1	1	0	1	0	0
1	0	1	0	0	1	0
1	1	1	0	0	0	0

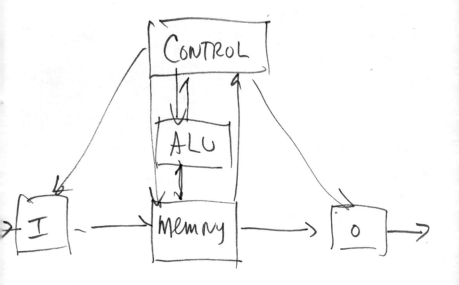